Abingdon in Context

Lantern of Long Alley Almshouse, first erected 1604-5. The original Fraternity of the Holy Cross had been chartered under Henry VI, and its successor, Christ's Hospital, under Edward VI.

Abingdon in Context

Small-town politics in early modern England
1547-1688

MANFRED BROD

2010

FASTPRINT PUBLISHING
Peterborough, England

www.fast-print.net/store.php

ABINGDON IN CONTEXT
Copyright © Manfred Brod 2010

ISBN 978-184426-888-7

First published 2010 by
FASTPRINT PUBLISHING
Peterborough, England.

An environmentally friendly book printed and bound in England by
www.printondemand-worldwide.com

Mixed Sources
Product group from well-managed
forests, and other controlled sources
www.fsc.org Cert no. TT-COC-002641
© 1996 Forest Stewardship Council

PEFC Certified
This product is
from sustainably
managed forests
and controlled
sources
www.pefc.org
PEFC/16-33-415

This book is made entirely of chain-of-custody materials

In memory of Mieneke Cox,

Historian of Abingdon

Contents

Time line

	National	Local/Regional
1547	Court of Surveyors merged into the Court of Augmentations (1 Jan). Chantries Act passed (24 Dec).	Roger Amyce becomes Receiver for Berkshire in the Court of Augmentations.
1548		Abingdon guilds dissolved
1549	Fall of Protector Somerset; Duke of Northumberland takes power.	
1551-2	Somerset tried and executed (Jan 1552)	Sir John Mason claims stewardship (Feb 1551). Pro-Somerset agitation in Abingdon, repressed by Mason (Nov 51).
1553	Death of Edward IV (6 July) and accession of Mary (19 July).	Charter for Christ's Hospital (18 May).
1554	Court of Augmentations merged into Exchequer	Amyce's survey clears the way for a municipal charter.
1556		Charter issued (24 Nov).
1558	Mary dies; Elizabeth succeeds (17 Nov).	Mason issues ordinances for the Hospital. (12 June).
1559	Earl of Leicester becomes Constable of Windsor Castle and *de facto* Lord Lieutenant of Berks.	
1563		John Roysse refounds Abingdon School.
1564		Death of Mason; Earl of Leicester becomes High Steward but without a fee.
1571		Bloody affray in Abingdon between adherents of Norris and Unton families (2 Oct)
1581		Leicester granted a stipend as High Steward
1585-6		Squabbles in Hospital between cousins Lionell and Anthony Bostock lead to persistent factions.
1588	Death of Leicester.	Uncertain whether Sir Henry Norris succeeds Leicester as High Steward.

Time line (cont)

1597-8		More trouble in Hospital leads Francis Little to bring in Lord Keeper Egerton, who rules for the Little faction and against the Tesdales.
1601		Death of Sir Henry Norris. Sir William Knollys, later Earl of Banbury, is already or later becomes High Steward.
1603	Death of Elizabeth, accession of James I (24 March).	
1604		Sir Richard Lovelace, later Lord Lovelace, MP for Abingdon.
1610		Two charter updates (16 Feb, 3 March). Walter Dayrell becomes recorder.
1620		Another charter, to help the corporation finance street paving (21 June).
1624		Edward Roode becomes vicar at St Helens.
1625	Death of James I; accession of Charles I (27 March)	
1627	William Laud becomes Bishop of London and member of the Privy Council.	
1628		Death of Dayrell leads to factional conflict over a successor and appeals to the Privy Council. John Stonehouse is MP.
1629	Charles dissolves parliament; start of the 'eleven years of tyranny'.	Roode deprived, and replaced by Chistopher Newstead.
1630		Banbury resigns as High Steward; replaced by his kinsman, the Earl of Holland.
1632		Bulstrode Whitelocke becomes recorder, apparently acceptable to both parties.
1633	Laud becomes Archbishop of Canterbury (Sept).	Sir George Stonehouse becomes son-in-law of Lord Lovelace.

Time line (cont)

1634		William Lenthall acquires Appleton and Besselsleigh.
1639	First Bishops' War against Scots	
1640	Second Bishops' War; disorders in London and throughout the country. Short Parliament (April) and opening of Long Parliament (Nov). North-east under Scottish military occupation.	Stonehouse defeats Whitelocke in Spring parliamentary election; unopposed in Autumn. Army recruitment is resented; county opposition to government centred west of Abingdon where Marten interest is strong. Roode returns as vicar, ousting Newstead.
1641	Parliament begins dismantling royal prerogative; Strafford executed, Laud to Tower; peace treaty with Scots (August). Irish rebellion.	John Richardson's poem (after Sept).
1642	War; Oxford becomes Royalist capital (Nov).	Mayor Franklyn humiliated by Parliament for posting a royal proclamation (Sept). Abingdon a Royalist garrison (Nov). Roode leaves Abingdon.
1643		Typhus epidemic.
1644	Royalist anti-parliament meets at Oxford (Jan). Stonehouse (probably) participates, and is dismissed from Westminster parliament. Laud executed.	Parliamentarians take Abingdon (26 May). Demolish market cross. Richard Browne is garrison commander. John Pendarves becomes vicar of St Helen's.
1646	King leaves Oxford and becomes prisoner of Scots (April-May). Fall of Oxford (13 July) marks effective end of First Civil War.	Surrender of Wallingford (27 July) ends fighting in Thames Valley. Parliament approves charity collections in favour of impoverished Abingdon (18 June). William Ball, a protégé of Henry Marten, becomes MP.
1647	Widespread army mutinies and confrontations with parliament. Rise of Cromwell as a major political figure.	Garrison disbanded (Jan). Mutinous troopers of Rainsborough's regiment re-occupy the town (June).
1648	Second Civil War. Army coup (6 Dec) clears way to king's execution.	

Time line (cont)

1649	King executed (30 Jan). Institution of a republican regime with unicameral parliament; Henry Marten works closely with Cromwell.	Earl of Holland executed (9 March) but not replaced as High Steward. Henry Neville, another Marten associate, is MP (Sept).
1650		Purged corporation purchases fee-farm rent (11 June). Pendarves becomes a Baptist. John Tickell replaces him as vicar of St Helen's.
1651	Third Civil War ends at Worcester (3 Sept).	
1653	Cromwell's coup d'état (20 April); he becomes Lord Protector (16 Dec) after failure of 'Barebones Parliament'.	
1654	First Protectorate Parliament (opens Sept).	Thomas Holt is MP.
1655	Institution of Major-Generals as local agents of government.	St Nicholas under attack for its religious conservatism. Defended by John Lenthall among others. William Goffe is M-G for Berkshire.
1656	Second Protectorate Parliament (opens Sept).	Death of Pendarves; major disorders at his funeral (Sept-Oct). Thomas Holt re-elected but is excluded from parliament as disaffected.
1658	Death of Cromwell (3 Sept); Richard Cromwell becomes Protector.	Agreement to save St Nicholas from demolition.
1659	Richard's Parliament (Jan- April). Richard resigns (25 May). Regime begins to disintegrate.	John Lenthall becomes MP, but with return of pre-1653 parliament Neville re-takes seat (7 May).
1660	The Restoration: Charles II enters London (29 May). Duke of York marries Anne Hyde (3 Sept). Her father Edward Hyde becomes Earl of Clarendon (April 1661).	Lenthall sent to Convention parliament (25 April), but dismissed (23 May) in favour of Stonehouse. Lord Lovelace becomes Lord Lieutenant of Berks (28 Aug). Corporation begins to purge itself.

Time line (cont)

1661	Venner's rising (6 Jan). Cavalier Parliament opens (May). Corporation Act (Dec).	Abingdon Baptist meeting raided after Venner's rising (13 Jan). Stonehouse MP. Clarendon becomes High Steward (31 July).
1662	Act of Uniformity becomes effective (24 Aug).	Mayor Franklyn takes action against Dissenters.
1663	Campaign for renewal of town charters at its height. Sheldon Archbishop.	Lovelace's commission purges Abingdon Corporation. New municipal charter, giving Crown additional rights (3 Dec 1663).
1664	First Conventicles Act (May).	A 'Commission of Association' makes Stonehouse and four other Berks gentry JPs in Abingdon. (Aug).
1667	Seth Ward Bishop of Salisbury. Fall and exile of Clarendon.	
1670	Second Conventicles Act.	
1672	King issues Declaration of Indulgence (15 March).	Presbyterians and Baptists register for Indulgence.
1673	Indulgence withdrawn: First Test Act (effective 1 Aug). Thomas Osborne becomes Lord Treasurer.	
1674	Osborne, now Lord Danby, makes Lord Norreys Lord Lieutenant of Oxon.	Death in exile of Clarendon (9 Dec).
1675		Death of Sir George Stonehouse; his son John replaces him as MP (19 April). Clarendon's son, the second earl, replaces him as High Steward (20 April). Thomas Medlicott replaces Holt as Recorder (July-August).
1678	'Popish Plot' hysteria; start of Exclusion Crisis.	
1679	Cavalier Parliament dissolved (24 Jan). First Exclusion Parliament (March-May).	Stonehouse returned for both Exclusion Parliaments, but count disputed for the second.
1680	Second Exclusion Parliament first meets Oct 1680 and dissolved Jan 1681.	

Time line (cont)

1681	Third Exclusion Parliament meets at Oxford, 21 March; dissolved 28 March. Start of the 'Tory reaction'. Lord Norreys wins credit for successful outcome of the Colledge trial (Aug). Start of a new campaign to remodel municipal charters.	Stonehouse MP. Lord Norreys begins to work on Abingdon Corporation, with George Winchurst as his tool.
1682	Norreys and Jenkins organise a quo warranto against Oxford, which it decides to oppose. Norreys becomes Earl of Abingdon (Nov).	Winchurst in correspondence with Secretary of State Leoline Jenkins. Whig midsummer parade in Abingdon. Municipal celebrations when Norreys chooses Abingdon as his title.
1683	Oxford gives up opposition to quo warranto (Aug).	Disputed mayoral election; Winchurst defeated and complains to Jenkins.
1684		Quo warranto against Abingdon (June).
1685	Death of Charles II and accession of James II (6 Feb). New Parliament (May). Monmouth rebellion (June)	Surrender of municipal charter (9 Nov). Stonehouse MP.
1686	King uses dispensing power in favour of Dissenters.	New charter (9 March) brought in by Stonehouse. Nine outsiders, of whom three from Oxon, to be JPs for life. Dissenters acquitted at the Assizes (July) after Medlicott procures royal dispensations.
1687	James's first Declaration of Indulgence (4 April). 'Regulation' of Corporations.	King purges Corporation and names replacements (Dec).
1688	Widespread dismissals in favour of Catholics. King seeks support in abolition of Test Acts. But under threat of William's invasion, all changes to municipal charters since 1679 are revoked (17 Oct). James flees (11 Dec), William takes over.	William, Prince of Orange, stops briefly in Abingdon on his way from Exeter to London (11/12 Dec).
1689	Convention Parliament accepts William as William III (13 Feb).	Medlicott represents Abingdon at the Convention, over the protests of Stonehouse who would eventually prevail.

Preface

Of making many books there is no end.

Ecclesiastes 12:12

Abingdon has been remarkably well served by its local historians. From the early effort of Francis Little in the seventeenth century to the contributions of a half-dozen or more talented researchers in the twentieth, the work that has been reported would do credit to a town of much greater size.

Why then another book?

There are a number of reasons. One is that the practice of history moves on, and much of what exists may seem today to be outmoded. Local history started as antiquarianism, and only in the last few decades has it left behind the recording of genealogies and individual events as important in themselves rather than as indicators of deeper processes; has it learnt to put concerns at the parish pump into a wider context; has it accepted that a major part of its role is providing the footnotes for higher order histories of the nation, or of the continent, or the world. What I have tried to do here is to use the history of a single locality, Abingdon, as a kind of microscope, hoping to see sharply, albeit only in part, what a study of small towns in general would leave diffuse.

Secondly, there is at the basis of this book, as at that of my earlier work on Reading, a question that many years ago as a teenager I put to my elders.[1] It was why our local councillors, when they stand for election, do so wearing the colours of one or other of the national political parties. Surely, I innocently suggested, local and national concerns could not be linked in such a simple parallelism? That the opening hours of the local swimming pool should be governed by the state of the parties at Westminster seemed to me to smack more of astrology, 'as above, so below', than of rational government. I forget what answer I was given, but I am still looking for one that will satisfy me, and this book is a part of the search. What it deals with is the process over two or three generations by which local politics ceases to be locally based and becomes simply an outgrowth of national movements. What my microscope is focussed on is a small part of the field that some historians term state formation: the centralisation of power that had previously been dispersed; bureaucratisation; the alignment of status with function, and the identification of function with office.

In the introduction to my earlier work on Reading, I tried to pre-empt criticism by pointing out the rule of thumb that declares that the number and quality of sources for urban history increases more than proportionately with the size of the town. In the period covered by this book, Abingdon was barely a third the size of Reading, and the rule holds very well. There are corporation minutes, but they are concerned mainly with the management of corporation property, of which there was a good deal. Many events of the greatest importance are either not mentioned or referred to in coded language that can be understood only by those in the know. It may be assumed that the most significant business was transacted in closed groups, often no doubt by the mayor and the two bailiffs for the time being, in private. The minutes rarely list who was present at a given meeting, and it is not always clear who was on the corporation at a given time. There are lists of men admitted to the freemanship, but they are scrappy and certainly incomplete.

Thus in order to understand the political history of the town it is necessary to supplement local sources with more general ones. In this, I have had the great advantage over my predecessors of electronic finding aids and digital availability of sources that were unthinkable even a dozen years ago, and will no doubt seem primitive a dozen years in the future. I was confident in undertaking this work that I would be able to establish a good number of facts and connections unknown previously, and this has proved to be the case. Nonetheless, it is necessary to insist that I also came upon facts that needed nothing more than the old-established calendars and indexes to bring to light. No one, for example, seems to have noticed that Abingdon got a new municipal charter in 1663, nor that it was forced to relinquish it by a writ of quo warranto in 1684. That such significant matters did not already figure in the published literature of Abingdon history must be put down, not to the lack of application of my predecessors, but to the different angle from which they were approaching the subject.

I have made much use of existing secondary material, as will be plain from the footnotes to the text. Most useful has been the enormous archive left behind by A.E. Preston, who died in 1942. This is now deteriorating in the Berkshire Record Office as his notes in soft pencil become illegible, and his bundles of unmatched sheets of paper, once held together by pins which have been removed for reasons of safety, become separated. It is a matter of the greatest regret that Preston left all but a little of this material in its raw state, and never produced the authoritative multi-volume work on Abingdon and North Berkshire history for which it would have more than sufficed. Some of his predecessors similarly laboured for little eventual gain – John Richards, whose notes and transcripts from the nineteenth century are in the British

Library, and the Reverend Stephenson in the eighteenth, whose collection is in the Bodleian.

Of the many individuals who have made this work possible, the foremost has undoubtedly been Mrs Jackie Smith, honorary archivist both to the Abingdon town council and to Christ's Hospital. Her unrivalled knowledge of the Abingdon records has been put unselfishly at my service, and she has shown a near-miraculous knack of finding exactly what I wanted at just the moment when I first knew I wanted it. Thanks are due also to Dr Felicity Heal and the Oxford University history faculty for the academic visitor status that gave me access to the Bodleian Library, its manuscripts, and its digital facilities. As also to Mr Chris Nutman and the Master and Governors of Christ's Hospital for access to the Hospital's archives. I have nothing but good to say of the staffs at other libraries and archives I have used – mainly the National Archives, the British Library, and the Berkshire Record Office, but occasionally also Oxfordshire Studies (Oxstud) at the Westgate in Oxford, the libraries at Harris-Manchester and Regents Park Colleges, the Oxfordshire Record Office, and at Lambeth Palace, Friends' House, and Dr Williams' Library in London. Drafts of the book have very kindly been read by Dr Christine Jackson as a working historian and by my wife Jessica as an interested amateur. I am grateful to both for their helpful comments, which have led to significant improvement, but retain responsibility for all faults that remain.

The book consists of two parts. The first and larger is an attempt at a narrative history of the politics of Abingdon from the Chantries Act of December 1547 to the Revolution of 1688-9. Throughout, I have tried to put events into their context. With the passage of time, themes develop and pass by. I point out, for example, that Abingdon was only one of many towns granted chartered status in the confused period between the dissolution of the monasteries and the accession of Elizabeth, and that this had as much to do with the needs of the crown as with those of the borough. Abingdon was never, of course, a democracy, and I discuss the closing down of entry to the corporation at the end of the sixteenth century, which turned it deliberately into an oligarchy. Such a development does not fit well with twenty-first century notions of constitutional propriety, and I have tried to explain that it had an intellectual basis which was not totally reprehensible. About the same time, factions were forming within the town's élite, and we see these as based both on family connections and on ideological preferences. The conservative faction, led by Francis Little and the extensive Mayott clan, tended to be connected with the smaller of the two local churches, that of St Nicholas, and dominated the charity of Christ's Hospital, while the more radically Protestant group successfully infiltrated the main church of St Helen's. The civil war was traumatic and destructive to the town, and its aftermath saw attempts to set up a Puritan hegemony that never quite succeeded. In the restoration period, the gentry of the surrounding rural areas took charge, while in the 1680s it was the new-made Earl of Abingdon who bullied and manipulated the corporation into giving up its charter and the rights that had gone with it. By the time of the 'revolution' of 1688, Abingdon's local politicians had lost the degree of independence that had lent interest to their previous activities.

A subsidiary aim of this account has been to record the contribution to Abingdon history of particular individuals, and I have tried to establish their motivations from their actions, their associates, and, where possible, their writings. Unfortunately, the vagueness of the local records means that policies and people can often not be connected, and the absence of much by way of private letters is a limitation. Few of the characters of this narrative will appear as more than two-dimensional, in spite of my best attempts at empathy. Nonetheless, I have been able to include special studies of, among others, Francis Little and John Pendarves, both emblematic of different and, indeed, opposing strands of local tradition. Unlike most of my predecessors, I have assigned continuing importance to the interaction (or lack of it) between Abingdon and the nobility and gentry of its hinterland, and devoted considerable space to this topic.

The second part of the book arose almost by accident. It had been my intention to provide a sort of index of persons, with brief comments, for the benefit of readers overwhelmed by being introduced to too many new acquaintances in a brief period of time. This developed almost in my despite into a mini-dictionary of local biography, with articles of, typically, some 500 words on individuals and families. These articles come from my own pre-existing notes or from previous publications. Their relative length reflects the information available rather than the importance of the person described, and I have tried not to duplicate what is already given in the main text. The principal sources for the information are given, but detailed references, in general, are not. I hope this section will prove of value independently of the main narrative.

---

[1] Manfred Brod, *The Case of Reading: urban governance in troubled times 1640-1690* (Abingdon, 2006).

Part One

1. The Commonwealthmen

> I praie youe, tell vs youre mynde what should be the occasion of this decaye of the good townes of this Realme, and of all the bridges, highe waies, and hospitalles; and how the same may be remedied and releved againe?
>
> Sir Thomas Smith, *The Common Weale of this Realme of England* (1549), p. 125

Abingdon owes the political structure that in some respects it has even to this day, with local administration divided between a town council and the charitable institution of Christ's Hospital, to two charters granted respectively in 1553 and 1556. How and why did these charters come to be granted, and who was responsible for them?

Existing accounts tend to describe the grants as isolated events, needing little context or discussion.[1] In fact, there was an upsurge in such grants at the time, and Abingdon was only one of a number of towns to benefit; on the other hand, there were numerous other urban settlements that were not incorporated until later, if at all. Abingdon's problems, like those of other towns, stemmed from contemporary national political movements; and the manner of their resolution depended on the resources available to the townsmen. Of these resources, the most important was the relationship they had with men of higher status than themselves, members of a small and tightly-knit administrative and governmental élite. Only such people could influence the central authorities on Abingdon's behalf. It will be part of the argument of this chapter that Abingdon was fortunate in the patronage it was able to attract at that time, and that the results were to its lasting benefit.

Henry VIII died in January 1547. His reign had been momentous, but towards the end both tyrannical and ineffectual.[2] The succession was adroitly managed. The new ruler, under the title of Lord Protector, would be the Duke of Somerset, uncle to the infant Edward VI. He was supposed to rule in collaboration with a powerful council, an arrangement that would prove difficult and lead eventually to his overthrow. The new government would have much to do. The social and economic situation was serious. The two defining features of the century would be monetary inflation and population increase, and both were well under way. The first was visible enough, distorting and depressing trade, and rendering the maintenance of public institutions and infrastructure unaffordable. The second showed itself in vagabondage, in masterless men and sturdy beggars, a perceived threat to the respectable of which the true cause was unsuspected and incomprehensible. And, as was usual for new regimes, this one needed to prove its credentials by pursuing the war that was already in progress against Scotland. Like all governments then or later, its most urgent need was for money.

The fashionable intellectual movement of the day was that of humanism, which had come into England about the turn of the century with the great publicist Erasmus of Rotterdam. Its bases were the writings of the Roman republicans; its principles were demystification and rationalism. In religion, these led to the Protestant reformation, depriving the creed of its traditions and ceremonial, and declaring that if it wasn't in the Bible, it wasn't Christian. In politics, the equivalent was the idea of the Commonwealth, an English rendering of the Latin res publica, suggesting that part of the rationale for government was the benefit of the governed.[3] This was not in itself new, but it now came with a platonic insistence that government was the business of a suitably educated élite, not one in which the participation of ordinary people should be encouraged.[4] The Privy Council became in 1540 a formally constituted body, its membership reflecting proven administrative ability rather than landed wealth and military power.[5] The new regime of the Duke of Somerset loudly proclaimed its commitment to enlightened humanist principles. This was largely an attempt to distance itself from its predecessor, but was not altogether false. In the wave of protests and revolts that shook the country in 1549, Somerset was seen as reluctant to shed blood. While this raised his reputation among the common people, it was regarded as weakness by others, and was one of the reasons for his later overthrow.[6]

That the late 1540s was a time of social and economic stress was impossible to ignore. It was a common perception that towns were especially hard hit. Food prices were rising even when harvests were good. Business was contracting as tradesmen could no longer pay a living wage to their journeymen. Maintenance of infrastructure and of such social services as existed was becoming impossible. There was an ingress of vagabonds who had no resource but to beg. Intellectuals attempted to diagnose the trouble. Foremost among them was a prominent Cambridge academic turned public servant, Sir Thomas Smith, secretary of state under the Duke of Somerset and especially well informed. In a brilliantly argued essay of 1549, he analysed the problems with a degree of sophistication remarkable for the period.[7] He concluded, no doubt correctly, that the main cause of inflation lay in the government's continuing debasement of the coinage.[8] This view put his career at risk; it was unacceptable to the regime he served, which preferred to assign the blame to human greed and ran an intense campaign against 'covetousness', a new propaganda term easily applicable to any group trying to defend its economic interests.[9] Behind the scenes, however, such economic thinking spread rapidly. Two members of Smith's circle were William Cecil, future minister to Elizabeth I, and Sir John Mason, an Abingdon man who had risen high in the government's service. In a private letter to Cecil in 1550, Mason attacked the government's current economic strategy based on stringent price controls; he predicted that if it worked at all it could result only in dearth. He would, of course, be proved correct.[10]

The new government's war-chest should have been well-furnished, but was not. The dissolution of the monasteries had brought to the crown an enormous windfall of landed property. These lands were rapidly being sold off, but there were limits to the rate at which even the most active land market could absorb them. The rulers looked for new sources of wealth, and found them in the multitude of associations that a vibrant civil society had thrown up. They had already determined on a forward strategy of religious reformation, abandoning the hesitations of Henry's latter years, and many of the institutions in their sights were devoted to prayer for the souls of the defunct, an observance now labelled superstitious. Even those of a primarily secular purpose, maintaining bridges or dykes, or succouring the poor, would invariably have a chaplain or two and be dedicated to some saint or relic. All were to be dissolved, and their assets fall to the government. There had already been an attempt to do this in 1545, but it had hung fire.[11] New legislation was prepared to be rushed through parliament, with a target date for completion before Christmas 1547.[12]

The passage proved difficult. Everyone, it seemed, had a favourite institution and a good reason why it should be protected. The colleges of Oxford and Cambridge, with their well-placed graduates, were easily enough saved. The livery companies of London were untouchable. Towns represented in parliament used delaying tactics in favour of their local interests. A bargain was struck with the members for Coventry and King's Lynn; if they gave up their opposition and let the bill pass, the properties they were interested in would be restored to them afterwards. They agreed, and the bill passed into law on 24 December 1547. The government duly observed its side of the arrangement, which may be an indication of its insecurity.[13] Corporate identity and parliamentary representation did not necessarily go hand in hand, but Abingdon at the time had neither. Thomas Denton, whose local interests were extensive, sat as a knight of the shire for Berkshire, but will not have been sympathetic. He had already begun to involve himself in surveying the properties to be taken over.[14] Abingdon's guilds and brotherhoods, including the Fraternity of the Holy Cross which was responsible among other things for the upkeep of the bridges and highway towards Dorchester and for a certain number of impotent poor, would not be exempt.

The uncertainties that were now perceived to beset civil society led to an increase in the demand for charters of incorporation. At the very least, a charter would enable a town to manage its own economy and to make some attempt to keep out poor immigrants who would undercut local tradesmen. There were twenty-one new incorporations of boroughs from the advent of the Tudors in 1485 to the end of Henry's reign in 1547, but thirty-six from then until the death of Mary eleven years later.[15] These do not include the many old charters that were reconfirmed or updated. No one seems yet to have counted the charitable and educational incorporations, but the number may have been even greater. Abingdon's charters were among those that date from this period.

The initial impetus for the charters must have come from the leading Abingdon townsmen, but of these we know little beyond their names and some family relationships, and of their individual actions almost nothing. The same family names, often the same individuals, were prominent both before and after incorporation; Richard Mayott, among the last masters of the Holy Cross fraternity, would be the first mayor of the Borough of Abingdon, and the Mayotts, already leading townsmen in the fifteenth century, would still hold that position at the end of the seventeenth. Such people might be substantial and well-educated, but by themselves could have no access to the channels of authority by which alone a royal charter could be delivered. For this, they would need the help of a patron already well established in the governmental apparatus.

Ws know much less than we would like about Abingdon's emergence as a chartered town. All in all, there are no more than half a dozen contemporary documents of relevance; but they do make it plain that there were two men who were prime actors in the setting up of the Hospital. These were Sir John Mason and Roger Amyce. Most of the surviving papers had, in fact, been drawn up by Amyce. For the incorporation of the borough, which came later, we have absolutely no information, apart from Amyce's survey of 1554 which was plainly preparatory to it. It is probably safe to assume that Mason was also involved in this in spite of having earlier opposed it, but it must be emphasized that there is no written evidence. By the same argument, it may be inferred that certain other individuals had a hand in the process even if the exact part they played must remain a matter for speculation. This account will attempt to set out what little we know, and perforce eke it out with some educated guesswork.

Who were Mason and Amyce, who were their friends, and what drove them?

Amyce had emerged from a great nursery of enlightened administration, the service of Henry's minister, Thomas Cromwell. Since in his career he produced numerous 'surveys', and is often referred to as a surveyor, he has sometimes been seen as a subordinate figure. This is anachronistic and incorrect. The days of a surveyor as a technician with rods and chains were still to come. Amyce certainly understood lands and buildings, but at that time the term denoted an essentially financial administrator of landed property. The General Surveyors, later the Court of Surveyors, looked after the king's settled estates and was separate from the Court of Augmentations, set up more recently by Cromwell to deal with those of the dissolved monasteries. Before taking up responsibilities that included Abingdon and while still in his mid-twenties, Amyce had acted as Cromwell's receiver for the abbeys of Glastonbury and Reading.[16] This was no sinecure, since in both, unlike Abingdon, the dissolution had taken place over the dead bodies of the abbots. It was because of the irregular nature of these dissolutions that Amyce at this time was working within the General Surveyors and not in Augmentations. He also served several times in parliament, and was given various miscellaneous functions as a trusted middle-ranking official under Protector Somerset.[17]

Behind Amyce and at an altogether higher social and political level was Sir John Mason. In spite of a social origin which was more than dubious – the identity of his father remains a mystery – Mason had worked his way by a combination of intellectual ability and personal affability to almost the highest reaches of the administration. A good linguist and negotiator, he was often abroad on diplomatic missions, and proved no less capable in financial matters.[18] His elevated position in the central government made him a gatekeeper and facilitator for Amyce's efforts.

There was a third man, not too hard to identify. Thomas Denton was wealthy and well-connected, a rising lawyer who had been at court, sat regularly in parliament, and who had married into the Fettiplace family of Appleton.[19] His interests were wide-ranging, but he does seem to have been trying to develop his regional influence. His involvement with Abingdon was twofold. His crown appointment as under-steward of the dissolved abbey meant that he was responsible for the local courts and, ultimately, for law and order; and, coming from a family of substantial landowners, he was engaged in building up a property portfolio of his own, much of it from the former abbey estates. A significant proportion of his purchases was in the town of Abingdon, where by 1554 he owned some forty properties, about one tenth of the total stock. Some of these he had apparently acquired as agent for the current tenants to whom they were eventually sold on, while others show a pronounced preference for unbuilt sites that could be developed.[20] He must have been working in close collaboration with Roger Amyce, and it is unfortunate that there is no evidence on whether their relationship was harmonious or otherwise. If only to safeguard his own interests, he can not have stood aside from any negotiations concerning the town's future.

What is important to note about Mason, Amyce, and Denton, was that all of them were within the new intellectual culture of humanism and involved in social networks that were imbued with humanist principles. All of them had worked for Cromwell at some time and in some capacity. For Mason, his first patron as an adult had been Thomas More, from whose fall he must have drawn useful lessons. He had exchanged letters with Thomas Starkey, one of the earliest of the great humanist political writers, although this correspondence might have had more to do with diplomacy than philosophy; and he had married one of his stepdaughters to another of the great humanists of his day, John Cheke, academic and tutor to the young Edward VI. When Amyce came to write his will in 1573, one of his two overseers was Edward Fettiplace, a stepson of Thomas Denton, and the other was 'my well beloved and trusty friend, the right honourable Sir Thomas Smith, knight, Principal Secretary to our Sovereign Lady, the Queen's Majesty'.[21] This was the commonwealth writer already mentioned, another leading humanist and one who, it will be argued, is likely to have influenced Amyce and Mason in their work for Abingdon. Smith and Mason worked closely together in their governmental functions and on at least one diplomatic mission. It is no doubt significant that Mason, Cheke, and Smith have all been identified as members of the circle of William Cecil, Elizabeth's future minister.[22] Denton is not so listed, but had been associated with the future lord keeper Nicholas Bacon in a report of 1540, sponsored by the king himself, on the training of lawyers.[23] Bacon was Cecil's brother-in-law.

The dissolution of the Abbey of St Mary in 1538 may have left something of a void, but it was not a catastrophe. The abbot's authority was not immediately extinguished; it was now exercised by John Wellesborne, who had been sent in by Thomas Cromwell to oversee the dissolution and who survived his patron's fall.[24] Thomas Denton, as under-steward, ran the quarter sessions; Thomas Meadowe, the bailiff, continued to collect rents, although they now went to the king's chamber and not to the abbot.[25] There may well have been some satisfaction among townsmen, for it had long been the ambition of many unchartered communities to exchange their local masters for a more distant royal one.[26] But the situation was unstable. Wellesborne would die in 1548.[27] It can only have been Denton who continued to represent the royal authority that had taken the abbot's place.

In principle, Abingdon had been a seigniorial borough under the abbot's lordship, and a long history of conflict shows that successive abbots were understandably reluctant to give up any part of their authority. Nonetheless, the fact that there was conflict indicates that the townspeople were well able to organise themselves. As far back as the 12th year of Richard II (1388-9), there were proctors responsible for the rood in St Helen's church, and when in 1397 the same monarch sent his agents round the country to raise loans from his reluctant subjects they assessed the probi homines of Abingdon at 100 marks, exactly the same as the abbot.[28] Proctors and probi homines are terms that describe an élite class, bearing authority.[29] Later town rent-rolls show that a proportion of local properties were held by burgage tenure, paying only a quit-rent, so that the abbey might have retained formal ownership but not the control that normally went with it.[30] In a memorandum to the drafters of the 1556 charter, Roger Amyce stated that the town had, 'time out of mind', had its own annual lawday, distinct from that of the Hormer Hundred, in a specially erected house in the middle of the market place, and two constables who 'had th'order rule and government of the said towne'. The house in the market place can only have been the abbey's court-house. Inhabitants 'keep watch and ward within the town, pay scot and lot, and bear and execute all manner of offices when they be thereunto elected and chosen'.[31] Thus, even before the dissolution of 1538, the townsmen were running their own affairs to a significant extent, with at least the acquiescence and probably the active encouragement of the abbey. This indicates an organisational structure of some kind, which is most probably to be found in the town guilds.

It seems to have been common for townsfolk in seigniorial boroughs to use their guilds as proto-corporations.[32] Guilds were the typical associations of medieval and early modern civil society. They could act judicially, settling local disputes by way of mediation or arbitration which would be binding on their members, and, since they could handle money, could organise charitable and infrastructure collections and disbursements. If chartered, they could hold funds in their own name; otherwise they would have to act less directly through feoffees. The Fraternity of the Holy Cross in Abingdon was well established by the sixteenth century; its two most recent charter renewals dated from 1441 and 1483 respectively, and the latter document had been reconfirmed as recently as 1509, at the accession of Henry VIII.[33] There is no direct evidence that it extended its administrative activities beyond its formal brief of maintaining the highways and bridges and caring for certain almspeople, but it would have been surprising if it did not.

The dissolution of the guilds and chantries and the appropriation of their properties had been widely expected, and administrative preparations were made. A major reorganisation took place on 1 January 1547, a few weeks, as it happened, before the king's death. The Court of Surveyors was merged into Augmentations, which would in future be responsible for all crown properties however acquired. Roger Amyce was compensated for the loss of his function, but was immediately taken on again by the new organisation.[34] This would no longer work by allocating the estates of specific monasteries to individual functionaries irrespective of where they lay, but on a county by county basis, with Amyce as surveyor for Berkshire. The guilds, of course, were much greater in number although individually smaller than the monasteries, and would be hard to fit into the old system.

When it finally came at the end of 1547, the act was a classical case of dissonance between the spin that its purpose was purely religious and the reality that the government wanted money. It stated that only such properties and funds were to be taken over as were used for 'superstitious' purposes, meaning the maintenance of priests and the rites of the old religion, and that these were to be applied to charities, to the funding of universities, and to the erection of grammar schools.[35] Needless to say, this is not what happened.[36] For each county or group of counties, there would be a commission 'to enquire into what colleges, chantries etc have come to the King by the Dissolution Act, and certify into Court of Augmentations'. It would be composed of gentry and magnates with local interests whose role would be mainly supervisory, but with a small number of full-time administrators who would do the actual work.[37] That for Berkshire brought together Sir John Mason, Amyce, and Denton.[38] Amyce would no doubt be the effective operator. In Abingdon, the Guild of Our Lady and the Holy Cross Fraternity ceased to exist, and their revenues went in their entirety to Amyce as receiver for the Court of Augmentations. But he will have had a fair degree of flexibility to meet existing commitments. It is not necessary to take too seriously a later statement that the poor ceased to be relieved and the bridges to be maintained.[39] A hiatus in poor relief would certainly have led to disorder, and Amyce is said to have approved bridge repairs in 1552, which might well have been justified as providing the poor with employment.[40] He seems to have taken a broad view of his local responsibilities, and it was no doubt under his urging that in 1551 the Court of Augmentations approved a subsidy to a skilled Breton who was teaching Abingdon tradesmen 'the weaving of poll davies and "olerounds"'.[41] This was exactly the sort of urban industrial development for which Thomas Smith had argued in his 'Commonweal'.[42]

But the important point was that Abingdon now had no formal framework for its government. At some time by early 1551 the townsfolk petitioned for a charter of incorporation. It would have seemed a natural thing to do. Smith's solution for the decay of towns was enhanced powers for municipal bodies to regulate trades, employment, prices, and above all the quality of manufactured goods. Such regulatory authority must be kept out of the hands of trade guilds whose sectional interests would be fatal to the common weale.[43] At the same time, the danger of social unrest was plainly greater in the towns than in the countryside, requiring firmly entrenched and well accepted local institutions.[44] Delay might be dangerous, since the abbey's local properties were steadily being sold off, and already in 1545 the Court of Augmentations had received a tentative offer for the whole of the town of Abingdon from Richard Andrews, a large-scale speculator in monastic estates.[45]

The scheme for a charter foundered. It is not certain who the townsmen used as intermediary, but Denton seems the only likely candidate. Amyce must have had some involvement but was probably of too low a status to have the necessary access. Denton had local knowledge, legal expertise, and the governmental contacts that will have come from his legal practice and court and parliamentary experience. Someone told Mason, who was abroad on government business. But the proposal did not meet with his approval. By now he was a member of the Privy Council in his own right, and at the end of one of his routine ambassadorial reports expressed a mildly-worded distaste and a strategic scepticism.

> I am advertised that the town of Abingdon sueth unto your Lordships for a corporation and for the farm also of the house and domain of the late Abbey whereof during my time I have the keeping and am steward of the town wherein I was also born. There is no one thing that more continueth a daily hurt to the realm than corporations neither was there ever any privilege of that nature sued for but for an ill intent. Nevertheless if your Lordships shall see such considerations as you shall think their request in this matter meet to be hearkened unto I beseech your

Lordships so to pass the thing as respect may be had to the continuation of my poor interest.[46]

This does not ring true. Patrick Tytler, who printed the letter in the nineteenth century, fastened on the threat to Mason's property rights as his motive. It is true he had now succeeded John Wellesborne as general steward of the abbey properties and had acquired a rent-free life tenancy of the abbey site, and the latter would be among the properties the proposed corporation would take over.[47] But nothing would have been easier than to protect these rights in the detail of the charter, as was actually done five years later by which time the abbey site had passed into the hands of the miller and entrepreneur from Swallowfield, William Blacknall. The criticism of corporations was disingenuous; it is true that they tended to arouse the suspicion of civil lawyers as damaging to the prerogatives of the prince, but this seems never to have been taken as a serious argument against their establishment.[48] In this case, the comment may best be seen as a personal one, hinting that the originators of the request may have had ulterior motives. It seems most likely that Mason, seasoned negotiator as he was, was putting down a marker. Abingdon was his birthplace, and he was, or claimed to be, its steward. Nothing should be done for Abingdon without his personal involvement. Nothing, therefore, was done. If indeed the petition had been motivated by the local ambitions of Thomas Denton, they had received a check; thereafter, he would turn his attentions elsewhere, and in 1554 it was Denton who obtained a municipal charter for the town of Banbury, becoming its first parliamentary burgess.[49] But if the problems of his native town had so far escaped Mason's attention, he had had a sharp reminder. He would now be obliged to justify his action by proving that he could get Abingdon a better deal than anyone else would have got for it.

Mason returned to England in September 1551 and would remain in the country until October 1553. He was now regularly attending the Privy Council, which was busy with the bringing down of the former protector, Somerset, and his replacement by the Duke of Northumberland. Somerset was arrested in October 1551, and the populist rhetoric of the years of his power meant that he still enjoyed much support among the common people. The position in Berkshire was critical; Somerset was a major property owner there, and was still lord lieutenant of the county, in command of such militia forces as it had.[50] In the disturbed summer of 1549, Berkshire gentry had been ordered 'to have trustworthy spies, especially in thoroughfares and market towns'.[51]

Mason seems still to have had such agents on his payroll. They warned him of possible unrest in Abingdon, and the expenditure of £5 gave him the names of the ringleaders. Thomas Denton and a number of other local legal gentlemen were named as a commission of oyer and terminer to look into the matter, and the Berkshire sheriff of the time, William Hyde, was ordered to transport the prisoners to London. Nothing more is known of their identities or their eventual fate.[52]

Once that emergency was over, Mason seems to have begun to work seriously on behalf of the town.[53] The timely transfer of his allegiance from Somerset to Northumberland meant that there were favours he could call in.[54] At a meeting on 1 March 1553, he got the Privy Council to agree that the Abingdon rents that had been intended for maintenance of the bridges and the local charities should never have been impounded 'upon coullor that the same were within the compasse of th'act of chauntries'. They were to be restored to the townsmen, and instructions to that effect were sent to the Court of Augmentations.[55] Letters patent issued on 18 May 1553 set up the charity of Christ's Hospital to take on the non-religious functions of the fraternity.[56]

The documents listing the main properties with which the charity was to be endowed and giving their values were complete by 4 May 1553, and delivered to Mason on 28 May. Mason and Amyce together, on behalf of the town, were given legal possession.[57] The endowment included most or all of the guild properties that had not yet been sold, as well as a few that had belonged to the abbey, with the right to acquire further properties and hold them in mortmain. As at 14 February 1548, soon after the Chantries Act, the Fraternity's annual outgoings had been assessed at £81 13s 10d p.a., including £6 6s 8d for each of the two chantry priests.[58] The necessary expenses for non-religious purposes were thus just over £69, or might be a few pounds less if all properties were tenanted.[59] The properties granted as endowment were valued at £65 11s 10d per year, and the decision of the Privy Council meant that they were given outright, free of encumbrances.[60] Immediate expenses recorded in the Christ's Hospital accounts and recognisably attributable to the grant total £27 14s 1d, most of which was borrowed from the future governors.[61] Mason had justified his earlier conduct by getting a more advantageous deal for the town than it could reasonably have hoped for.

Twelve men were named to run the Hospital; Mason was the first master and would retain the office for life, with a fee of £4 per annum. The second name listed was that of Roger Amyce, whose tenure was also indefinite. He would receive £2 per annum as auditor. The other men were governors; they were to be replaced by co-option, and after the death or departures of Mason and Amyce, masters would be chosen from among the governors and would serve for one year. Unlike the other governors, neither Mason nor Amyce would be bound to reside in Abingdon; Mason's home was in Hampshire and Amyce was an alderman and MP for New Windsor.[62] One of the early governors, Oliver Hyde, was later designated by Mason as his deputy. This was fitting, since Hyde was a member of an old-established Berkshire gentry family, and outranked any mere tradesman.[63] It was a simple and effective scheme, so far as it went.

In spite of the encomia of its later historians, Christ's Hospital was by no means a re-foundation of the old Fraternity. The Master and Governors were no more than a board of trustees, charged with the administration of a portfolio of properties and the allocation of the revenues to specified charitable purposes. Unless the Fraternity had been quite untypical of such institutions, it will have included in its membership the quasi-totality of the respectable tradesmen and merchants of the town and of their families.[64] Certainly, the refoundation of 1484 had specified that it would be for 'secular persons of either sex', and in 1509 it was collectively designated as 'the master, brethren *and sisters* of the Holy Cross in Abendon'.[65] Its officials will have been able to speak authoritatively for the town as a whole. There was still a need for such a body, and only a borough charter could provide one.

The charter of incorporation was not issued until 24 November 1556, and the main reason for the delay was probably that Mason was in Brussels as ambassador to Charles V for two years until the summer of that year.[66] If his earlier denunciation of corporations was sincere, and it probably wasn't, his opinion changed radically once he could be sure his personal interests and authority wouldn't suffer. It seems that Roger Amyce had once again been a key participant in the process, since his survey of 1554 listing all landed properties in the town became the basis for the properties to be granted to the new corporation.[67] Producing this survey had not been a straightforward process, involving many knotty problems of ownership and tenure that he had to settle.[68]

Town charters by this period were reasonably well standardised as to format; they contained all the legal niceties that were necessary in a logical order. But they differed greatly in substance, being individual documents tailored to local needs and produced by negotiation among the interested parties.[69] The preamble is always to be examined with care, for beneath its deliberate vagueness may be a clue to the underlying motivation. Abingdon's charter starts, after the usual formal recital of the king's and queen's various styles and titles,

> Whereas our Town of Abingdon, in our County of Berks, is an ancient and populous Town, and Inhabited by many poor people, and which Town is the Capital Town in our said County of Berks, and is in so great ruine and decay for want of repairing of the Houses and Buildings within the same, that it is very likely to come to extream calamity (as we are credibly informed) if remedy thereof be not by us provided.[70]

The remedy turns out to be granting the inhabitants' request for incorporation, although quite how this will result in the repair of buildings is not explained. In fact, the timing of the charter is significant and the length of its gestation period may have been due to more than Mason's absence and Amyce's local difficulties. There had been over several years a debate within government on the management of the crown lands, a debate of which both Mason and Amyce must have been aware, and in which they may have participated.[71] Essentially, it had been an inter-office argument in which Augmentations was accused of inefficiency and corruption in the repair and maintenance of the properties in its keeping. It was the Exchequer, under the elderly Marquess of Winchester, that won. The new policy was that the crown and its agencies should not be directly responsible for maintenance. Rural leases should be written so that tenants would keep the properties in repair; urban property should be handed over to the town authorities, who would hold it on behalf of the crown, paying an annual fee-farm rent which would in principle be equivalent to the rental income after maintenance costs. Abingdon's desire for incorporation dovetailed with the crown's wish to be rid of the burden of property repairs and to receive a fixed annual income from the surprisingly many properties of Abingdon Abbey that remained unsold. In his memorandum to the drafters of the charter, Amyce was still optimistic that he and Mason or Denton might retain responsibility for repairs that the townsfolk would finance:

> And finally be yt remembered that upon graunte of the premysses to be made to the Townesmen of Abingdon it be reserved that the Surveyor and Steward maye have place and authoritie to sit in their courtes specially at there lawe daye within there and there to peruse and oversee the reparacions of the king and quenes majesties tenements and houses within the same at thonly costs and charges of the said Towneshipp during theire abode there.[72]

But in 1554 the Court of Augmentations had been abolished, and Amyce was now employed by the Exchequer, which was interested only in hard cash. He would retain no such function.[73]

Abingdon's charter is unique in its time for the sheer volume of property which was to change hands.[74] It has been estimated that the Hospital and the Corporation between them would own some 250 separate properties, representing more than half the total by number, if not by value, in the town.[75] The annual fee-farm rent would be £102 16s 7d.[76]

The charter says emphatically that it is to be 'made and sealed without fine or fee, great or small, to us in our Hanaper or elsewhere', but documents of such a degree of complexity do not come cheap, and there must have been a whole regiment of lawyers and other functionaries about the court who will have been demanding their fees and gratifications; the new-made burgesses must have spent heavily to get their charter but it will no doubt have seemed a good investment.[77] In fact, although this was still barely understood by contemporaries, the century being one of inflation, the investment would prove very much better than they had calculated.

November 1556 was an important milestone in Abingdon's history. In the time of the abbey, however oppressive its rule, Abingdon townsfolk had known their place and had known to whom to appeal if they had a problem. After the dissolution, there was a steward and there were still the guilds. When these disappeared from the scene, the townsmen had entered, for all legal purposes, a state of collective nonentity, a mere agglomeration of individuals, with no one to speak for them and no certain entitlements. From this they had now emerged into the definite and understood status of a corporate town with its own mayor and bailiffs. Mason and Amyce, in their respective stations, had both shown themselves true benefactors. Even those of the townsfolk who did not stand to gain financially must have experienced a feeling of relief.

---

[1] James Townsend, *A History of Abingdon* (1910), pp. 107-11; Mieneke Cox, *Medieval Abingdon* (Abingdon, 1989), pp. 138-142; Mieneke Cox, *Peace and War* (Abingdon, 1993), pp. 1-7.

[2] Robert Hutchinson, *The last days of Henry VIII* (2005).

[3] S.T. Bindoff, *Tudor England* (1960), pp. 129-36; G.R. Elton, *England under the Tudors* (3rd edn, 1991), pp. 184-90; Diarmaid MacCulloch, *Tudor Church Militant: Edward VI and the Protestant Reformation* (1999), pp. 125-6.

[4] The classical exposition of late medieval town government is in Charles Pythian-Adams, *Desolation of a City: Coventry and the urban crisis of the late middle ages*

(1979), part 3. The paradigm shift brought on by humanist thinking is analysed by Ethan H. Shagan, 'The two republics: conflicting views of participatory local government in early Tudor England' in John F. McDiarmid (ed), *The Monarchical Republic of Early Modern England: Essays in response to Patrick Collinson* (2007).

[5] Penry Williams, *The Tudor Regime* (1979), pp. 423-5.

[6] Barett L. Beer, 'Seymour, Edward, duke of Somerset (c.1500-1552)' in *DNB*.

[7] (Sir T. Smith), *A Discourse of the Common Weal of This Realm of England* (1549, ed. E. Lamond, Cambridge, 1893). M. Dewar, 'The Authorship of the "Discourse of the Commonweal"', *The Economic History Review,* 19 (1966), pp. 388-400; Ian W. Archer, 'Smith, Sir Thomas (1513–1577)' in *DNB;* Neal Wood. 'Foundations of political economy: the new moral philosophy of Sir Thomas Smith' in Paul A. Fideler and T.F. Mayer (eds), *Political Thought and the Tudor Commonwealth* (1992), pp. 140-168.

[8] (Smith), *A Discourse of the Common Weal,* esp p. 16 .

[9] MacCulloch, *The Tudor Church Militant,* pp. 151-156.

[10] Patrick Fraser Tytler, *England under the reigns of Edward VI and Mary* (1839), I 339-42.

[11] Ethan H. Shagan, *Popular Politics in the English Reformation* (Cambridge, 2003), p. 244.

[12] A. Kreider, *English Chantries - the Road to Dissolution* (Harvard, 1979), Chap. 8.

[13] *APC* 1547-8, pp. 193-5 (6 May 1548).

[14] *L&P* 21 ii (1546-7) No 775 p. 451 (20 July 1546). His work must have been on a serious scale, since he was paid £40 by the Court of Augmentations for it.

[15] Robert Tittler, 'The emergence of urban policy, 1536-58' in Jennifer Loach and Robert Tittler (eds), *The Mid-Tudor Polity c 1540-1560* (1980), p. 93; Martin Weinbaum, *The Incorporation of Boroughs* (1937), pp. 132-38.

[16] *L&P* Vol 13 ii (1538) No 1184 p. 497 (undat); Vol 14 ii (1539) No 12 p. 3 (2 August), Nos 532 p. 186 (undat), 782 p. 328 (23 Dec); Vol 15 (1540) No 282/113 p. 116 (26 Feb); Vol 17 (1542) No 880 pp. 474-5 (1 May-30 Sept 1542); Vol 20 ii (1545) Appx No. 13 p. 555 (undat).

[17] *HoP 1509-58*, I, p. 319; *1558-1603*, I, pp. 342-3.

[18] *HoP 1558-1603*, I, pp. 29-31; P. R. N. Carter, 'Mason, Sir John (c.1503–1566)', *DNB*; D. Hurd, *Sir John Mason 1503-1566 Distinguished Son of Abingdon* (Abingdon, 1975).

[19] *HoP 1509-58*, II, pp. 30-31.

[20] Berks RO, draft letter Agnes Baker to A.L. Rowse (undated), D/EP7 94; Janey Cumber, personal communication.

[21] TNA, PROB 11/56. We cannot know when Amyce and Smith first became acquainted, but in 1549 Smith, in temporary disfavour, was resident at Eton College of which he was provost, and Amyce was probably already living in Windsor. By the 1560s, both were landowners in Essex.

[22] David Loades, *The Cecils: Privilege and power behind the throne* (2009), p. 41.

[23] Clare Rider and Celia Charlton, 'The 16th century Inns of Court in Context', www.innertemplelibrary.org.uk/news/conference.doc (n.d.)

[24] *L&P* 15 (1540) No 1032 pp. 539, 565 (17 Dec).

[25] BRO, D/EP7 94

[26] D. G. Shaw, *The Creation of a Community: The City of Wells in the Middle Ages* (1993), pp. 115-7; S. H. Rigby, *English Society in the Later Middle Ages: Class, Status and Gender* (1995), p. 165.

[27] A.E. Preston, *St Nicholas Abingdon and other essays* (1928), p. 295.

[28] C. D. Cobban (ed), *Francis Little: A Monument of Christian Munificence* (1871), p. 2; *CPR* 21 Richard II, i p.178 (20 Sept 1397).

[29] J. Tait, 'The Origin of Town Councils in England', *English Historical Review,* XLIV (1929), pp. 177-202.

[30] BRO, D/EP7 86. On the political significance of burgage tenure, see S.H. Rigby, *English Society in the Later Middle Ages* (1995), p. 160.

[31] BRO, D/EP7 141, final membrane. This document, wrongly identified by A.E. Preston as a separate survey of 1555, lists the properties that were to pass to the new borough in the order in which they would be mentioned in the charter. There is a modern transcript in the same file.

[32] W. Potts, *History of Banbury*, (2nd Edn, rev by E.T. Clark, 1978), pp. 29-37; B. R. McRee, 'Religious Gilds and Civil Order: The Case of Norwich in the Late Middle Ages', *Speculum,* 67 (1992), pp. 69-97; Shaw, *The Creation of a Community*, pp. 104-140.

[33] ? Griffith-Boscawen, *Endowed Charities (County of Berks) Report of the Charity Commissioners, Parishes of Abingdon St Helen and Abingdon St Nicholas* (July 1908), p. 83; BRO, Preston Papers, D/EP7/53; *CPR* 1476-1485, p. 386 (20 Feb 1484); *L&P* 1 i, p. 247 (10 August 1509).

[34] TNA, E 315/218, Minute Book of the Court of Augmentations, (4 August 1547), fo. 59.

[35] *SR*, 1 Edw VI, c.14. An abridgement is printed in J.R. Tanner, *Tudor Constitutional Documents 1485-1603* (2nd edn, 1930), pp. 103-7.

[36] Paul Slack, 'Social policy and the constraints of government, 1547-1548' in Jennifer Loach and Robert Tittler (eds), *The Mid-Tudor Polity c.1540-1560* (1980), at pp. 98-9; A. Kreider, *English Chantries – the Road to Dissolution* (Harvard, 1979), pp. 186-206.

[37] Williams, *The Tudor Regime*, p. 414; S.J. Gunn, *Early Tudor Government 1485-1558* (1995), p. 119.

[38] *CPR* Ed VI 2 vii p. 136 (14 Feb 1648). The nine-man commission was responsible for both Berkshire and Hampshire, and as far can be ascertained only Amyce and Denton were currently Berkshire residents.

[39] Cobban (ed), *Francis Little,* p. 41.

[40] BRO, Preston papers, D/EP7 94. Preston's reference for this information is 'PRO p. 129', which has proved impossible to locate.

[41] *CPR* Edw VI 3 v p. 310 (22 March 1550); see also *APC* II 1547-1550 p. 109 (20 July 1547). Poldavy: 'A coarse canvas or sacking, originally woven in Brittany and formerly much used for sailcloth' – *OED*.

[42] (Smith), *A Discourse*, pp. 126-9.

[43] (Smith), *A Discourse*, pp. 129-130. It is significant that one of the stated duties of the corporation of Barnstaple, like Abingdon chartered in 1556, was 'to make laws … for

the government and rule of the Artificers of the Borough...'

[44] Robert Tittler, 'The emergence of urban policy, 1536-58', in Jennifer Loach and Robert Tittler (eds), *The Mid-Tudor Polity c 1540-1560* (1980), esp. pp. 80-83.

[45] *Ninth Report of the Deputy-Keeper of the Public Records* (1847), Appx II, p. 154. A Richard Andrews or Androys, possibly the same man, had worked for Thomas Cromwell in the preparations for the abbey's dissolution – *L&P*, 8 (January-July 1535), No 689 p. 259 (8 May); 7 (1534), No 1205, p. 466 (29 Sept), Nos 1213 and 14 p. 471 (undat); 10 (January-June 1536), No. 378 p. 153 (undat).

[46] Tytler, *Edward VI and Mary,* pp. 361-2 (modernised spelling).

[47] TNA, E 315/220/178. The site had been granted to Lord Seymour of Sudeley, the protector's brother, but became free again at his attainder. According to A.E. Preston (D/EP7 82, fo. 66v) Mason had at some time exchanged another office for the 'chief stewardship' of the abbey lands paying £20 p.a. In his memorandum to the drafters of the charter (D/EP7 141), Amyce describes Mason as chief steward and being paid £5 p.a. which may be an estimate of the proportion of the fee which the townsmen should be expected to bear. This was crossed out on the document, presumably indicating that it was not to be allowed for in calculating the fee-farm rent.

[48] Kreider, *English Chantries*, pp. 203-4..

[49] *VCH Oxon,* Vol. 10, 'Banbury: Local government', pp. 71-89; J.S.W. Gibson and E.C. Brinkworth (eds), *Banbury Corporation Records: Tudor and Stuart* (Banbury, 1977), p. 5.

[50] John Strype, *Ecclesiastical memorials* (1822), II ii, p. 201; *APC* 1550-52, p. 258 (13 April 1551). As late as August 1551, he had led his forces into Wokingham to put down unrest there – *DNB* sub nom.

[51] *CSPD* Edw VI No 306 (24 July 1549).

[52] *APC* 1550-1552, p. 421 (21 Nov 1551); p. 423 (same day); p. 443 (13 Dec 51). A commission of 'oyer and terminer' was normally to 'hear and conclude' cases, or refer them upward to higher courts.

[53] *CPR,* Edw VI, 4 iv pp. 188-90 (28 Dec 1551); 5 ii pp. 18-19 (5 May 1553).

[54] D.E. Hoak, *The King's Council in the reign of Edward VI* (1976), p. 61.

[55] *APC* 1552-1554, pp. 226-7

[56] The name may have been chosen in emulation of Christ's Hospital in London, set up in 1552 for the benefit of foundling children, but where all outdoor relief for the poor was later centralised. It was currently fashionable for towns to set up hospitals - Tittler, 'The emergence of urban policy', pp. 74-93.

[57] TNA, Particulars for grants, E 318/31/1776. The document bears Amyce's signature and appears to have been prepared and written by him with data taken from the relevant chantry certificate which also seems to have been his work – TNA, E 301/3 no 9.

[58] Griffith-Boscawen, *Endowed Charities (County of Berks): Report of the Charity Commissioners,Parishes of Abingdon St Helen and Abingdon St Nicholas* (July 1908), p. 83.

[59] The accounting convention seems to have been that unpaid rents were regarded as an expense.

[60] According to a list made by A.E. Preston and Agnes Baker, the number of properties awarded to the new Hospital was sixty-one, while twelve Fraternity properties, seven

belonging to the dissolved Guild of Our Lady, and three that had been held by each of the Abingdon churches for obits, had been sold off earlier. However, the *Calendar of Patent Rolls* mentions twenty-four Fraternity and seven Guild properties as having been sold off to twelve distinct purchasers. Berks RO, Preston Papers, D/EP 7/47, (unfol); *CPR* Edw VI: 2 i pp. 192 (25 March 1549), iii pp. 301-2 (undat), iv pp. 333-4 (19 May 1549), v p. 382 (15 Jan 1550), vi pp.404 (1 April 1549) and 424 (8 April 49); 3 ix pp. 102 (21 July 1549), 4 vii p. 375 (15 May 1550); ix p. 4 (12 March 1550); 5 ii p. 30 (25 June 1553), v p. 104 (12 May 1553), ix p. 194 (3 Feb 1553). The count was made on the basis of parcels in individual tenure, even if these were of multiple tenements in different places. It is not possible from the Calendar to determine the value of the individual holdings.

[61] Based on an unpublished analysis by Janey Cumber, whom I thank for the information, Richard Mayott lent 40s, Thomas Jennens 20s, Oliver Hyde £5, and Thomas Tesdale £10.

[62] *HoP 1509-1558*, I, p. 319.

[63] A.E. Preston, *Christ's Hospital, Abingdon* (1929), p. 43. Oliver Hyde was either the son or the brother of the William Hyde who as county sheriff had cooperated with Mason in the arrests of 1551– *HoP 1558-1603*, II, pp. 364-5. He was noted also as a trustee of Our Lady's Chantry of Abingdon, also of course dissolved, and which had held about half as much property as that of the Holy Cross – TNA, E 301/3 no 9: Chantry Certificates.

[64] Preston, *Christ's Hospital,* pp. 11-26; G. Rosser, 'Solidarité et Changement Social: les fraternités urbaines anglaises à la fin du Moyen Age', *Annales ESC,* 48 (1993), pp. 1127-1144.

[65] *L&P* 1 i (1509-10) p. 247 (10 August 1509).

[66] Challenor, in his *Selections from the Borough Records* (1899), wrongly ascribes the charter to 1555. It is clearly dated the 3rd and 4th years of Phillip and Mary. Hurd seems to have been misled by this error into the view that Mason could have had nothing to do with the charter because of absence abroad; in fact he was briefly in England in March 1556 and permanently after the summer. It is inconceivable that the charter could have been granted if he had not, at the very least, withdrawn his earlier opposition – Hurd, *Sir John Mason,* p. 33.

[67] There are what appear to be contemporary copies of the survey in the archives of Christ's Hospital, Abingdon (with a transcript in BRO, D/EP7 82), in the National Archives (LR 2/187/196-215), and in the Cambridge University Library (Gg.iv.21). It is dated to 2-6 October 1554.

[68] Not least among Amyce's headaches was the aggressive stance taken by the miller William Blacknall against anyone claiming water rights in the Thames upstream of his mills. Amyce himself had to become a party to litigation in the Court of Augmentations when Thomas Reade sought vainly to protect the fishery attached to his manor of Barton – TNA, E 321/41/136,188.

[69] R. Tittler, 'The Incorporation of Boroughs, 1540-1558', *History* 62 (1977), pp. 24-42.

[70] The quotations are from the version of the charter published by Challenor in his *Selections from the Borough Records* (1899). He attributes the translation to Recorder Holt in 1658.

[71] W.C. Richardson (ed), *The Report of the royal commission of 1552* (1974), esp pp. 46, 68, 131, 182; J. Alsop, 'The Revenue Commission of 1552', *The Historical Journal*, 22 (1979), pp. 511-533.

[72] BRO, D/EP 7 141 (Para 61 of the accompanying transcript).

[73] The Marquess of Winchester, who may have been born as early as 1475, was an old man in a hurry, but would have at least fifteen years of active life left to him – L. L. Ford, 'Paulet, William, first marquess of Winchester (1474/5?–1572)', in *DNB*.

[74] Richard Hoyle, 'Introduction: aspects of the Crown's estates c. 1558-1640' in R. Hoyle (ed), *The Estates of the English Crown 1558-1640* (Cambridge, 1992), pp. 1-57, esp. p. 39. It is an interesting point that some properties in the grant had belonged to chantries, or had been given to the two town churches for obits. Although Philip and Mary were now sharing the throne and the old religion had been re-established, there was no suggestion that these might be restored.

[75] Janey Cumber, 'The Society and Economy of the Town of Abingdon, c. 1520-56', unpubl. M.Stud. dissertation, Oxford University (2001), p. 49.

[76] A.E. Preston totalled the rental value of the properties listed by Amyce at £88 16s 3d plus, rather charmingly, a pound of cumin and a needle without an eye. He believed that surviving copies of the survey were actually early drafts – BRO, D/EP7 82, loose sheets headed A2.

[77] Sybil M. Jack, *Towns in Tudor and Stuart Britain* (1996), p. 87; R. Tittler, *The Reformation and the Towns in England: Politics and Political Culture C. 1540-1640* (1998), p. 95. According to Tittler, the Beverley charter of 1573 cost £233, and travel and incidentals came to almost £130 more.

2. The structure of government

> ... so in a cuntrey, city, or towne, ther ys perfayt cyuylyte, ther ys the true commyn wele, where as al the partys, as membrys of one body, be knyt togyddur in perfayt loue and vnyte; euery one dowyng hys offyce and duty ... and without enuy or malyce to other accomplish the same.
>
> Thomas Starkey, *A dialogue between Pole and Lupset* (1532)[1]

Charters of incorporation were not new in the sixteenth century, and well before that period lawyers had developed standardised formats with all the essential material in a more or less logical order. An incorporation, be it for civic or charitable purposes, created as a legal fiction an artificial person that could perform certain defined functions without being limited by the unpredictable duration of a human life. The charter would normally have a preamble that stated reasons for the incorporation, although these might be distorted by the needs to conceal previous political failures and to emphasize the generosity of the sovereign in making the grant. The institution to be set up would have to have a style or title – in Abingdon's case, the Mayor, Bailiffs and Burgesses of the Borough of Abingdon in the County of Berks – and be permitted to have a common seal; these would be equivalent to the name and signature of a real person. It would have to be able 'to plead and be impleaded' – to sue and be sued in a court of law. It would have to be able to acquire, hold, and manage property, and the limits of such rights would be defined. It would normally have some sort of hierarchical structure, with the senior members exercising certain rights of discipline; and there would need to be a mechanism for replacing members who dropped out by death or for other reasons. There would normally be an outside visitor to check, either regularly or when appealed to, that the institution was being properly run in accordance with its charter and rules. For a municipal corporation, the visitor was theoretically the sovereign, and his function would devolve at need on the court of King's Bench. Charitable foundations should have a visitor specified, although in the case of Christ's Hospital the rules left it to John Mason to nominate such a person and he never did so, an omission that would be regretted later in the century.[2]

Borough charters were always designed to maintain a delicate balance between representation of the population as a whole and actual government by the 'better sort', and no two towns had identical ideas on how to achieve this. In Abingdon, the mayor would be elected each year at the beginning of

September, and would enter into his office at Michaelmas. All burgesses and 'men of the inferior sort' could attend the election, and they would nominate 'two of the more discrete and grave men then being Principall Burgesses'. The mayor, bailiffs and other principal burgesses would choose one of the two to be the next mayor. The outgoing mayor would nominate one man, who might be either a capital or secondary burgess, to be one of the two bailiffs for the coming year, and the secondary burgesses and the 'inferior sort' would nominate one secondary burgess to be the other. Anyone who refused to take on an office to which he had been duly elected could be fined and, if need be, imprisoned.

The charter defined a structure for the town government that had obviously been the subject of much thought. There were to be twelve principal or capital burgesses, which number would include the mayor and possibly one of the two bailiffs, and they would be able to elect sixteen or more others as secondary burgesses. The whole would be the common council of the borough. It was emphasized that these councillors were to be chosen from among the 'better, honester, and discreeter' townsmen, and there are occasional mentions of 'other the Burgesses and Men of the Inferior sort in the said Borough, Inhabitants' to make it plain that the usual social hierarchies would be maintained.

As was usual with incorporations, both those of the hospital and of the borough list the initial governing members. These lists define the town élite of the 1550s. It was by no means a new élite. Of the twelve masters of the Holy Cross fraternity at its dissolution, five survived and were all named to the hospital, although one of these died before he could take his place.[3] Two of the old guild-masters were appointed to the new corporation, one of them, Richard Mayott, as the first mayor; and altogether five of the ten new hospital governors also feature on the list of principal burgesses. The overlap in membership between the hospital and the corporation would continue. Almost all the leading families of Abingdon would be represented both among the masters of the hospital and the mayors of the town, mostly by the same individuals.

The mayor would also be coroner, and would be sole justice of the peace for the town. No other justice of the peace 'from henceforth shall intermeddle himselfe or enter or come in to do any thing which to a Justice of Peace there belongs'. It was this provision that confirmed the legal independence of the town from rule by the gentry of the surrounding region, but there was an immediate and important qualification: 'except our Justices ... by Comission or

Comissions of us ... from time to time to be assigned, nominated and authorized ...'. It would not be until the next century that the full import of this clause would become clear.

The mayor would have a staff to help him. There would be a town clerk, no doubt legally qualified; a chamberlain, who would look after the corporation's financial affairs and who would in practice be a member of the corporation elected annually, and two serjeants-at-mace to act as ceremonial escorts for the mayor, and as messengers, enforcers, and general progress chasers. The clerk of the market would have a significant workload, since there would be a market each Monday, and no fewer than five yearly fairs which would bring money into the town and, by tolls and fines, to the corporation in particular. It was the lucrative rights over markets and fairs that had been one of the most consistent sources of conflict between the townsmen and the abbey, and gaining these was probably second only to the property portfolio among the economic advantages conferred by the charter.

The bailiffs were important member of the council, since it would be they who would run the court of record that would sit every Tuesday and could deal with cases up to a value of £5. This proved unsatisfactory in practice. Some years later, in 1565, the mayor and corporation surrendered this part of the charter in the court of Chancery and received a new document whereby the court of record would henceforth be held before 'the Mayor, or his sufficient Deputy or Deputies'. The argument was that since no one who had already held the mayoralty could be a bailiff, there was difficulty in recruiting well-qualified men.[4] Some who had occupied the position had proved 'very unfit to decide and determine ... to the great scandal and disgrace of the said Court'. There must at some point have been dissatisfaction with one or more of the court's decisions but no indication survives of the details. However, the function of the bailiffs remained significant. It was they who were responsible for finding and paying the fee farm rent, and, in view of the manner laid down for their selection, which continued to be observed, they probably formed a sort of inner cabinet with the mayor. One bailiff would be concerned to ensure continuity with the policies of the previous year, while the other represented the views of the lesser members of the town community.[5]

There were no particular duties laid down for secondary burgesses other than attendance at the yearly common council meetings where mayors and bailiffs were to be nominated. There must also have been occasional extraordinary meetings with all the burgesses present to discuss particularly difficult or urgent matters. One such was held on 20 July 1599 at the initiative of the then mayor, Francis Little, to promulgate a revised set of 'acts and orders' – i.e. procedures, rules and by-laws – that would guide the work of future councils.[6] There had been an original set produced in the early years of the borough, but this was apparently considered obsolete. The new protocol named the mayor, two bailiffs, twelve principal and twenty secondary burgesses. The number of corporation members had thus increased somewhat since the original charter. Most of those named must have been present, although no signatures have survived. Among the new rules was one making it clear that only principal burgesses would attend the regular council meetings, which were to be held quarterly; but another specified the hierarchical order in which mayor and burgesses were to be seated and this did provide for the presence of secondaries. The latter were understood to be divided into two groups, with those who had already served as bailiffs taking precedence over those who had not. There seems to have been some disquiet about the numbers and quality of secondary burgesses, from among whom the future principals would be recruited. The meeting agreed that there should never be more than twenty of them and to continue the system whereby on entry to the corporation each one was to pay a fee of 20s.[7] This would be amply enough to discourage ordinary tradesmen, for whom it might represent several weeks' wages.

In one clause of its charter Abingdon was unusually fortunate. A disadvantage of chartered status was the obligation to send a number – normally two – burgesses to Parliament. Parliaments were irregular, and their duration uncertain. Only in the unlikely event that it wanted a special act, or had problems that needed to be aired in a national forum, would its parliamentary representation be of any great interest to a town. If it were to send its own men, they would have to be paid. Otherwise, it would be necessary to agree with some local gentleman with parliamentary ambitions to nominate him in exchange for a reduced salary, or with a more distant magnate to give a seat to some kinsman or client to whom he owed a favour. Either way, a powerful outsider would gain influence in the town which might or might not be to its advantage.

Town charters usually took parliamentary responsibilities for granted, and Abingdon's was unusual in mentioning them. It was even more unusual in specifying a single parliamentary burgess instead of the usual two. Abingdon would be one of only four boroughs in the country in that position.[8] Furthermore, the burgess was to be local, 'a discreet and honest man of the said Borough'. This had no doubt emerged from the negotiations that preceded the issuance of the charter; it will certainly have suited the interests of Mason and Amyce that they had a parliamentary seat available to them should they need it, but that there was no opening for an outsider to use this means to set up a competing interest in their bailiwick. In fact, Mason sat regularly and Amyce occasionally in parliament although neither ever represented Abingdon.[9] Mason used the seat for patronage. The first occupant was Oliver Hyde, whom Mason had named as his deputy at the Hospital, and he does not seem to have required any payment.[10] In 1559, the seat went to Robert Byng, who came from Kent and should have been disqualified, but had been the husband of Mason's deceased stepdaughter.[11]

The charter talks much of burgesses but does not mention freemen, although the corporation minutes make it clear that such a status existed. The two terms cannot have been quite synonymous, since the orders of 1599 specify the freemanship as a prerequisite for becoming a secondary burgess. Only freemen could exercise trades in the town other than as apprentices and servants, and only the mayor and corporation could grant freemanship.[12] It was assumed from early on that the different trades would come together in fellowships or guilds, but it does not seem that this ever happened to any significant extent. An ordinance of 1609 includes a full set of rules for a fellowship of shoemakers and cordwainers, including the oaths to be taken by the master, wardens and ordinary members, but there is no evidence that such a guild actually existed at this time.[13] The rules probably existed to ensure that any guilds that might be set up would be under the ultimate control of the corporation.

The only other formal authority structure was the two parishes of St Helen's and St Nicholas. St Helen's was, of course, the main town church, and then as now by far the bigger of the two. In the decade 1611 to 1620, there were 546 baptisms recorded at St Helen's, against only sixty-three at St Nicholas, suggesting that the sizes of the congregations were in the same proportion.[14] St Helen's was relatively wealthy; a taxation in 1606-7 raised almost £50. Its churchwardens and vestrymen were of prominent local families, and in most years the churchwardens' accounts were signed off by the current mayor. There were some wealthy and prominent men who lived in St Nicholas parish, but the churchwardens there who signed a bond in 1620 were Robert Harwood, clothworker, and William Cooke, cordwainer, neither of whom is otherwise known.[15] Francis Little, several times mayor, although he lived in St Nicholas and was occasionally a churchwarden, also held the same function at St Helen's and went there to have knells rung when family members died and for their burials. As will be seen, the two churches in the seventeenth century became associated with different factions in the town.

There is no full record of all the men who became secondary or primary burgesses in Abingdon between the grant of the charter and the Civil War, but it is a fair assumption that most or all who entered the corporation and survived long enough would eventually become principal burgesses and eligible for the mayoralty. The list of mayors for the period shows that the office was dominated by no more than a dozen families who also provided masters of the hospital, with something of a change-over about 1600. In twelve years out of eighty-one, the mayor's surname was Mayott; in seven each it was Tesdale and Orpwood; in five it was Payne. Bostocks and Braunches held the mayoralty five times each and Hydes four times, but these names are restricted to the sixteenth century. The twelve Mayott mayoralties represent at least five distinct individuals; there were four distinct Tesdales, with a fifth to come in 1642. Mayotts were intermarried with Paynes and Orpwoods; Tesdales were intermarried with Paynes and a few of the other mayoral families, notably Stevenson and Clempson. It is dangerous to attribute political action to families as such, rather than to individuals within them, but, as will be seen, it would be rare to find Mayotts and Tesdales on the same side in a political conflict; Orpwoods would go with Mayotts as would most Paynes, but Francis Payne and Laurence Stevenson, both with Tesdale wives, would follow that line. The consistency is all the more remarkable in that the Mayotts – a family so large and complex that it defies genealogical analysis – were divided into cousinages of which at least two were separately armigerous.[16]

Roger Amyce seems never to have involved himself with the corporation, and he ceased to be resident in Berkshire in the late 1550s, retiring to a property he had bought in Essex. When Mason died in 1566, Amyce took over the nominal mastership of Christ's Hospital, perhaps to the annoyance of the governors. A surviving letter of December 1566 from Amyce at home to the governors in Abingdon, all mentioned by name, points out rather caustically that they have given him so little notice of a forthcoming audit that they obviously don't want him to be there. Nonetheless, he does intend to visit after the Christmas season, and 'peruse all the accounts that have been since (by my meanes) the hospital was established. God willing, who preserve you all and the same hospitall to Gods glory and the benefit of the poore.'[17] He continued as master until 1569, when he was replaced by the venerable Richard Mayott, who had been a master of the Fraternity in 1547. He made a brief return in 1573-4, perhaps on a nominal basis, and died in the latter year.[18]

Thus by the later sixteenth century Abingdon had taken on the political structure that, in at least some particulars, it would keep for several centuries. Two institutions, the corporation and the hospital, administered a high proportion of the landed property in the town. They were run by a small élite of leading families. There must always have been differences of opinion and clashes of interest both within the élite and between it and the 'inferior sort'. The following chapters will consider the evolution of ideas about how these differences might be dealt with.

---

[1] pp. 54-5.

[2] William Blackstone, *Commentaries on the Laws of England* (various editions), Vol 1, Chapter 8.

[3] James Townsend, *A History of Abingdon* (1910), p. 57.

[4] The charter has no such limitation on the choice of the mayor's bailiff, although it does seem to have been observed. No doubt it had always been understood, but accidentally omitted by the draughtsmen.

[5] ATCA, Register of Ordinances, Chapter 29, fo. 6v. The bailiffs were allotted certain rents for the fee farm – BRO, D/EP7 86.

[6] ATCA, Register of Ordinances, title page.

[7] ATCA, Register of Ordinances, Chaps 8-11, fos 2v-3, 4, 12v.

[8] *HoP 1558-1603*, I, p.32; Jennifer Loach, 'Parliament: a 'New Air'? ' in Christopher Coleman and David Starkey (eds), *Revolution Reassessed: Revisions in the history of Tudor government and administration* (Oxford, 1986), p. 125.

[9] Mason sat at different times for Reading, Taunton, and Hampshire; Amyce for Reading and New Windsor.

[10] *HoP 1509-1558*, I, p. 32. Hyde was a younger son. His father and brother, both named William, of Denchworth, were county gentry and also MPs.

[11] *HoP 1509-1558*, I, p. 524.

[12] ATCA, Register of Ordinances, Chapter 12, fo. 3.

[13] ATCA, Register of Ordinances. Chapter 48, fos 19v-21. Interestingly, the members were assumed to include both 'brothers' and 'sisters'.

[14] From parish registers. The numbers indicate a total population in the region of 2000.

[15] BRO, D/A2 C.182, fo. 14, Sequestration bonds.

[16] When in 1664 Elias Ashmole, as Windsor Herald, was making his visitation of Berkshire, only one of the armigerous branches was willing to pay his fee, and the other, therefore, was not written up – H. Rylands, *The Four Visitations of Berkshire, 1532, 1566, 1623, 1665-6* (Harleian Soc: 2 vols, 1908), II p. 178

---

[17] BRO, D/EP7 94. Amyce must have been preparing for his retirement as Surveyor of Berkshire. This office was passed on in June 1567 to Edward Marten − *CSPD* 1547-80 p. 295 (June 1567); *CPR* 1566-9, Eliz part vii, p. 77 (17 June 1567).
[18] BRO, D/EP7 49. The Fraternity had twelve masters at any time − *CPR* 1476-1485 (20 Feb 1484).

3. The Oligarchs

Leaders of the people by their counsels and by their understanding.
Ecclesiasticus 44:4

The Corporation and the Hospital, once they had got themselves organised, were working in a complex political space, and within an intellectual framework that was less than totally appropriate to it. Above them, politically, were such gentry and magnates as deigned to take an interest in them or in their town; below, the population at large. Their own preference, no doubt, was to concentrate on the management of the properties that their incorporations had given them. The fee farm had to be paid and any surplus would be the return on their investment in the grant of the charter. But there was a town to be administered, the almspeople to be supported, and the bridges maintained. Failure in these departments would bring on them the active displeasure of such bodies as the court of Chancery, should any townsman choose to appeal to it, or even of the Privy Council, which had urban peace and tranquillity as one of its constant concerns.

The prevailing mindset was an unstable amalgam of two distinct sets of principles. Social harmony was always the aim, and this could only be maintained if each member of society performed his function as he should, with deference for his betters and condescension towards those below. The rhetoric from the centre was that this depended on an unquestioning obedience to superiors in a social order that narrowed towards the top, where stood the single figure of a sovereign whose authority was absolute.[1] But against this was an older tradition where questioning was possible, where negotiation occurred, and where even men in a humble station had an active part to play. Town councils fitted by their nature better into this second tradition than the first.[2] Inevitably, disagreements developed in the councils, and factions formed. What must be remembered, for there is little mention of it in the archives, is that these disagreements will have echoed beyond the walls of the Guildhall and the governors' hall of the Hospital, and divided the lower orders as well as the more solid citizens. The fear of trouble on the streets must have constrained the debates and limited the options of the élite. The authoritarian principle would have led to the simple exclusion of dissenting groups and the suppression of their views, but this was never possible. The language that was used in local political argument often betrays a dissonance between absolutist rhetoric and political reality.

Relations within the élite were never perfectly harmonious. As early as 1561, it was found necessary to order that 'there shall be no manner of unseemly words stirred, raised or multiplied within the common council'.[3] A feud that was to continue through several generations of Abingdon's social leaders seems to have been in progress by December 1585. In that month, a squabble erupted among the Hospital governors.[4] Lionel Bostock, currently master, accused Anthony Bostock of 'dissention, strife and variance'; he had 'unquietly behaved himself' and addressed 'high words' to his fellow governors. The 'ordinances' set down by John Mason in 1558 provided that 'a sower of debate or discorde' might be expelled by the master and a majority of the governors.[5] The minute book has a long essay detailing Bostock's alleged faults, along with angry marginal rebuttals, later crossed through.. Among much else, he had publicly accused John Fisher of granting hospital leases for favours, thus depriving the poor of £100 that should have gone to them. When challenged, he refused to withdraw the slander. Anthony Bostock was supported by at least three of the governors, but his dismissal was forced through, and he was replaced by Anthony Tesdale, whose uncle Richard Tesdale was already a governor. The three dissentients, William Braunche, Thomas Smythe (or Smith), and Thomas Mayott, boycotted the next meeting, for which they were fined. Anthony Bostock appealed to Chancery, with no obvious effect. All these men were of leading Abingdon families, in at least their second generation of service in the fraternity or the hospital. Anthony Tesdale became master in 1588, which was an unusually rapid progress to the top position. A few years later he was joined as a governor by his brother Christopher. It would later be claimed that Anthony Tesdale had fabricated the accusation against Bostock to ensure his own election.[6]

The Hospital management was now split, at least partly on family lines. There seem to have been three factions, although one of them consisted of John Fisher alone. Each levelled at the others accusations of dishonest practices and of enriching themselves and their friends at the hospital's expense, but only in the case of John Fisher were the allegations against him detailed and specific. The Tesdales joined in the criticism of Fisher, but tended to ally with him politically.[7]

Time did not heal the rifts, and the next phase of the quarrel centres on perhaps the most interesting figure in the early history of the borough, Francis Little, or Francis Brooke, for he used both names. His origin is uncertain, but he may have had a Tesdale connection. The patriarch of the Tesdale family, still alive at that time, was Thomas Tesdale, whose considerable wealth had enabled him to move out of Abingdon to reside on his estates at Kidlington and later at Glympton. He had married the widow of an Edward Little alias Brooke, who had killed himself for reasons that have not come down to us. Francis Little may have been a son of the earlier marriage, or a relative of the suicide. He became a governor in 1592, in the same year that he was first elected to the mayoralty, and was master four years later. He would prove to be a tenacious opponent of the Tesdale interest.

Little's mastership was interrupted by the calling of a parliament; he was elected as Abingdon's MP, and will have been away from October 1597 until the following February. The Tesdales took the opportunity of his absence to elect another family member, Laurence Stevenson, son-in-law to Anthony, as a governor.[8] He would replace the deceased Paule Orpwood, brother-in-law to Thomas Mayott, so that the balance would move in favour of the Tesdale faction.[9]

Little, when he returned, ruled that an election held in the absence of the master was invalid. It is certainly the case that John Mason's ordinances insisted that such elections should be 'by the consent of the saide master and the more parte of the saide gouuernours'.[10] The normal procedure for settling the dispute would have been to appeal to the visitor, whose responsibilities would include maintaining the actions of a chartered institution within their legal bounds.[11] Every institution was supposed to have a visitor, and Mason's rules had provided for him to nominate one who would inspect every three years. However, no appointment had been made.[12] Little petitioned Thomas Egerton, Keeper of the Great Seal and head of Chancery, to take on the responsibility.[13] He emphasized the danger if the Hospital were to be dominated by a single family, and this was supported by a certificate signed by twenty-three prominent Abingdon people, including the bailiffs of the time, the constables and the churchwardens, to the effect that 'wee knowe the sayd Laurence to bee a man farr inferior unto divers other of the saide towne to supplie the place...' . The Tesdales, they alleged, had blocked the election as governors of seven named men who would have been more suitable (and of whom five would, in fact, be elected within the next three years). They were offering bribes and inducements to potential supporters. Making a strong, but probably insincere, propaganda point, Little offered to recognise Stevenson's election on condition that the Tesdales were prepared to accept a new statute that would prohibit governors from issuing leases to themselves and their relatives.[14]

Egerton accepted the petition. He nominated a commission of local gentlemen to investigate. These were Sir Thomas Parry of Hampstead Marshall, Henry Marten whose mother was from Lyford, John Dolman of Shaw, and Edward Clarke of Ardington. Marten was a rising star of the legal profession. They met at Wantage to take depositions. The report was signed by Marten, Dolman and Clarke, and Little's action was vindicated.[15]

The Tesdale faction was unhappy. Egerton's letter of 12 April 1598 ordering the dismissal of Stevenson crossed with one from Anthony Tesdale to Egerton requesting that judgement be held over pending a private meeting. As the current mayor, he could not absent himself from the town, and the meeting would have to be after Michaelmas when his term would come to its end. A biblical quotation emphasises Tesdale's godly credentials and suggests that Egerton had not been told the full story: 'against an elder receive not an accusation but before two or three witnesses'.[16]

It did not help. In a flurry of faction meetings the Tesdales sought to replace Stevenson with another of their party, the dyer John Winsmore, as against Little's nominee, John Blacknall. Winsmore was described as 'unlettered and much inferior', and was plainly not of the traditional town élite; Blacknall was a son or grandson of the William Blacknall who in John Mason's time had turned the abbey site and its mills into the town's main industrial area.[17] The factions were now meeting separately, each claiming to be the legitimate court of governors. Little's group chose Lionell Bostock as master, and brought in another Mayott in-law, the lawyer Paule Dayrell, as a governor. On 30 August 1598, there was a further appeal to Egerton. Bostock claimed that the Tesdale group had broken open the cupboard where documents were kept and had taken and still held the Hospital's muniments. They purported to have chosen John Fisher as master, and were trying to elect a new set of governors who were 'alehouse keepers and men of mean condition'.[18] Egerton sent another even higher-powered commission, under Thomas Shingleton, vice-chancellor of the University.[19] Shingleton was principal of Brasenose, Egerton's own college. The other commissioners were the academic lawyer John Weston, John Dolman of Shaw, Alexander Chock of Avington, and a William Crane esquire who I have not been able to identify. They gathered in the hospital hall, and, after having heard all sides, again ruled against the Tesdales.[20] Noisy disputes continued until, in 1602, Fisher and Christopher Tesdale were forced to resign.[21]

It is now impossible to judge the validity of allegations of dishonesty, but what is certain is that malpractices were taking place. The custom both for the

Hospital and the Borough was to write head-leases to a nominal twenty-one year period. It should have been possible when each lease fell in to re-write the terms to reflect changing rental values, and thus to maximise the income for the charitable works of the Hospital and the necessities of the Corporation. In fact, leases were never allowed to expire. Instead, it was expected that they would simply be rolled over, either to the same leaseholder or to his assignees, without any change in the terms. Renewal was taken to be due at fourteen years, and for every additional half year the lease ran the entry fines were increased by 2½ %, which may be understood as a penalty for late payment. The holders of the head-leases, relatively wealthy people, often the governors themselves or their relatives, would profit from the increase in rental values from their level at the mid-sixteenth century.[22] A new set of ordinances was brought in under Thomas Orpwood as master in 1605. These explicitly forbade renewal of leases more than one year before their expiry.[23] It seems they were ignored. The malpractices would continue until the nineteenth century, when government charity commissioners would bring them to the notice of the attorney-general, and the governors of that time would once again find themselves in the court of Chancery to be pilloried for systematically infringing their own rules.[24]

The quarrel was not, of course, limited to the Hospital but raged also in the Corporation, where many of the same individuals sat. In November 1591, it was found necessary to issue an ordinance forbidding members to call each other knave or to use other terms of reproach, on pain of a fine of 5s or five days in prison without bail or mainprize.[25] In 1592, there seems to have been a shouting match between Fisher and William Braunche, and the mayor, William Hulcott, introduced a new standing order insisting on politeness and the observance of hierarchy in council meetings.[26]

Anthony Tesdale was mayor in 1597-8, and a campaign was mounted to get Christopher Tesdale promoted from secondary to principal burgess. Allegedly, Laurence Stevenson was offering a bribe of £10 for each vote.[27] At the end of Anthony's term, Christopher got his promotion, along with another Tesdale supporter. The incoming mayor was, once more, Francis Little, and there was another eruption, but he was faced with a fait accompli that he was powerless to change.[28] But Little was a man of infinite resource.

In 1599, while Little was still mayor, the Tesdales felt it necessary to petition the Privy Council against a new charter that the Corporation was said to be seeking. It was, they complained, intended to reduce the element of popular participation in local elections and to further the financial misdoings of the faction. Little and his friends were, they said, taking illicit profits from both the Hospital and the Corporation, and were 'greatly oppressing the inhabitants by rack renting'. The Tesdales claimed also that the proposed new charter would restrict the entry of 'foreigners' to trade in the town, and 'do other things hurtful to the Corporation'. It seems that they were positioning themselves as spokesmen for the lower orders in Abingdon, who would suffer, rather than profit, from rent increases and might welcome the ingress of outside traders bringing employment opportunities. The later 1590s was a period of high prices and low industrial wages.[29] The appeal was not pursued, but it had its effect; the idea of a new charter was dropped. John Winsmore was dismissed from his status as a secondary burgess 'for settinge his hand unto the peticon ... and for ioyninge him self (being a sworne member of this incorporac'on) wth dyvers factions and troublesome persons whoe have maliciously and slaunderously exhibited the said petic'on to the privy counsell'.[30]

Little's anger was unconcealed, but he was not yet at a loss. Instead of a new charter, there would be a revision of the basic ordinances that the Corporation had made in its early days but which were now, he said, 'perished & defaced' and 'some of them holden contrary to the Lawes and statutes of this Realme, and the residue not thought so fitt & convenient for this tyme as for the tyme when they were made and ordeyned'.[31] There were forty 'chapters' promulgated at a common council meeting held on 20 July 1599, and another twenty-nine would be added to them in the next thirty years.

The 'Book of Ordinances' that was issued in 1599 was large, and neatly and clearly written.[32] It started by listing the mayor, the bailiffs, and the twelve principal and twenty secondary burgesses of the time, although it is not clear that all of them approved. It is not, however, a purely partisan document, since Little would be succeeded as mayor by Christopher Tesdale and it was not withdrawn. Its first 'chapter' repealed all former acts and orders made by the common council, and the following chapters represent a point-by-point revision of these, according to what must have been the current preoccupations of both parties. Some are matters of routine administration, forbidding trading on the Sabbath, assigning responsibility for street repairs and fire prevention, and limiting the number of bakers and publicans; it may be that these were more contentious at the time than now appears. Most are fundamental, defining the governance of the town in some detail, and may have been taken over directly from the abandoned charter. The order in which points are handled may indicate the preoccupations of the drafters.

Chapter 2, from its position, its length, and the language it uses, is plainly the one closest to Francis Little's heart. It is concerned with standing orders for council meetings and rules of debate. According to the preamble, it is

> for the avoiding of all contention that may arise …. Which doth many tymes not only breake the band of charitie amongst them [the burgesses], But is also a great hynderaunce to the busyness and causes in hand'.

It sets up a platonic ideal of conciliar practice. The burgesses are to sit in order of seniority starting with the mayor, but the two bailiffs will share a bench with the town clerk, one on each side of him,[33]

> And they being all thus placed every one shall quietly, soberly and discreetlie propose such things or answer such questions or gyve such holsome counsel as by occasion shalbe offered or in his wisdom shalbe thought fitt to be declared, and in all thinges behave himself as a grave & worthy Counseller of that howse'.

Meetings over the last few years had obviously not met that desirable standard. The chapter goes on to forbid 'termes of Disgrace' or 'of intent and purpose to hurte, prejudice, disgrace or disquiet any of the persons so assembled' and prescribes a fine of 12d and possible imprisonment in the Gatehouse for infringement. Judgement in such cases is to be given, not by the mayor, but by the 'major parte of the common council then present'.

Other chapters define the freemanship, which is open to freemen's oldest sons and to others who have served their apprenticeships within the borough. Freemen need to pay entry fines and be formally registered. Those already working in the borough who have not registered must do so. Freemanship ceases if a man leaves the borough.[34] Secondary burgesses are to be selected from among the freemen, and principal burgesses from among the secondaries.[35] Secondary burgesses must pay 20s to the chamberlain at entry as a 'benevolence', and there must never be more than twenty secondaries.[36] Principal burgesses must attend at least four council meetings each year, at quarter days.[37] The bailiffs, who handle public money, must provide sureties, and the chamberlain a bond.[38]

Perhaps most significant, in view of what had gone before, are a chapter that forbids the mayor and burgesses to make unauthorised use of corporation funds, even for charitable purposes, and one that compels the mayor to give effect to orders made by the council and punish offenders against them, on pain of a fine which is to be decided by the *next* mayor and a majority of the principal burgesses.[39] The intended effect was, plainly, to reduce the freedom for a mayor to use his term of office as a period of unchecked reversal of his predecessors' policies and of absolute rule by his faction, and it underlines the wisdom of those who drafted the charter of 1556 in providing for one of the bailiffs to be nominated by the outgoing mayor.

Numerous authors have drawn attention to a 'rise of oligarchy' in towns at this period. Barriers to entry into corporations, which had always been high, are raised still further; entry becomes virtually impossible for men from outside a limited social circle, and the elevated status of councilmen is emphasised by civic rituals and ceremonial.[40] Little's chapters can easily be incorporated into such a picture. Corporation members, wearing their gowns, accompany the mayor to church on high days and holydays; aspiring freemen take their oaths of allegiance before the mayor and his brethren, and the status of secondary burgess is open only to a limited number of the more affluent residents. But the real closing of the corporation was effected by a further chapter, passed in 1604 in the mayoralty of John Blacknall. It may be relevant to note that Blacknall's wealthy nephew, also John, was like Little a resident of St Nicholas. Little was Blacknall's tenant for several properties in the old abbey precinct, and they were neighbours.[41]

The original charter had distinguished between the burgesses and 'men of the inferior sort', but all of the latter could join in the nomination of two candidates for the mayoralty and of one of the bailiffs. The innovation of 1604 was to divide the commonalty into two classes, the higher of which would be the 'common electors', while the rest would in future be totally excluded from the electoral process.[42] It was a major step to take and of doubtful legality under the charter, and is justified at considerable length in the chapter (which is printed below as Appendix 1).

There was, it was plain, some political opposition to the corporation or to its majority, and the purpose of the chapter was to neutralise it. The individuals concerned were described as of a rebellious underclass:

> Certayne disordered persons within this Borough some of them neither having wherewith all to lyve, nor yet using any honest or lawful courses or trade of life whereby to manteyne themselves, but living in riot and disorder offensive to the godlie quiet and peaceable government of the said Towne.

Can this really be a description of men like the dyer John Winsmore, who had actually been a secondary burgess allied with the perhaps obstreperous but certainly respectable Tesdale family, or might it rather apply to those who were idle because they were unemployed? However much the Tesdales might claim to speak for the lower orders, they evidently accepted that the lower orders should not speak for themselves. Whoever they were, these disorderly persons attended mayoral elections and might

> often tymes ... combine and confederate them selves to nominate, chuse and assign such person or persons unto the said Offices or places as either they suppose or ymagine will more favorably tolerate and beare with their disorders and misrule orells [or else] such as for some other sinister and undewe respectes they shall like to prefer thereto.

In other words, the opposition was organised, and favoured candidates according to their political positions. What was worse, their preferred candidates often won, even in spite of themselves:

> ...sometime preferring, electing and nominating suche as were not fitt, and rejecting those which were fitt, sometymes in ymposing these offices and charge and burthen of them upon some especial persons more often than was fitt or perhaps than they or their Estates were well able conveniently [to] beare.

It was true that the mayoralty was expensive; the mayor received an allowance of £20, which might well not cover all the costs of keeping up suitable appearances, but there was a long-established pattern whereby principal burgesses became mayor more or less in turn, in cycles of seven to eleven years depending on mortality rather than election. A more credible objection was that

> in assemblies of such people is very usual some mutinous tumults, uprores, quarrelinges, civill Dissentions and other disorders have happened and befallen...

Elections were becoming raucous and rowdy occasions, no longer corresponding to the decorum specified earlier by Little for council meetings, and which one may doubt was actually achieved.

It was difficult for the town élites to admit that their administration could be questioned from below, and it was a commonplace of the time that political dissent could only be a sign of depravity in the dissenter. In any case, 'tumults, uprores and civill dissentions' risked bringing down on the borough and its corporation the wrath of the central authorities. The answer was to nominate

> Forty persons or more ... of the gravest, wisest and most sufficient men of the said
> other burgesses and inhabitants of the lower sorte

who would, together with the secondary burgesses, perform all the electoral duties specified in the charter. We have no reliable numbers for the population of Abingdon at this time, but the number of adult males must have been five hundred at the least. There was now a political class of just seventy-five chosen individuals; everybody else had simply to obey what the council pleased to command, but would have no part in its selection or – at least in principle – any influence over its decisions.

The names of the forty trusted inhabitants are listed. They start with an Esquire - Walter Dayrell, son of Paule, and soon to be Recorder of the Borough. Then come six 'gents' - including John Blacknall's aged father William, and William Bostock, soon to be master of the Hospital. Such men are not likely to have involved themselves in riotous activity. Some of the electors may well have been of the 'lower sort' but remarkably many seem to have been chosen from among relatives of the elite. An additional eighteen names were added at some later stage, presumably to replace men who had died.

It might be expected that this narrowing of the electorate even for the limited number of matters within its competence would satisfy the principal burgesses, but it did not. In 1614 with Christopher Tesdale again mayor, there was renewed concern. This time it was the very principle of a choice between two nominees for the mayoralty that was at issue, and again the preamble was enormously long.[43]

> ... some tymes some men are and have beine more often chosen unto yt [that] place
> than others. And thereby much spleen, discontentment, Devision, and Distraction
> hathe happened ... it seemed unto Divers they were neglected, disgraced and helde
> unworthy or unfit for suche office ...

This in turn has led to

> dissention devision and distraction to be aboute the choice of men unto the places of
> Secundary Burgesses, electors and the like places, eche one accordinge to his fancey
> and effection being carried to make choice of such as they conceaved would be
> reddieste to concur and joyne with them in those elections and in the like busines.

In short, the device of a closed electoral group had failed to ensure the quiet harmony that Francis Little had hoped for. The whole messy business of elections and electioneering, the articulation of issues, the forging of alliances, tactical voting, uncertainty of outcome – all this was intolerable to the Abingdon élite. These were men, it must be remembered, who were wealthy, successful, and by necessity much occupied with their own affairs; they undertook the onerous duties of council membership largely for the honour and respect it carried; and to have their opinions and actions subjected to public scrutiny or to be the loser in an electoral contest meant a loss of face which was unacceptable to them.

It was noted that other towns in a similar situation had instituted a formal *cursus honorum* and, with the stated consent of both the corporation and the common electors, it was decided to follow suit. Future elections would be a sham; the secondary burgesses and electors would list principal burgesses in order of the time since they had last been mayor, and send up the first two, of whom the Council would invariably choose the first. Only at the death of an ex-mayor could a junior principal burgess accede to the list by way of replacement, and he would then have to wait for a whole cycle to be completed before he could take office. The effect would be to entrench a gerontocracy. There was no special dispensation for men who had been passed over in earlier contests, confirming that that consideration had been no more than a pretext. The only exceptions to the general rule were to exclude men for 'notorious or schandolous Crime', or incapacity, or if a man 'shalbe of soe pore estate as he shall not be able to beare that porte'. John Fisher, now presumably aged, was stated to be too poor to act as mayor 'in such sorte as maye stand with the creditt and reputacion of this Boroughe' and was to be omitted from the list. The emoluments of the mayor were increased; to the traditional 20s per annum were added the tolls of the corn market, but this would still obviously leave the mayor severely out of pocket.

For added certainty, the next eleven mayors were listed and indeed all of them served as planned except for John Francis, who died before 1621 when his turn should have come round.[44]

There was still a loophole that seems to have been noticed on review. A faction among the electors with minority support in the council might get a man chosen as a secondary burgess, and then fast-track him into a bailiff position. This option was closed by a further provision that a man could not become bailiff until he had served at least a year.[45]

Thus, after much travail, Little and his friends, who now seemed to include even the previously obnoxious Christopher Tesdale, had triumphed. Oligarchy was complete. Abingdon as a political entity was embodied in a self-perpetuating circle of rich men from half a dozen intermarried families, who sat in olympian detachment to deliberate on what they considered the good of the town, free of any need to pander to the misguided self-interest or malicious special pleading of the commonalty outside. It was, of course, an illusion.

The rules for the mayoral succession did not retain general approval, and indeed seem to have broken down in 1625, when it should have been the turn of Thomas Orpwood but Thomas Clempson was elected for the first and only time.[46] During his mayoralty, the system was abrogated.[47] The next year, the rules for choosing electors were revisited. Each year, shortly before the mayoral election, the list was to be revised, and electors replaced if they had died, removed, or if they might 'combygne themselves to disturbe the Eleccion or for any other iuste cause'.[48] There was a completely new list of forty electors which has no names in common with that of 1604. This list was again later augmented with seven more names, perhaps replacing electors who had died in the years immediately following. There was then a third list which is dated 1636, has an overlap of twelve names with that of 1627, and is again augmented in 1640 and 1641.[49] The electoral system obviously continued at least until the Civil War. [50]

The new rule also allowed for 'scrutators' who, in the event of a contest, could take names as the electors came down out of the council house into the hall. The principle of majority voting was gaining acceptance, albeit within a restricted electorate. In 1629 it was found necessary to forbid bribery and intimidation at elections.[51]

But the Little faction was unhappy. On 1 April 1630, the lords of the Privy Council considered a petition from John Mayott, Francis Little, and 'divers others Inhabitants of Abingdon'. In view of 'many disorders committed by the Commons', the corporation had established an order for the election of the mayor. But now 'some factious persons by a new act of Common Council had repealed (it) ... whereby divers inconveniences had ensued.'[52] Their Lordships referred the matter to Sir William Jones and Sir James Whitlock, judges of assize for Berkshire, to settle on their next circuit. The petition seems to have failed, since most of the mayors of the 1630s had not previously held the office, and Benjamin Tesdale served in 1634 and again in 1637.[53] In August 1630, Little was threatened with dismissal from the corporation he had served for forty-three years. The reason may have been sickness rather than anger at his part in the recent petition. He died a few months later.[54]

The disputes dragged on. At the mayoral election of 1634, the scrutators found that the votes were equal for two slates; Richard Barton's name appeared on both of them, but in one he was partnered by John Mayott and in the other by Benjamin Tesdale. Somehow, Tesdale ended up as mayor, and there was another appeal to the Privy Council.[55] As late as October 1640 the Council again received a petition which was once more referred to the assize judges to deal with:

> ... concerning the complaint therein made against John Mayot gent for detaining and suppressing of an order made (upon a former reference from this Board) by the then Justices of Assize for the regulating of the proceedings from time to time in the election of the mayor of that Corporation, as also concerning the differences arising between the principal and the secondary Burgesses (as they call them) touching the leasing and granting of the lands and revenues belonging to the Corporation.[56]

John Mayott had been mayor in 1639-40, and had just been succeeded by his kinsman Robert Mayott; their opponents were crying foul. The judges' decision is unknown, but would soon be rendered nugatory by the general catastrophe of the Civil War.

Without any doubt, it is Francis Little who was the outstanding citizen of Abingdon at the turn of the seventeenth century. He was woollendraper, brewer, innholder, and even property developer at different times of his life, yet his main interest always seems to have been in public service as he and his contemporaries saw it. He became a freeman in 1587, and in the same year a secondary burgess and the bailiff nominated by the outgoing mayor, Lionell Bostock. Five years later, in 1592, he began the first of four terms as mayor, and at the same time became a hospital governor; he would be master in two successive years, 1596 and 1597. He was also a churchwarden of St Helen's several times in the 1590s in spite of his residence in St Nicholas parish, and the anonymous presenter to the former church of a silver flagon for communion wine weighing 47 ounces. He served as parliamentary burgess in 1597-8, and was always ready take on any odd job that might need doing – auditing the hospital accounts, going to London to negotiate a new charter which would allow the Hospital to acquire additional properties in mortmain. He was responsible for the refurbishing of the hospital hall in the years around 1605, and the acquisition of the portraits of donors and benefactors that grace it to this day.[57] It has been suggested that the double portrait of the builders of the Abingdon bridge, where each of those worthies has the same imagined features, actually shows likenesses of himself. He was equally involved in the rebuilding in 1605 of the market cross, observing current proprieties by replacing at least some of the old religious images with the heraldry of local gentry families, and contributed £30 of his own towards the project. Most importantly for posterity, he was the first serious historian of Abingdon; his manuscript of 1627, published in the nineteenth century as 'A Monument of Christian Munificence', describes the development of the Holy Cross Fellowship and of the Hospital, and praises their benefactors down to his own time.[58]

Paul Slack deservedly made something of a hero of Francis Little in his 1995 Ford Lectures in Oxford. Christ's Hospital, for Slack, was 'one of the bridges across what might have been the great caesura of the English Reformation', and Little himself was cast as a late upholder of the mid-sixteenth century commonwealth tradition, of the idea that it was an élite responsibility to see to the public good.[59] No doubt this is correct, and he might well have agreed. But a great part of the tradition he upheld was in fact a much older one: the holistic idea of a harmonious urban community where all men counted, each according to his degree, but where rule was the concern of a minority who alone were qualified by wealth and experience to exercise it. A properly conducted council would reach optimal decisions irrespective of its individual members, and there should be no reason for acrimonious elections or canvassing for individual candidates. Civic office was both an honour and a burden, but should give no scope for the furtherance either of private advantage or of a particular ideology. To Little, there were no problems that could not be settled by discussion and compromise, no conflicts that were not amenable to arbitration and reconciliation.[60] The whole history of his lifetime as religious divisions widened should have taught him otherwise, but neither he nor most of his contemporaries had yet understood the lesson.

What comes through the records is the impression that he must have been a formidable committee man, hard-working, well-briefed and persuasive; that he was an able politician, for the survival of his Book of Ordinances shows that he must have obtained support for it both from within his own party and the opposition; but above all that he was an idealist who had his vision of how things ought to be. A common council ought to be a place of quiet, rational, debate, untroubled by passion; leadership meant the exercise of authority, not the seeking of a popular mandate; the lower orders would do best to express their concerns quietly in private; and, especially, the proper return for benevolence was commemoration. Bede-rolls – lists of deceased individuals to be remembered in prayer – had disappeared with the guilds and chantries, but just as the fraternity had returned in the guise of a hospital, so Little adapted the bede-roll to a changed time; if it could no longer be on parchment, it was in paint on the hospital walls, in stone on the market cross, and on paper in the hospital chest. Francis Little was a monument in his own time.

[1] On the opinion of James I, see the extract from his *True Law of Free Monarchies* (1598) in J.R. Tanner, *Constitutional Documents of the Reign of James I 1603-1625* (1930), pp. 9-10. For local proponents of this view: W. Dickenson, *The King's Right, Briefly Set Downe in a Sermon* (1619); J. Overall, *Bishop Overall's Convocation-Book, MDCVI Concerning the Government of God's Catholick Church, and the Kingdoms of the Whole World* (1606, 1690). Dickenson was rector of Appleton and Besselsleigh, within a few miles of Abingdon; Overall was rector of Hinton Waldrist, in the Vale of White Horse, between 1599 and 1602, although he must have been an absentee, having academic duties to attend to in Cambridge – Leeds University Library, Marten-Loder Papers, Vol 14.

[2] Charles Pythian-Adams, *Desolation of a City: Coventry and the urban crisis of the late middle ages* (1979), part 3; John Guy, 'The 1590s, the second reign of Elizabeth I?' in J. Guy (ed), *The Reign of Elizabeth I: Court and Culture in the last decade* (1995), Chap. 1; Paul Slack, *From Reformation to Improvement* (1999), pp. 27-8; Paul Withington, 'Citizens, Community and Political Culture in Restoration England' in Alexandra Shepard and Phil Withington (eds), *Communities in early modern England* (Manchester, 2000), esp pp. 136-140; David Loades, *Tudor Government: structures of authority in the sixteenth century* (1997), pp. 9-10.

[3] ATCA, Corp. Minutes i fo. 7v.

[4] Agnes C. Baker, *Historic Abingdon: fifty-three articles : parliamentary history and notes on M.P.s., 1588-1714* (Abingdon, 1963), p. 50 sqq

[5] BRO, Transcript, D/EP 7/53, paras 11, 21, 22.

[6] CH, Minute Book I, fos. 22-23v; BRO, Preston Papers, D/EP 7/47 fos 23-4; D/EP 7/51 fos 22-4.

[7] CH, Misc letters and papers, 1034/26.

[8] BRO, Christopher Tesdale's will (1631), D/A1/16/233.

[9] Harry Rylands, *The Four Visitations of Berkshire, 1532, 1566, 1623, 1665-6* (Harleian Society, 1908), II p. 186.

[10] CH, Minute Book I, fos. 8-12; . The ordinances are transcribed in Berks RO, D/EP 7/53 - see para 22.

---

[11] William Blackstone, *Commentary on the Laws of England* (Various edns), Chapter 8.

[12] CH, Minute Book I fos 8-12; Berks RO, D/EP 7/53, para 17..

[13] The office of Lord Keeper was absorbed into that of Chancellor when there was one, but at this time there was not. The next man down in the hierarchy was the Master of the Rolls, whose role was more 'hands-on'.

[14] CH, Miscellaneous letters, 1034/14 A-C.

[15] CH, Misc letters, 1034/15. The CH accounts for 1598 claim a suspiciously round figure of £10 for the entertainment of this and the following commission, miscellaneous clerical costs, and the travelling expenses of Little and Lionell Bostock. They also explicitly, if incorrectly, describe Egerton as 'visitor of this hospital'.

[16] CH, Misc letters, 1034/16 and 17; 1 Timothy 5:19.

[17] Not to be confused with 'the great' John Blacknall, who died in 1625 and was his nephew. The uncle died in 1611.

[18] CH, Misc letters, 1034/24, 26

[19] CH, Misc letters, 1034/25.

[20] CH, Minute Book, fos. 37v, 38. Baker, *Historic Abingdon: parliamentary history*, p. 57 et seq; BRO, Preston Papers, D/EP 7/48.

[21] CH, Misc letters, 1034/28; John Carter and Jacqueline Smith, *Give & Take: Scenes from the History of Christ's Hospital, Abingdon, 1553-1900* (Abingdon, n.d.), pp. 86-7.

22 They would have to ask the Hospital or the Corporation for a license to sub-let, but it is not clear either on what terms such licenses were granted, or what happened to the proceeds, if there were any. This is a subject on which further research would be valuable. A detailed study for the town of Barnstaple shows that similar abuses were current there, and gives estimates of the value lost to the poor and gained by the élites as a result, which run over the years to some £5000 − J.B. Gribble, *Memorials of Barnstaple* (1830), pp. 158-94. But it is also true that systematic raising of rents and entry fines in the sixteenth and seventeenth centuries was always legally questionable and politically unpopular − J. Chartres and D. Hey, *English Rural Society, 1500-1800: Essays in Honour of Joan Thirsk* (Cambridge, 1990), esp pp. 73-124.

[23] CH, Minutes I, fols 13-15.

[24] Law Reports, *The Times*, 13 November 1841.

[25] ATCA, Corp. Minutes i fo.17v.

[26] ATCA, Corp. Minutes i fo.19v.

[27] BRO, A/AZ 3; CH, Misc letters, 1034/14B.

[28] BRO, A/AZ 3; Baker, *Historic Abingdon: parliamentary history*, pp. 50 sqq.

[29] Lionel Munby, *How much is that worth?* (1989), pp. 26-30.

[30] ATCA, Corp. Minutes i fo. 20v; Robert Tittler, *Reformation and Towns in England: Politics and Political Culture 1540-1640* (Oxford, 1998), pp. 191-2.

[31] ATCA, Corp. Minutes i fos. 3-9. There had been some piecemeal revision of the early ordinances in recent years.

[32] In Abingdon Town Council Archives. There is a partial transcript in Bromley Challenor, *Selections from the records of Abingdon* (Abingdon, 1898) as an appendix.

[33] Perhaps to check the accuracy of his note-taking?

[34] ATCA, Book of Ordinances, Chapters 14, 15, 17, fos 3, 3v.. The most prominent freeman who had left the borough while still maintaining his interests in it was, of course, the patriarchal Thomas Tesdale.

[35] Chapters 5, 12, fos 2,3.

[36] Chapters 8−11, fos 2-3..

[37] Chapter 37, fo 9.

[38] Chapters 28, 29. fos. 6-6v.

[39] Chapters 30, 35 fos. 7, 9.

[40] J. T. Evans, 'The Decline of Oligarchy in Seventeenth-Century Norwich', *The Journal of British Studies,* 14 (1974), pp. 46-76; Sybil M. Jack, *Towns in Tudor and Stuart Britain* (1996), pp. 77-80; Peter Clarke, '"The Ramoth-Gilead of the Good" Gloucester 1540-1640' in Jonathan Barry (ed), *The Tudor and Stuart Town: A Reader in English Urban History 1530-1688* (1990), pp. 244-273 esp at pp. 259-261.

[41] Baker, *Historic Abingdon: parliamentary history*, pp. 40-48.

[42] Chapter 41, fo. 13.

[43] Chapter 49 fos 22-25.

[44] Buried at St Nicholas, 17 May 1617 - (Parish Registers).

[45] Chapters 50, 52 fos 23v, 24v.

[46] He held the position briefly in 1631, when John Payne died in office.

[47] Chapter 66, fo 31v. Clempson was a governor of Christ's Hospital from 1624 and master in 1626, lived in St Nicholas parish, and seems to have been close to Little and the Mayotts so the change in the rules may have been against his will − Little, *A Monument* p. 86; BRO, Will of Robert Payne (1628), D/A1/11/153.

[48] Chapter 68 fo. 32.

[49] An additional two names are carried over to 1636 from the seven additions to the 1627 list. For the list of 1636 and its additions, see the end pages of the Register of Ordinances. A death rate of 70% in nine years seems improbably high even for this period, and would suggest that electors might be removed from the list for reasons other than death. Some were certainly selected as secondary burgesses.

[50] Chapter 68, fo. 32

[51] Chapter 69, fo. 33.

[52] *APC*, May 1629-May 1630, p. 358 Item 1150 (21 April 1630).

[53] See Chapter 68, fo. 32.

[54] A. E. Preston, *Christ's Hospital, Abingdon* (1929, repr. 1980), pp 35-6.

[55] *CSPD* 1634-5 No. 48 (27 Sept 1634).

[56] *Privy Council Registers* 12, Oct 1640- Aug 1645, p. 41.

[57] The portraits, and probably the biblical scenes depicted on the outside walls of the hospital, are by Sampson Strong from Oxford, whose reputation derived from his commemorative depictions of college founders − Robet Tittler, *Civic Portraiture and Civic Identity in Early Modern England* (Manchester, 2007), pp. 72, 80.

[58] Baker, *Historic Abingdon: Parliamentary History*, pp. 40-8; C. D. Cobham (ed), *Francis Little: A Monument of Christian Munificence* (Oxford & London, 1871). Urban history writing was much in vogue at the time, but Little's work stands out for its

emphasis on the commemoration of charitable benefactions as against political or civic achievements – Tittler, *Reformation and the Towns*, pp. 279-294.

[59] Paul Slack, *From Reformation to Improvement* (2000), pp 25, 165-6.

[60] S. H. Rigby, *English Society in the Later Middle Ages: Class, Status and Gender* (1995), pp. 170-7; D. G. Shaw, *The Creation of a Community: The City of Wells in the Middle Ages* (Oxford, 1993), pp. 167-176. The term 'urban holism' to express ideas of this sort is used by H. Swanson, *Medieval British Towns* (1999), pp. 92-3.

4. The Magnates

> The powers that be are ordained of God.
>
> > Romans 10:1

> As to the Authority in the Nation; to the Magistracy; to the Ranks and Orders
> of men – whereby England hath been known for hundreds of years? A
> nobleman, a gentleman, a yeoman; the distinction of these: that is a good
> interest of the Nation, and a great one!
>
> > Oliver Cromwell, Sept. 4, 1654

Abingdon's charter guaranteed a limited degree of self-government, but the town was by no means free to ignore either the minor potentates of the region or the great officers of state that came within its purview. One reason was economic. Much of its income came from its function as a market and social centre and from the provision of services to its hinterland. In 1577, Abingdon's working population included nine innkeepers, two taverners and twenty-six alehouse keepers.[1] The Corporation and the Hospital owned several of the inns, and at least two of the principal burgesses, Richard Ely and Thomas Orpwood, were licensees.[2] If the county gentry as a body decided to hold their quarter sessions elsewhere, or if landowners individually were tempted to resort to other towns to market their produce and buy their necessities, Abingdon would suffer. Then, as now, it did not do to alienate one's customers.

A more important reason was political. The idea of a Tudor revolution in government, as promulgated by Geoffrey Elton in the 1950s, has long been abandoned; but the century was undoubtedly one in which the state developed and government became both more pervasive and more centralised. The over-mighty barons with their private armies faded from the scene, and their successors found themselves integrated into a ruling hierarchy. Those near the top could strut about the court, advise the monarch in the Privy Council, or travel abroad on diplomatic missions; those further down ruled their 'countries' or their estates in accord with instructions received or with what they knew, or imagined, or hoped, were the monarch's desires.

The position of towns in this political space was difficult to define, even perhaps anomalous. Merchants and tradesmen did not fit into the medieval division of society into those who prayed, those who fought (and incidentally governed), and those who tilled the soil. Mayors and bailiffs were outside the chain of command that linked the smallest rural leaseholder, through greater and greater landlords, to the crown. It was easy enough to ensure that they received their instructions and orders, but difficult for them to send up the line the information, the reports, the requests, that would make the system work as effectively for them as it did in the villages around. In practice, what linked towns to the regional and central government was the formal or informal patronage of senior figures within that system.

Catherine Patterson has written a sensitive study of the delicate relationship between a town and its gentle or noble patrons.[3] Every town, if it was to thrive, needed the favour of a magnate with access to the highest reaches of government, although ideally such a figure should not be so highly placed as to be too busy or too often unreachable. He should hold estates in the locality, so that he might have first hand understanding of local problems and would fear for his prestige if he failed in resolving them. And, most importantly, he should be a man with whom it was possible to develop a personal rapport. The relationship would be initiated and maintained with entertaining, feasting, and gift exchange. The rituals and discourse would express a bond of affection between unequal parties, the patron condescending, the town deferential. The patron would be expected to be open to requests by the town to help it in its relations with other magnates or with governmental authorities, and would act to an appropriate extent as its proxy at court or in Westminster. This, of course, was exactly the function John Mason had fulfilled in getting the Privy Council to grant the Christ's Hospital charter. In return, the patron would expect the town to provide what political support it could, and to grant jobs or other favours to his friends and relations. Both sides would derive honour from the arrangement, the town by being patronised by a prestigious magnate, the patron by the respect in which he was held. The patron, in addition, would gain credit for the extent of the influence he could bring to bear to maintain harmony and good governance in the country. If the relationship was healthy, it was not one of naked power or dominance, with the patron seeking to infringe the town's traditional or chartered liberties. Rather, it was one of infinite flexibility, with each request in either direction likely to lead to an ad hoc renegotiation.[4]

Mason had done well for Abingdon, but there are reasons for thinking that after his time the town was not well served by the patronage system. In the 1580s and '90s, as we have seen, the corporation was riddled with faction, which led to appeals to Chancery and to the Privy Council to settle local conflicts. The custom of making such appeals would continue until the outbreak of the Civil War.[5] These were matters that should normally have been dealt with by the town's patron or high steward. The present chapter will consider the regional patronage networks in the sixteenth and early seventeenth centuries and Abingdon's place within them.

Long before Abingdon became a chartered town, the townsfolk will have benefited from the prominent people who were made members, no doubt honorary members, of the Holy Cross Fraternity.[6] But the later institution of high stewards as town patrons seems to have developed out of the stewardship of landed estates, in Abingdon's case that of the abbey. The stewardship of monasteries by the sixteenth century had become a complex and puzzling matter. The man who was responsible at Abingdon before its dissolution in 1538 for the actual work of stewarding, and whose own money was at stake if he failed in his well-defined duties, was John Audlett.[7] Audlett was a man of local status and influence in his own right, and there were sums in dispute between him and the abbey in the 1630s that amounted to close to a year of the abbey's revenues.[8] Yet several other individuals also claimed to be stewards of the abbey. The stewardship in this sense had become a purely artificial device by which the king could reward his servants, courtiers and ministers at the abbey's expense, and the abbot seems to have had no alternative but to accept the nominations. The salary was £10 per year – perhaps £50,000 today – and courtiers amassed large portfolios of such offices which could be bought and sold and, taken together, could make them very rich.[9] There were no fixed duties, or if there were they could be carried out by deputies, but the post did allow oversight and influence. One holder was Sir Thomas Fettiplace, of a prominent local family, in 1522.[10] In 1528, the soldier and courtier William Lord Sandys wrote to the chancellor Thomas Wolsey about 'my brother Essex desiring the stewardship of Abingdon lately held by Compton'. Sir William Compton was another courtier recently deceased, and brother Essex was presumably Sir William Essex of London and Lambourn who was building up his Berkshire interests at the time.[11] Henry Norris, courtier, alleged lover of Anne Boleyn, and father of the Sir Henry Norris who will figure largely in this chapter, was a steward.[12] The arch-conservative Duke of Norfolk was another, apparently partly at the same time.[13] So was the Viscount Beauchamp, later Protector Somerset.[14] When the entrepreneur William Blacknall and his associates applied to Somerset for a relaxation of the terms on which he could run his fulling mill in the old abbey precinct, it may have been in the latter's capacity of steward rather than as regent for the infant king.[15] But by 1551, as we have seen, Sir John Mason was claiming the stewardship, and was extending its reach to cover the town as a whole. It is unclear what right he had to the formal title of High Steward of Abingdon, but no one seems to have doubted that this was what he was until his death in 1566.

In spite of his tenure of the abbey site, John Mason never lived in or near Abingdon. He preferred his estate in Hampshire, and his name usually figures in commissions of the peace for that county.[16] The founding document of the Hospital did not require him or Amyce to be resident in the town, although all other governors had to be inhabitants. Only one Berkshire gentry family seems to have taken any interest in the fate of Abingdon in Mason's time, that of Hyde, with its seat at Denchworth in the Vale. This was one of the few such Berkshire families that were of long continuance in their estates; it was highly prolific, and younger sons seem often to have come to seek their fortunes in Abingdon. Hydes were members of the Holy Cross fraternity from the early fifteenth century until its dissolution.[17] Their status was recognised by Mason when he made Oliver Hyde his deputy as master of the Hospital, and it must have been by Mason's favour that he was returned to Parliament in 1558 and 1563. His father had sat several times for Berkshire, and in 1563 his brother William was also a member.[18] His father had been sheriff of Berkshire in 1551, when he had worked with Mason to suppress the demonstrations planned in favour of the Duke of Somerset; his nephew Humphrey would acquire Northcourt and be mayor of Abingdon four times before the end of the century.[19] But the Hydes never attained the independent prestige that might have permitted them to rival Mason in the services they could render.

In fact, as Christopher Durston has pointed out, Berkshire was remarkably deficient in well-established gentry or noble families. No doubt the extensive holdings of Abingdon and Reading abbeys will have made it difficult for others to develop the landed basis necessary for regional authority.[20] Mason himself never sought to set up a power base in Berkshire, and his last recorded activity in Abingdon was to promulgate a set of regulations for the Hospital in 1558. He would die in 1566, by which time a new regional political structure had appeared, dominated by families of recent arrival in the district and active across county boundaries.

These families were the Norrises, based at Rycote near Thame, and the Knollyses, whose main residence was at Rotherfield Greys, near Henley in Oxfordshire. There is no suggestion of overt hostility between the two groups, and indeed they cooperated perfectly well in regional administrative tasks, but contemporaries had no doubt that a certain rivalry existed.[21] The situation was complicated by the power and influence of Robert Dudley, earl of Leicester, official favourite from early in Elizabeth's reign until his death in 1588. Leicester's power came from his office as lieutenant and from 1562 constable of Windsor Castle. He seems to have been regarded by the Privy Council as lord lieutenant of Berkshire even when no such position formally existed.[22] He was allied to the Knollyses by shared religious convictions, and his second wife, Lettice Devereux, countess of Essex, whom he married in 1578 after she had long been reputed his mistress, was a daughter of that family. [23]

Sir Henry Norris owed his wealth and position to his father-in-law, Baron Williams of Thame, who had died in 1559. Williams had started his career as a functionary of the Court of Augmentations. His background seems to have been very similar to that of Roger Amyce; his first important assignment had been as receiver for the dissolved abbey at Thame, as Amyce's had been at Reading and Glastonbury. But his career took a different turn.[24] By 1540 he had acquired the Thame abbey complete, as well as what would be his residence at Rycote and a Berkshire estate at Wytham. In 1544, he became treasurer of the court, and the way was open to some serious enrichment.[25] In 1553, he was among the first to proclaim Queen Mary over the pretensions of Northumberland and Jane Grey, and he personally raised a force said to be of six thousand men in her support. But he was also prescient enough to protect his position with Elizabeth by personal kindness to her when she was a prisoner at Woodstock, and may have provided a covert link between her staff and the rebels of 1554 who sought to depose Mary in her favour.[26] Elizabeth's gratitude would carry over to his daughter Margery and her husband.

Sir Francis Knollys came from a line of prominent courtiers and had proved his ability in a number of military and political roles. His wife was first cousin to the queen.[27] He had gone into exile during Mary's reign, but at Elizabeth's accession returned to rapid advancement. On the death of Lord Williams, he replaced him as custos rotulorum for Oxfordshire and became high steward of the city of Oxford.[28] It was probably he who arranged for Leicester to replace Mason as chancellor of the University, and he himself succeeded Mason as treasurer of the queen's chamber.[29] He was also an efficient parliamentary manager on behalf of the crown. His position in Oxfordshire enabled him to hold the senior county seat and to have some of his many sons sit as MPs for Oxford city; other relatives sat for Reading.[30]

Henry Norris was less of a courtier, and a diplomatic posting to France was unsuccessful.[31] Like Sir Francis, he had many sons. They were, however, of very different character from the younger Knollys generation; in the words of a later commentator, 'they (the Knollysses) were of the court and carpet, and not led by the genius of the camp'.[32] The Norrises, in other words, were soldiers, who made names for themselves for turbulent indiscipline, ruthlessness, and a high degree of military skill.[33] Five of the six would die on active service, until Elizabeth finally heeded the pleas of their distraught mother by withdrawing the survivor, Edward, from his exposed post in Ostend. [34] But before then the second son, John, had done the family fortunes no good by quarrelling in the Netherlands with Leicester, his superior officer, and making enemies of that worthy and of his stepson, the Earl of Essex.

Abingdon was a place where Knollys and Norris influence overlapped; the chamberlains' accounts show civic entertainment and gift exchange with both whenever they visited.[35] But the authority of the Earl of Leicester was overriding. At Mason's death, Leicester moved fast, sending his trusted associate Anthony Forster with gifts to the Abingdon corporation, and, it seems, was accepted to fill the vacancy as high steward. Forster immediately became Abingdon's parliamentary burgess, even though he lived outside the town, at Cumnor. For the second time, it was the town that had been chosen by a patron rather than the other way about. Leicester was high steward of no fewer than thirteen towns including four in Berkshire — Windsor, Reading, Wallingford and Abingdon — but took little interest in them. There is no evidence that he saw his high stewardship as anything other than a means to get parliamentary seats for his friends and relations, or — which is not quite the same thing — to ensure that local seats went only to men who would give no trouble to the government. The relationships were always one-sided and, as his biographer Simon Adams has commented, 'more that of a lord of the manor than a high steward'.[36] Local parliamentary seats were shared out among the magnates; Abingdon was represented several times by Forster and, after his death in 1576, by another Leicester man, Richard Beake, who had married into the Reade family of Barton. In 1584 and 1589, the member for Abingdon would be Edward Norris, third son of Henry, Lord Norreys of Rycote, as he by then was. In 1586, the seat went to Miles Sandys, brother of Edwin, Archbishop of York. Edwin Sandys, and possibly Miles Sandys as well, had during Mary's time been in exile with Francis Knollys.[37]

There will have been little enthusiasm in the corporation for Leicester's services. A remarkably clumsy intervention in the 1571 election, when Norris, no doubt against his better judgement, was obliged to support Leicester's carpet-bagging candidate for the junior county seat, caused hostility between the Norrises and the followers of the defeated candidate, Sir Henry Unton of

Wadley. This led to a serious affray in the Abingdon market place at which John Norris and several others were wounded and one man killed. At least two young members of the Abingdon élite, Thomas Tesdale and Richard Smith, were drawn in on the Unton side.[38] It was not until 1581 that Mayor John Fisher and the bailiffs formalised Leicester's appointment as high steward, granting him a stipend of five marks per year.[39]

Even this, however, was not enough to put the relationship onto a firm basis. In 1584-5, Leicester on his passages through Abingdon when travelling to and from his home at Kenilworth seems to have had to do without civic entertainment and to open his own purse for the customary bell-ringing and musical serenades.[40] In May 1584 Mayor Thomas Smith wrote to Francis Walsingham, Elizabeth's secretary of state, asking that Abingdon might have its own militia commission 'according to ancient privilege'.[41] Having its own militia commission was a matter not only of economy but also of honour for a town corporation.[42] Walsingham passed the request to the county commissioners, who blankly refused.[43] It was not usual for a mayor to write directly to a secretary of state; such matters would be within the normal province of a high steward, especially if the high steward was also effectively the lord lieutenant of the county who could have made the decision on his own authority. That Leicester was being bypassed in this way shows firstly that the Abingdon mayor and corporation were dissatisfied with his services and secondly that they did not care if he felt affronted by their action, as well he might.[44]

When Leicester died in 1588, it was Lord Norreys who must have seemed the most likely candidate for the succession as high steward, but there is no certain evidence that the office was ever granted to him. In fact, the Norris family was entering a period of decline, as the sons died prematurely in battle leaving the bereaved father with their debts to settle. It was unfortunate that, as we have seen, the same period saw the development of intense factionalism in Christ's Hospital and the Corporation. With no figure of authority that could be appealed to, the warring parties seem to have had little alternative but to resort to the distant and less satisfactory mediation of the court of Chancery or the Privy Council.[45]

The only noticeable, and in fact successful, outside intervention in this period was that of Thomas Egerton in 1598.[46] He had no formal position in Abingdon, but stepped at Little's request into the vacant function of visitor of the Hospital. The setting up of investigatory commissions of local gentlemen was standard Chancery practice, but it is plain from the records that he was acting informally by his own authority as Lord Keeper, and that there was no involvement of the court hierarchy. To have had two such commissions set up successively and reporting within a total of nine months would scarcely have been possible had normal Chancery procedures been followed.

It does seem probable that the involvement of Egerton was an act of patronage, possibly by Lord Norreys, who was then, if anyone was, high steward, but more likely by the future high steward, Sir William Knollys, son and successor to Sir Francis. Both families had connections to Egerton. In 1593 or 4, Edward Norris, Lord Norreys's son, had incurred Egerton's displeasure by receiving from the queen a lucrative clerkship of the petty bag in Chancery which should have been in the Keeper's gift.[47] Two years later, in making his will, Henry Norris would 'humbly entreat' Egerton, 'if it would please his lordship', to act as overseer and accept £100 for so doing. There were complications in his inheritance that might need the help of a top lawyer.[48] But Egerton's link with the Knollyses was much closer; he was a friend and advisor to the Earl of Essex, and had been granted a Knollys parliamentary seat before his elevation.[49] Egerton and Sir William Knollys were among the more assiduous attendees at meetings of the Privy Council. When the trouble broke out in Christ's Hospital, Francis Little and William Knollys were sitting together in parliament, and the balance of probabilities would seem to be that it was there and then that Egerton's aid had been enlisted.

In this period, also, it was townsmen who were representing Abingdon in parliament. No doubt this was what had been envisaged by the men who had drafted the charter, but the fact is that from the start the town's MPs had been nominees of its patrons: of Mason, and then of Norris or Leicester. But in 1593, the parliamentary burgess was William Braunche, a draper and maltster, a former mayor; in 1597, it was Francis Little; in 1601, a Robert Rithe of whom so little is known that, according to the History of Parliament, he was probably the son of the man with whom he is usually identified.[50]

Lord Norreys died in 1601, and Sir William Knollys took over several of his administrative functions. At some time, he became high steward of Abingdon.[51] He certainly seems to have acted in that capacity in obtaining the two charter revisions of 1610, which would work to the advantage of his old fellow parliamentarian, Francis Little.[52] But as he aged, his influence followed that of the Norrises into decline.[53] He gave up his high stewardship of Abingdon in 1630 and died in 1632, aged about 87 years. His successor would be his great-nephew, Henry Rich, Earl of Holland. Like Leicester, Holland had no property in Berkshire but was constable of Windsor Castle.[54]

The rising power in Berkshire in the early seventeenth century would be the Lovelaces of Hurley. Sir Richard Lovelace made a fortune, or so it was said, under Howard on the Spanish Main. In 1598 he married the widow of William Hyde of Denchworth, head of a family that had long been active in county and Abingdon affairs, and he and his new stepson (who was his senior by two years or thereabouts) became the two knights of the shire for Berkshire. In the parliament that sat from 1604 to 1611, Lovelace, rather than a Knollys nominee, would be the member for Abingdon. He would sit later for New Windsor, and be ennobled in 1627 as Baron Lovelace of Hurley.[55] It would be men connected with his family who would be politically dominant in Abingdon for much of the rest of the century. But by then, as will be seen, patronage would have become less a mutually beneficial relationship than one of tutelage and control

Urban self-government seems a laudable ideal to a modern historian as it did in the sixteenth century, but in the context of that time it had its limits. In spite, or perhaps because, of the lack of definition of the office, the high stewardship was an important part of the governance of an early modern town. Properly exercised by the town corporation, by the crown, and by the high steward himself, it kept the town integrated into the wider county and national community and mediated conflicts both internal and external. The lack of proper patronage in the later sixteenth century was damaging to Abingdon in that it gave scope for the unchecked growth of factionalism, and this, in its turn, would contribute to further difficulties in time to come.

---

[1] TNA, SP 12/119 fol 44 (30 Dec 1577).

[2] BRO, D/EP 7 49; Jacqueline Smith and John Carter, *Inns and Alehouses of Abingdon 1550-1978* (2nd edn, 1989), pp. 101-118 and passim.

[3] Terms like 'gentle', 'noble', 'aristocratic' have given rise to much debate over their exact definition. For the present purpose, I use 'magnate' to designate anyone of sufficient status to act as a broker in the relationship between a town and county or national authorities.

[4] Catherine Patterson, *Urban Patronage in Early Modern England* (1999).

[5] Above, Chap. 3, and below, Chap. 5.

[6] Mieneke Cox, *Medieval Abingdon* (Abingdon, 1989), p. 102.

[7] Cox, *Medieval Abingdon*, pp.112, 114-9, 136, 137.

[8] BRO, Preston Papers, D/EP7 33 (unfol).

[9] The figure of £50,000 is arrived at from runs of incomes over time. Purchasing power is much harder to estimate, but gives an equivalent of some £4000 in present money. See http://www.measuringworth.com/index.html. For a good example of the miscellaneous nature of the wealth built up by courtiers, see the list of properties of Henry Norris, drawn up after his attainder in 1536: *L&P* Vol 10 1536 No. 878ii (Mich. 1536).

[10] TNA, Military Survey of 1522, E 315/464 (I am grateful to Dr Margaret Yates for this reference); 'Sir Thomas Fettiplace', www.berkshistory.com. According to the Survey, Thomas Fettiplace, who was an elderly man by then and will have retired from the court, actually did have defined practical responsibilities, and also acted as steward for other landlords, including the crown. He was buried in the Abbey church – W. Harry Rylands, *The Four Visitations of Berkshire* (1907) I p. 1.

[11] It is not clear that Sir William Essex ever did become high steward – *L&P* Vol 4 1526-8 no. 4454 (2 July 1528); G. W. Bernard, 'The Rise of Sir William Compton, Early Tudor Courtier', *The English Historical Review* 96 (1981), pp. 754-777; *VCH Berks* shows Essex as holding eight, and Compton two, Berkshire manors.

[12] *L&P* Vol 10 1536 No. 878ii (Mich. 1536); Walter C. Richardson, *History of the Court of Augmentations, 1536-1554* (Baton Rouge, 1961), p. 289.

[13] *L&P* Vol 8 1535 No. 401 (17 March 1535).

[14] TNA, Decrees of the Court of Augmentations vol 105 fo. 56 (12 Feb 1537), transcript in Berks RO, Preston papers, D/EP 7 39 (unfol); *L&P* Vol 12 i no 246 (26 Jan 1537).

[15] TNA SP 46/2, fols 200-206.

[16] *CPR* Edw VI 1 iii p. 84 (22 March 1647); 2 vii p. 136 (14 Feb 1548), where Mason and Amyce appear both for Berks and Hants; Vol 5 Appx 1 p. 358 (16 Dec 1550).

[17] Mieneke Cox, *Peace and War* (Abingdon, 1993), pp. 21-2; James Townsend, *A History of Abingdon* (1910), p. 57

[18] *HoP 1509-1558*, I, p 32; II, pp. 430-1; *HoP 1558-1603*, I, p. 114; II, pp. 364-5.

[19] A.E. Preston, *St Nicholas and other Papers* (1928), p. 432.

[20] C.G. Durston, 'London and the Provinces: The association between the capital and the Berkshire county gentry in the early seventeenth century', *Southern History* 3 (1981), pp. 38-53.

[21] James Caulfield (ed); *The Court of Queen Elizabeth: Originally Written by Sir Robert Naunton, Under the Title of "Fragmenta Regalia."* (1814), pp. 57-62.

[22] BL, Addl Ms 41809 (Yelverton XIX), fos. 282v-3, 293v-4v; Simon Adams, *Leicester and the Court; Essays on Elizabethan politics* (Manchester, 2002), pp. 200-2, 385.

[23] Simon Adams, 'Dudley, Lettice, countess of Essex and countess of Leicester (1543–1634)', in *DNB*.

[24] Sybil M. Jack, 'Williams, John, Baron Williams (*c*.1500–1559)' in *DNB*.

[25] S.J. Gunn, *Early Tudor Government 1485-1558* (1995), p. 158; Richardson, *Augmentations*, pp. 266-8.

[26] David Starkey, *Elizabeth: Apprenticeship* (2000), p. 259.

[27] She was the daughter of 'the other Boleyn girl', Anne's sister Mary, and may actually have been fathered by Henry himself - which would make Knollys the queen's brother-

in-law - Sally Varlow, 'Knollys, Katherine, Lady Knollys (*c.*1523–1569) in *DNB*; Jonathan Hughes, 'Stafford, Mary (*c.*1499–1543)', in *DNB*.

[28] The Custos Rotulorum was recognised as senior among the local members of the county commission of the peace. The position was therefore one of high honour.

[29] Intriguingly, Elizabeth Mason continued to function as treasurer and also as master of the posts for almost a year after her husband's death. One wonders whether she had the necessary competence, or simply relied on subordinate staff - Walter C. Richardson. *History of the Court of Augmentations, 1536-1554* (Baton Rouge, 1961), pp. 158-9.

[30] *HoP 1558-1603* II p. 408-20; Wallace T. MacCaffrey, 'Knollys, Sir Francis (1511/12–1596)', in *DNB*.

[31] BL, Stowe Ms 147, passim.

[32] James Caulfield (ed); *The Court of Queen Elizabeth*, p. 60.

[33] John S. Nolan, *Sir John Norreys and the Elizabethan Military World* (Exeter, 1997).

[34] Doran, 'Norris, Henry', in *DNB*.

[35] H. T. Riley. 'On the Abingdon Corporation and Christ's Hospital Records', in HMC 2nd Report, (1874), pp. 149-50; BRO, Chamberlains' accounts transcripts, D/EP7 83.

[36] BL, Add Ms 41809 (Yelverton XIX), fos 293v-4v; Simon Adams, *Leicester and the Court: Essays on Elizabethan politics* (2002), pp. 201-2.

[37] *HoP 1558-1603*, I, p. 411; II, pp. 135-6; III, p. 341.

[38] *HoP 1558-1603*, I, p. 113; III, pp. 580-581; TNA, STAC 5/N/10/11; STAC 5/N16/38; *CPR* Elizabeth 1569-72 No 3348 (15 Feb 1572). The affair gave rise to a proclamation against liveried servants – Paul L. Hughes, James F. Larkin (eds), *Tudor Royal Proclamations* (Yale: 1964-9), II pp. 350-352.

[39] Marquess of Bath (Longleat), Dudley papers Box 3, 55 (8 Aug 1581). I am grateful to the archivist at Longleat for a photograph of the patent. The wording makes it clear that Leicester had been high steward of Abingdon for some time but had not previously been paid for it. He was already noted as high steward in the 1566 Visitation – Rylands, *Four visitations* (1907) I 13-14.

[40] S. Adams (ed), *Household Accounts and Disbursement Books of Robert Dudley, Earl of Leicester, 1558-1561, 1584-1586,* (Camden Soc, 3 Ser, Vol 5, 1995), pp. 189, 216-8, 289; W.J.H. Liversidge, *Abingdon Essays: Studies in Local History* (Abingdon, 1989), p. 66.

[41] *CSPD* 1581-1590 No 93 (27 May 1584). Expenditures on the militia are detailed by Liversidge, *Abingdon Essays,* p. 68.

[42] Robert Tittler, 'The emergence of urban policy, 1536-58' in Jennifer Loach and Robert Tittler, *The Mid-Tudor Polity c1540-1560* (1980), pp. 74-93 at pp. 86-7.

[43] *CSPD* 1581-1590 No 11 (7 June 1584). It seems that in 1569 the Berkshire militia was mustered in Abingdon and marched to York to help put down the Northern Rising. There is a record that Reading and Windsor were reimbursed for equipping their men, but not Abingdon. If correct, this will have rankled. *CSPD* 1601-3 Addenda p. 502 No 65 (noted as 'May 1560?', but probably after 1569).

[44] It is unlikely to be coincidental that the letter was dated a few days after Leicester had left for a holiday trip to Denbigh and Chester – Adams, *Leicester and the Court*, pp. 324, 386.

---

[45] For many examples of the role of high stewards in settling such conflicts, see Patterson, *Urban Patronage* pp. 88-106.

[46] Above, p. 30.

[47] W.J. Jones, 'An Introduction to Petty Bag Proceedings in the Reign of Elizabeth', *California Law Review* 51 (1963), pp. 882-905 at p. 885. The petty bag was essentially the function that handled incoming mail and documents.

[48] TNA, PROB 11/98.

[49] *HoP 1558-1603*, I, pp. 80-3

[50] *HoP 1558-1603*, III, p. 294.

[51] From 1603, he was Baron Knollys of Greys; he would later become Viscount Wallingford and Earl of Banbury.

[52] Below, p. 67.

[53] His reputation was not improved by a late marriage to a teen-age daughter of the Catholic Howard family, who was, no doubt correctly, suspected of cuckolding him – Victor Stater, 'Knollys, William, first earl of Banbury (*c.*1545–1632)', in *DNB*.

[54] R. Malcolm Smuts, 'Rich, Henry, first earl of Holland (*bap.* 1590, *d.* 1649)', in *DNB*.

[55] *HoP 1558-1603*, II, pp. 360-1, 490-1.

5. Family factions

The lower and weaker faction is the firmer in conjunction: and it is often seen that a few that are stiff do tire out a greater number that are more moderate.

Francis Bacon, *Essay LI*

We have seen in a previous chapter the rise of faction in the Abingdon corporation, and have noted that it pitched families, or groups of families, against each other.[1] The Tesdales seem always to have been at the centre of one faction, hostile to that led by Little in his time and afterwards by members of the large and complex Mayott clan. It may be significant that the Tesdales arrived in Abingdon about the end of the fifteenth century with one member of the family, whose religious name was John Clyffe, serving as the abbey's sub-prior and master of its school.[2] The Mayotts by then were already well established as leading townsmen.[3] It may not be over-imaginative to see in the continued family competition some vestige of the age-old hostility in Abingdon between town and abbey. There were no doubt business rivalries, but these remain unclear. The conflicts that have left their traces in the historical record include some over municipal offices, but more often concern religion.

Few historical categories can have been subject to as much controversy and debate as that of Puritanism. That a historian of the stature of S.R. Gardiner could casually characterise the Civil War and its aftermath as the Puritan Revolution now seems incredibly naïve. Multitudes of later scholars of a literary or post-modern bent fastened on the imprecision of the term and analysed and deconstructed it until almost nothing was left. In the nineteen-nineties, research students were advised to avoid the term completely, for fear that finicky examiners and referees would focus on questions of definition and lose sight of the main subject of the thesis or paper. And yet, it is a category that the local historian cannot do without, and it is no less precise than that of the Left in discussions of the twentieth century, or the Greens for the present day. Like those, Puritans had their plethora of warring subgroups, their realists and fundamentalists, their militant tendency and their hooligan fringe. They might deplore the name under which they were forced to labour, but they knew who they were and what they stood for, and their opponents likewise knew who the Puritans were and what they stood for.

What they stood for was complex, but it was distinct from the desires of their neighbours. In religion, they wished to complete the Reformation by a general downgrading of ceremony in favour of bible study and preaching. In itself, this might not have been unduly divisive. But extended into politics, it meant that their priority was not social harmony but the legal entrenchment of their principles, even if this meant social conflict. Their principles included extreme sabbatarianism as well as such apparently irrational exotica as the abomination of stage plays, stained glass, and market crosses. Their greatest peculiarity was perhaps in the social connections they made; Puritans networked horizontally for political support among their fellows in the region or the nation, while their opponents tended to rely on the vertical structures of information and control preferred by successive monarchs and the majorities in their privy councils. It was this, above all, that earned the Puritans the distrust of the political establishment.[4] Until about 1640, as will be seen, Puritans were an increasingly irreconcilable oppositional group. At that time, they captured the political mainstream, only to lose it again within a couple of decades. This and the following chapters will describe these processes as they played out in Abingdon.

Abingdon was born as a chartered town into a period of religious confusion. For some twenty-five years past, governmental policy had been oscillating between religious conservatism and radical change. The radicals dominated the 1530s, but Cromwell had lost his head in 1540 and the direction had been reversed. With the death of Henry VIII and the accession of a boy king, the move towards Protestantism had been resumed, and the abolition of the guilds and chantries was one of a series of measures that were supposed to make a return to the old ways impossible. In 1556 Edward's Catholic sister and her Spanish husband were on the throne and the clock had, at least officially, been put back. But because of its geographic position, between London and Oxford, on the major waterway that was the Thames and on the highway that crossed it at the Burford Bridge, the new ideas had come early to Abingdon, and had appealed especially to the educated and literate. There seems to have been little enthusiasm among the town's élites for a return to the old religion.

For Protestants, but not for Catholics, listening to sermons was the main way of affirming their religious identity. The lawyer and property speculator Thomas Denton who died in 1558 financed what seems to have been the first regular endowed sermon in the town, to be delivered at St Helen's annually on Easter Day. In fact the endowment was sufficiently wisely invested to provide for two sermons by the next century.[5] Thereafter, it was by the increasing numbers of sermons or 'lectures' financed by individuals or by the town government that the development of Protestant beliefs, at least among the wealthier classes, can be gauged.

Thomas Denton was stepfather to Sir John Fettiplace of Besselsleigh. In 1577, Sir John joined with the rich woollendraper Lionell Bostock to provide a weekly Thursday lecture in Abingdon. It was designed to fit in with proceedings in the local sessions, and litigants were expected to attend the lecture while the justices decided their cases. There were to be two lecturers, learned divines of Oxford, who would be retained on a stipend of £10 each per year.[6] Earlier, in 1573, Ralph Segar, yeoman, had left 11s for a doctor of divinity to preach in St Helen's yearly on the Sunday next before Easter. In 1579, another woollendraper, Richard Mayott, left 6s 8d yearly for a 'learned preacher' to perform at St Helen's on the morning of the day on which the mayor was chosen, normally the first of September.[7] Lionell Bostock in 1600 left the surely over-generous sum of 24s for a Christmas afternoon sermon. Thomas Orpwood, Master of Christ's Hospital in 1604, endowed an annual founder's day sermon at Whitsun, which was inaugurated by the already controversial William Laud; and in 1616, Maud Tesdale arranged for the Hospital to have a preacher of at least M.A. standing every Sunday at 13s 4d per week. In 1619, a canopy was put over St Helen's pulpit, no doubt to improve the acoustics. In 1625, Thomas Mayott left an annual 13s 4d for a sermon to be given on Palm Sunday afternoons, and the same sum to the vicar of St Helen's for preaching in the morning; 6s 8d was available for preparations and for bell-ringing to bring in the audience. Presumably Segar's bequest of 1573 had run out.[8] In the same year, no doubt under Francis Little's influence, the council re-established a Good Friday sermon in honour of the town's benefactors; first on the list of those to be praised were, remarkably for the time, the Catholic monarchs Phillip and Mary, who had granted its charter.[9] Finally, Richard Wrigglesworth in 1647 endowed a regular weekly lectureship that would be split between Abingdon and Marcham, and was originally intended to provide a £30 p.a. stipend for the extreme Puritan minister, John Pendarves.[10]

But among the populace at large and among a proportion of the élite, the Catholic mindset persisted. At St Helen's, it was only in the fourth year of Elizabeth's reign that the rood loft was removed, and the holes in the wall where the joists had been fixed stopped up and painted over with scriptural verses.[11] When John Roysse endowed his school in 1563, he expressly provided that the master and scholars would, three times each day, go down on their knees and pray for his soul, singing the Ave Maria and the De Profundis. What he plainly had in mind was to bypass the laws forbidding chantries and prayers to speed the deceased through purgatory. The corporation feigned acceptance of his untimely condition, but added other provisions which effectively negated it.[12] It seems to have been especially the desire for commemoration of the dead that died hard in Abingdon. As we have seen, Francis Little was a great exponent of the commemorative principle, which seems to have been more strongly accepted at St Nicholas than at the larger church of St Helen's. John Blacknall's will of 1625 left ample funds to finance ceremonies at St Nicholas four times a year, of which two would be his birthday and the anniversary of his death. These would take place in the presence of the Provost of Queen's College in Oxford, the Recorder of Abingdon, and the Vicar of St Helen's 'or any two of them'. No doubt these worthies, who would be well paid for their attendance, would attest to the orthodoxy of the proceedings which might otherwise be questioned. There would be a sermon, charity money would be distributed to six poor men of the parish, and also

> ... a celebration of the blessed sacrament of the eucharist, or the holy communion of the supper of Our Lord .... and that at the said daies there shall such thankes giving to almightie God and such com'emoracon of me and this my guifte as I have thought meete. And that the said sixe poore inhabitants and such of the people present at the divine service at the said dayes as shall please to ioyne with them shall pray for the good and prosperitie of our sovereigne Lord King Charles and of the offspring and progenie of his body, and of the offspring and progenie of me John Blacknall and of William Blacknall Esquire deceased my father, and of William Blacknall gent my grandfather, and for the good of all faithfull people.[13]

The caution shown by John Blacknall, and that of Thomas Mayott whose will, also of 1625, provided a financial inducement for the Puritan vicar of St Helen's to accept a preacher chosen by the testator's friends at Christ's Hospital, suggests that their religious conservatism was under attack from a more enthusiastically Protestant faction.[14] The split between the 'hotter' Protestants and those less ready to leave the old ways behind probably dated back to the high stewardship of the Earl of Leicester in the previous century. Leicester was a great patron of the Puritans, and it seems that the Tesdales were among his active supporters. In 1573, Thomas Tesdale rented a part of Fitzharris to Leicester's protégé Richard Beake, who had married into the

Reade family of Barton and would replace Anthony Forster as the town's parliamentary representative three years later.[15] There was probably already a religious dimension to the conflicts between the Tesdale party and that led by Francis Little in the Corporation and the Hospital before and at the turn of the century, and it is remarkable that Little's pioneering attempt at local history has not a single mention of the earl, important though his influence must have been in Abingdon.

It is certainly the case that advanced Protestant ideas were being disseminated in Abingdon before the turn of the century. The Thursday lectures (moved to Tuesdays in 1609) seem always to have attracted Puritan preachers of very high calibre. The first lecturer in 1577 was Lawrence Humphrey, President of Magdalen, known for his ability as a speaker.[16] He was followed by John Rainolds, fellow and later President of Corpus Christi. Robert Abbott, brother of the future archbishop, fellow and later Master of Balliol, preached frequently until 1616 when he moved to Salisbury as bishop.[17] Perhaps the most remarkable of the lecturers was John Prime of New College, who in 1587 delivered a fortnightly course on Galatians which he later published as a book of some 350 pages. It is hard to imagine this course being appreciated by the average townsman of Abingdon; it makes no intellectual concessions whatever. In fact, the lectures seem to have attracted an élite audience from the region; the book's introduction includes a greeting 'to Abington and the Gentlemen & Justices neere adjoining'. Prime's exposition was thoroughly up to date, at the cutting edge of contemporary scholarship.[18] Thus, even before 1600, a full indoctrination into the prevalent religious ideologies was available to any townsman or woman who wanted it. Indeed, it may have been forced even on those who did not. From 1585, on pain of a fine, every household had to send one or more representatives, depending on its size, to each of the lectures. They were expected to pass what they had learnt on to their families.[19] By the turn of the century Sabbath observance was being tightened; and by 1607 the mayor was levying heavy fines for 'unlawfull games' on Sundays.[20]

Opposition to the trend towards an advanced or Puritan version of Protestantism came to be centred in the smaller Abingdon church, that of St Nicholas, and was led by Francis Little and John Blacknall. St Nicholas about 1600 was not in a prosperous state. It had suffered from a spate of lawsuits, and there was little money available to attract experienced ministers or even able curates. Some bequests came in early in the century, and in 1617 a Chancery commission ruled that certain properties in the town rightfully belonged to the church and their income could be used in part to pay a minister or a curate 'chosen by the parishioners or the greater part of them' and the rest for maintenance of the fabric. One of the members of the commission was Walter Dayrell, currently recorder of the town. He was a Mayott son-in-law and would be one of the overseers of John Blacknall's will, referred to there as his 'good friend'. The ruling was significant; henceforth the choice of a curate would be made by the church vestry and not by the rector, always an absentee, nor by the vicar of St Helen's who held, ex officio, the same position at St Nicholas. The vestry was dominated by Little, Blacknall, and Dayrell, and they appear to have had the support of the current vicar, William Kisbey.[21]

The amounts of money available for a curate at St Nicholas were still limited, but the church's finances were further improved in 1625 with the death of John Blacknall. His will added significantly to the endowments of the church and the emoluments of the curate. The properties that were to contribute to these funds were scattered throughout Berkshire and neighbouring counties, and included lands in Longworth, some six miles west of Abingdon. The rectory of Longworth was held by Samuel Fell, future Dean of Christ Church in Oxford, who was also rector of Sunningwell, nearer to Abingdon, and now began to take an interest in the town. John Stone, the curate who would benefit from Blacknall's legacies, was a former curate of his in Longworth, and in 1626 one of his parishioners there, Susanna Davis, provided an additional £20 towards 'bewtifying' the screen between church and chancel. Charles Tooker, Doctor of Civil Law, an official at the Berkshire archdeaconry and an Abingdon resident, provided an additional £5 for similarly 'bewtifying' the roof.[22]

By now, the split that had long existed in the English church between the advanced or Puritan tendency and the traditionalists was widening, and the nature of the conflict was changing. No longer could the Puritans see themselves as leaders of a movement where all travelled, albeit at widely different speeds, towards the same destination. With the accession of Charles I, the influence of the future archbishop William Laud and his allies became paramount in the church while the current archbishop, George Abbot, sometime friend of Thomas Tesdale, suffered eclipse.[23] Analysis of the division in doctrinal terms ceases to be helpful; Laud was, arguably, as much a Calvinist as any of his opponents.[24] The innovations he fostered were primarily ecclesiological; the church was to regain the dignity and the ceremonial that it had lost in its rejection of Catholicism; it was to aspire to 'the beauty of holiness'.[25] Puritans were appalled, and counter-attacked. St Nicholas with its newly acquired 'bewtifying' was among their objectives.

Among the items presented by Blacknall was a new communion table with a fine carpet to cover it. Communion tables were controversial; the Puritans saw them as purely utilitarian pieces of furniture to be placed wherever in the church was most convenient, while to the Laudians they were essentially altars and to be treated with respect, even bowed to at appropriate occasions. In 1628, a new set of chancery commissioners, with Samuel Fell among its members, made a number of orders enforcing Laudian norms at St Nicholas, including

> ... that the Table given by Mr. *Blacknall* should not by the multitude of People coming to Service, or otherwise by sitting or writing upon it, or by any other unreverent usage, be prophaned, spoyled, or hurt; We do order and decree, that the said Table shall continually stand at the upper end of the Chancell, upon which a Carpet (by him given) should be laid, where it shall continually stand close to the upper Skreen (there being of old within that Skreen a kind of Vestry for keeping the Plate, Books, and Vestments which belong to the Church) and there to be covered with the Carpet aforesaid, and in no place else.[26]

It was later commented that this was the only known instance of the altarwise arrangement of the communion table being ratified by a decree in Chancery.[27]

But while the traditionalists were victorious at St Nicholas, the struggle was raging at St Helen's. Kisbey resigned in 1624, no doubt through old age, and his replacement as vicar was a man who would set the whole town by the ears, Edward Roode. His origin was obscure, and he was not a graduate. It was perhaps no coincidence that in the same year the corporation discussed damage to the Guildhall at a performance by a troupe of players. Repairs being needed to windows, benches, and pavements suggest a protest that had got out of hand.[28] Puritans had a visceral objection to theatricals.[29] In 1627, with Joshua Tesdale one of the churchwardens, there was an unauthorised attempt to take down the chancel screen. Puritans, for whom the ideal church building was a simple preaching space, disapproved of chancel screens. This caused some stir; at the end of the year, Roode did not sign the churchwardens' accounts, and nor did Joshua Tesdale who had been replaced by his immediate predecessor, John Boulter. Two completely new men intruded their signatures between those of the current year's wardens and the edge of the page, and appended a 'memorandum that all those that set their hands to the taking down of the skryne shall pay to the [incoming] churchwardens Phillip Poffle and Henry

Langley two shillings a pece'.[30] The incident had brought big guns into play; Samuel Fell reported to Laud, now Bishop of London and a Privy Councillor, that the screen was firmly back in place. 'We have shaken the authoritie of there vestrye', he wrote, but complained that no penalties were being enforced on the guilty parties, and that the 'sectaryes' were 'serving his [Roode's] turne in the gouernment of the towne, & there Hospital'.[31]

Fell's language admirably captures the fear of Charles I and his counsellors that the Puritans were a force for subversion and anarchy.[32] Robert Mayott petitioned the Privy Council complaining that Roode was 'a great disturber of the peace and amitie of the town'; he 'interposed' in town affairs, and – most seriously – he had preached against the royal supremacy in religion. 'The Maior', said Mayott, referring presumably to John Bradford, 'neglects itt'.[33] Mayott was using tactics that were becoming standard in municipal factionalism, employing exactly the language that would arouse the concern of the central authorities.[34] Roode was taken into custody and brought before the Privy Council, but, perhaps surprisingly, was discharged.[35] The Privy Council probably simply passed his case to the ecclesiastical Court of High Commission, which deprived him in 1629 and replaced him with a reliable anti-Puritan, Christopher Newstead. His widow would later claim that he remained in prison for eleven years, although this seems unlikely.[36] The Puritans were not prepared to admit defeat. The borough council allowed Roode a property lease to enable him, or at least his family, to remain in Abingdon.[37] In 1630, he paid 5s for his wife to occupy one of the most prestigiously positioned seats in St Helen's.[38] In 1640, when power had passed from Laud and his bishops, Newstead's 'voluntary' resignation allowed Roode to be re-installed as vicar as though he were completely new to the cure.[39]

It was John Stone, no doubt rejoicing, who inducted Christopher Newstead to St Helen's in 1629, in an interesting inversion of the usual pecking order between the churches.[40] Newstead had travelled in Turkey as chaplain to Sir Thomas Roe's embassy, and had won the patronage of that gentleman and, through him, of William Laud himself. Stone had studied under Laud at St John's.[41] The new vicar was obviously not made welcome by some of his parishioners, and there are signs of friction. An item in the churchwardens' accounts concerning 'Mr Newstead's goods' is crossed out and then re-instated. These accounts and the following ones are not regularly signed and approved but were passed by Charles Tooker, the archdeacon's official, in September or October after their due date. In 1634, Tooker sued the churchwardens for alleged irregularities, unfortunately undefined in the available sources.[42]

Unusual amounts of new glass had to be used in church repairs – almost 200 feet and forty dozen 'quarrels' in the years 1629-31.[43] It would seem that old painted or stained glass was being replaced with plain, which suggests deliberate iconoclasm.

What may have happened during Newstead's eleven years in Abingdon can be glimpsed, but no more, from the proceedings of the Committee against Scandalous Ministers in Essex for March 1644.[44] It seems that he had not found another living until 1643, when his new parishioners at Stisted kept him out of their church with stones and fists.[45] Stisted was a Canterbury peculiar, and the parishioners could reasonably argue that, with Laud by then in the Tower, Newstead's presentation must have been irregular. Nonetheless, he obtained a declaration of the House of Lords in his favour. The parishioners appealed to the Committee for support, and the major part of their case against him was provided by evidence obtained, apparently by correspondence, from Abingdon. The details are frustratingly vague. In 1633, Newstead had a curate with whom he had a public disagreement, stopping a sermon in which he was explaining the Calvinist theory of grace and himself preaching the Arminian view that Christ died for all. The curate could not have been Roode himself, since the churchwardens had to buy him an M.A. hood.[46] Since Newstead continued to sign the accounts, there is no obvious reason why he should have needed a curate, and he would hardly have voluntarily employed one with Calvinist principles. There were clashes on the texts and mottoes to be painted on the church walls and on the attitude to be taken to the ceiling paintings in the lady chapel. Newstead was accused of observing Lent, and of burying the dead with crosses on their breasts. In 1640, he was manoeuvred into a position where he faced prosecution, and his resignation was the price of it being dropped. No details of this are given; had there been any real guilt, they certainly would have been. The account that the Puritans published of Newstead's removal was amusingly different from that given to their Essex friends. There had been, it was said, an amicable discussion, after which Newstead had seen the impossibility of his position and had resigned with no hard feelings on either side.[47]

Roode's return to the St Helen's cure would be of short duration. When the town was occupied by royalist forces at the start of the Civil War, he found it expedient to leave, although his family remained behind. As a trusted parliamentarian, he was intruded into two London church livings, those of St Mary Magdalene and St Benet Sherehog, replacing the royalist Matthew Griffith, but he also seems to have worked for the parliamentary authorities as a tax official in Essex and Suffolk.[48] He died in or before October 1643.[49] His widow was awarded a pension of 15s per week, which would have been generous had it ever been paid, and his son was imposed on Merton as a postmaster (undergraduate) when that college was purged in 1648.[50]

Walter Dayrell, a lawyer from Buckinghamshire, had in 1602 married a daughter of Thomas Mayott, twice mayor of Abingdon. He became legal counsellor to the town in 1604 and auditor of Christ's Hospital in 1606. As we have seen, he was a strong anti-Puritan. Nonetheless, he seems to have been accepted in his functions. It was apparently Dayrell who was the moving spirit behind two important charter revisions that were made in 1610.

In 1609, during the mayoralty of John Mayott who may have been Dayrell's brother-in-law, Francis Little was sent to London for negotiations.[51] James I was encouraging charter renewals; in spite of the usual statements that no fees were payable, they did bring in significant benefit to the royal finances.[52] The Abingdon renewal was in two parts. The first, issued on 16 February 1610, was an admission that, in spite of the vigilance of Amyce and Mason, numerous items of abbey, church and chantry property had hitherto been concealed from the crown. These were listed and valued at £12 12s 4d per annum, and were formally granted to the town for the remarkably low sum of £50 9s 4d, being exactly four years' purchase.[53] The more important document, for the town if not for the king, was dated 3 March 1610. Abingdon is to 'be and remain a Borough of the Peace, and quiet to the fear dread and terror of evil delinquents'.[54] To this end, the office of counsel to the corporation would be upgraded to that of recorder. Walter Dayrell would be the first holder of the new post.[55] Whereas originally it was the mayor who was the sole justice of the peace in the town, that function would in future be shared by the current mayor, his immediate predecessor, and the recorder. As well as the court of record, two additional weekly markets and two new annual fairs were granted, and all this without any payment beyond the traditional fee farm. It must have added up to a significant economic advantage for the town.[56]

The intermediaries are mentioned in the second charter. They were William Lord Knollys, the high steward; Sir John (actually Thomas) Parry, chancellor of the Duchy of Lancaster; and Sir David Williams, judge in the Court of Common Pleas. For once, patronage was being properly used. Parry was a Berkshire deputy-lieutenant under Knollys, resident at Hampstead Marshall; Williams had married a widow of the manorial family of Kingston Bagpuize and lived there when not occupied with his legal duties.[57] All three of them were, according to the charter, to become Abingdon JPs along with the three local men who would have that status. This should not be seen as an undue dilution of the town's privileges. It was common for commissions of the peace to have magnates and judges as honorary members; it was a demonstration of trust that they would not misuse the local influence the position might give them, and that influence in itself was one of the mechanisms by which a town or region was connected with the developing institutions of the central state. The Privy Council was tending to use assize judges as its ambulating agents, and David Williams was on the Oxford circuit which included Berkshire.[58]

There was a further charter issued on 21 June 1620 which confirmed the town's market rights and listed the rates of toll that could be levied on different sorts of merchandise 'for aid, help and assistance to pave the Borough aforesaid, and to repair and mend the Bridges and Ways of the Borough aforesaid'.[59] This was a period when the town was being 'improved' in many ways, with Little's restoration of the cross in 1605, the Hospital's remodelling of the New Almshouse in the same year, and almost continuous work on St Helen's culminating in the new spire in 1634.[60] Paving the streets would seem to have been the corporation's contribution.

Dayrell died in 1628. He and his family had apparently been on visiting terms with Samuel Fell and personally known to Laud.[61] The wording on his funeral inscription in St Nicholas makes his position on the religious controversies of the time quite clear:

> ... his Law was not opposite to the Gospell, the advancemt of the Clergy being his Joy, & the beauty of Gods house his delight.[62]

The Puritan faction in the town would want a candidate of their own to replace him.

The rules that John Mason had laid down in 1558 for the Hospital provided that the man chosen as its auditor should also become the town's counsel or recorder:

> '... always such a one as he might bee hable to serue the Town as recordour or as a counsailor besydes th'executing of th'offyce of th'audytorshippe for which seruyce the saide Towne hathe promised to the saide Sir John Masone to allowe unto him xl s. ouer and aboue th'audytors fee, the hole amounting to iiii poundes which promesse the said Sir John Masone requireth them may bee obserued so as one

suffycient man maye alwaye supplye bothe the saide offyces for otherwyse the fee wyll bee very lytle'. [63]

It seemed a practical arrangement, but the promise made by the town was never enshrined in any binding agreement. There was always the potential for conflict, and one now broke out.

The governors of the Hospital elected as Dayrell's successor his son-in-law, Charles Holloway of the Inner Temple, who had Fell's approbation. Following precedent, the corporation duly elected Holloway recorder. But in October 1628, with John Bradford as the newly-installed mayor, it changed its mind, claiming that the election had been irregular. Holloway was replaced with Thomas Tesdale of Gray's Inn, who had no fewer than three kinsmen among the new electors. [64] It was about this time that John Mayott was complaining of Roode and of Bradford's toleration of him, and for good measure the corporation now demanded that future curates at St Nicholas should be appointed by the Bishop of Salisbury rather than the parishioners. [65] The case went to the Privy Council and the individuals concerned were summoned to London to account for their actions; but Thomas Tesdale remained the borough's recorder and Holloway auditor for the Hospital. [66] The Privy Council's comment was to the point: 'the said Towne is troubled with faction, by means whereof things are not carryed in so direct and faire a manner as were fit'. [67] A resolution of sorts was achieved in April 1632 when Thomas Tesdale resigned, perhaps because of ill-health, and was replaced by the young Bulstrode Whitelocke who was already well known in the district through his father, one of the judges on the local assize circuit. [68]

In the early 1630s, there seems to have been something of a balance, with the Mayott party in control of the Hospital where Tesdale names do not appear among the masters, and the Tesdales and their friends narrowly predominant in the corporation. It has been argued that the public unpopularity of Puritans had less to do with their religion than with their instinctive desire to set up 'the city on the hill', where righteousness would be imposed by the godly, if necessary with whips. [69] It seems that in Abingdon whips were necessary. Among the few sets of chamberlains' accounts that survive are those of Phillip Poffley, who served in 1633-4, with John Haw, one of the Tesdale group, as mayor. A council sub-committee headed by Benjamin Tesdale took over Abbey House for use as a workhouse at a rent of £3. It was enlarged with a loft and two rooms 'fit to keep the prisoners in'. There was a £5 budget, and the equipment provided included staples, rivets, and shackles. The whipping post was refurbished with new irons and nails, and a ducking stool constructed using no less than 34 pounds of iron, and provided with a lock and key. And, inevitably, a wandering theatre troupe was given 10s to go away.[70] On the positive side, there was a special grant of £5 to Roysse's schoolmaster for teaching poor boys. But the traditional undeserving poor, doing what they traditionally did at and coming away from the alehouse, might find a hard life becoming even harder.

Thus Abingdon in what no one could yet have known was the run-up to the Civil War was a divided town, with conflict both in the council chamber and in the church vestries. As late as April 1642, there would be a complaint to the archdeaconry against the election of John Hanson as churchwarden at St Helen's. Hanson was 'a stranger lately come to the towne, much unacquainted with the estate of the town'. He was a tobacconist, 'which are accounted enemies of the common wealth'; he was 'not well affected with the liturgie of the church', and, like Roode, had spoken of pulling down the screen.[71] It was disingenuous to describe Hanson, grandson of a former mayor of Abingdon, as a stranger, and naive indeed to think that the archdeaconry in 1642 could still act against the religiously disaffected.[72]

It was probably this period that determined the nature of later developments in the Abingdon churches. St Nicholas had become what it would remain, a haven for traditionalists who might or might not be Laudians. St Helen's was a battleground between partisans of Edward Roode and those of Christopher Newstead. For the first time, there had appeared in Abingdon a congregation that had separated from the established church, owning no allegiance to the officially-recognised minister. But that congregation, arising within St Helen's, considered the church rightfully its own. From then until the Restoration, the dominant principle among the Puritans of Abingdon would be one of congregational independency, and one aim of the various groups as they formed would be to gain the sole possession of the main parish church.

---

[1] The family as a unit that persists through time seems to have been an unexpected consequence of the sixteenth century population increase. Earlier, urban families were much more likely to die out in two or three generations – D.G. Shaw, *The Creation of a Community: The City of Wells in the Middle Ages* (Oxford, 1993), pp.173-5.

[2] A.E. Preston, *St Nicholas, Abingdon, and other Papers* (1928), pp. 289-193.

[3] Preston, *St. Nicholas,* p. 68.

[4] It would be impossible here to give a detailed bibliography. The current state of the debate is well covered in John Coffey and Paul C.H. Lim (eds), *The Cambridge Companion to Puritanism* (Cambridge, 2008). The pragmatic local historian might restrict himself to a classic of the last generation but one: Christopher Hill, *Society and Puritanism in Pre-revolutionary England* (1964).

[5] C.D. Cobban,, *Francis Little: A Monument of Christian Munificence* (Oxford & London, 1871), p. 54.

[6] Cobban, *Little,* p. 55.

[7] It is worth noticing that these lectureships started very early. W.K. Jordan, in *Philanthropy in England, 1480-1660* (1959), p. 375, listed such endowments in eleven counties, unfortunately not including Berkshire. He found very few that started before 1581, and none at all before 1571.

[8] TNA, PROB 11/152; Cobban, *Little,* pp. 51-58, 94; Bodl., Mss Gough Berks 10 f.2 sqq; Berks RO, D/EP 7 61 Bundle 2 fols 154, 172, 174, 178..

[9] ATCA, Corp Mins I, fo. 143.

[10] Griffith-Boscawen, *Endowed Charities of Berks* (HMSO, 1912), I, part 1, p.37; part 2, pp. 1095-1112.

[11] Bodl., Ms Gough Berks 5, fos 237-290.

[12] The eleventh clause of the 'Laws and Ordinances' for the school prescribes the traditional Latin prayers, but the twelfth allows prayers to be in English, and the sixth appears to give the master the right to decide what prayers are said – Preston, *St Nicholas Abingdon and other Papers* (1929), pp. 386-392; Thomas Hinde and Michael St John Parker, *The Martlet and the Griffen: an illustrated history of Abingdon School* (1997), pp. 31-3

[13] TNA, PROB 11/147, 152; The Provost of Queens at the time was Barnaby Potter, rather Puritanical (see *DNB*). Earlier provosts, Airay and Abbot, had had good relationships with Abingdon.

[14] TNA, PROB 11/152. (Probate was granted in 1627).

[15] Preston, *St Nicholas*, pp. 426-8; Simon Adams, *Leicester and the Court* (Manchester, 2002), p. 209.

[16] (Sir John Pechell), *History of the University of Oxford from the Death of William the Conqueror to the Demise of Queen Elizabeth* (Oxford, 1773), pp. 224-6

[17] Julian Lock, 'Abbot, Robert (1559/60–1618)', in *DNB*.

[18] John Prime, *An Exposition and Observation on St Paul to the Galatians* (Oxford, 1587).

[19] Berks RO, D/EP7/84 fo. 207; Bromley Challenor, *Selection from the Borough Records* (1898), Appx Ch. 4.

[20] Challenor, *Selections,* Appx Ch. 3; ATCA, St Helen's Churchwardens Accounts, April-Oct 1606.

[21] Bodl., Ms Gough Berks 10 fo. 2 et seq; Preston, *St Nicholas,* pp. 174-9, 208-213. Kisbey was a local man, son of a former mayor and himself a governor and future master of the Hospital. There is a possible connection with Little in that both at different times lived at the Coosner's House in the parish of St Nicholas.

[22] Berks RO, D/EP 7 66, fos 3, 172.

[23] Abbot had been one of the overseers of Tesdale's will of 1610, which left large bequests for Abingdon scholars at Oxford and provided most of the endowment for the future Pembroke College – TNA, PROB 11/116.

[24] Anthony Milton, 'Laud, William (1573–1645)', in *DNB*.

[25] 1Chr 16:29; 2Chr 20:21; Psalms 29:2, 96:9.

[26] TNA, C 93/11/13; Peter Heylyn, *Cyprianus Anglicus* (1668), p.171; CH, St Nicholas Old Church Book, fos 10-13, 172; CH, St Nicholas Book of Decrees and Presentments, fo.12; Preston, *St Nicholas,* p. 217.

[27] Bodl, Mss Gough Berks 6, f. 264. The comment is attributed to a bishop of Lincoln, probably John Williams, who had ideas of his own on the placing of the communion table – Brian Quintrell, 'Williams, John (1582–1650)', in *DNB*.

[28] ATCA, Corp Mins I, fo.140v.

[29] William Prynne, in his closely-printed 1000-page anti-theatre treatise *Histrio-mastix* (1633), admirably demonstrates the deep fear of freedom, be it only that of the imagination, that is at the root of seventeenth-century Puritanism.

[30] ATCA, St Helen's Churchwardens Accounts, Vol 2, p. 43.

[31] Christ Church (Oxford), Letter, Fell to Laud, (13 August 1628), Ms Estates 141 fols 247v-248v. I am grateful to Mrs Judith Curthoys, archivist, for a transcript.

[32] Richard Cust, *Charles I: a political life* (2007), pp 86-103 and especially p. 95.

[33] *CSPD* 1634-5, no 48 (27 Sept 1634). The item seems to have been misdated in the preparation of the Calendar.

[34] R. Cust, 'Anti-Puritanism and Urban Politics: Charles I and Great Yarmouth', *Historical Journal,* 35 (1992), pp. 1-26; J.N. Langston, 'John Workman, Puritan lecturer in Gloucester ', *Transactions of the Bristol and Gloucester Arch Soc,* 86 (1945), pp. 219-232.

[35] *APC,* September 1627-June 1628, pp. 89, 106, 130.

[36] *CSPD* 1654 No. 15 (Sept 2 1654). A stay in prison of such length would have been unusual and would almost certainly have led to comment in print.

[37] ATCA, Corp. Mins I, fols. 151, 152v; Mieneke Cox, *Peace and War: The Story of Abingdon Part 3,* p. 216.

[38] ATCA, St Helen's Churchwardens Accounts, Vol 2, p.97.

[39] Berks RO, Induction mandates, D/A2 d.4 f.9.

[40] Berks RO, Inductions, d.4 f.8.

[41] Joseph Foster, *Alumni Oxonienses 1500-1714* (1892), p. 1428.

[42] ATCA, St Helen's Churchwardens Accounts, Vol 2, pp. 107, 110, 135, 247, 249.

[43] ATCA, St Helen's Churchwardens Accounts, Vol 2, pp. 85, 105, 106. Quarrels are small diamond-shaped pieces of window glass.

[44] BL Add Mss 5829.18ff.

[45] A.G. Matthews, *Walker Revised* (1948), p. 160; *LJ,* vi, pp. 59, 97; House of Lords Record Office, HL/PO/10/1/50, fos 173, 196; *HMC 5th Report,* Appendix, pp.18, 20, 87, 91. Stisted was in the area of the Stour Valley riots of the time, when Arminian clergy were commonly mobbed and beaten up – John Walter, *Understanding Popular Violence in the English Revolution: the Colchester Plunderers* (Cambridge, 1999).

[46] ATCA, St Helen's Churchwardens Accounts, Vol 2, p.217.

[47] G. Gulter, *The Archbishops Crueltie, Made Knowne in a True Story of One Mr. Edward Rood, Who Was Minister at Saint Helens in Abingdon, and Dismissed of His Meanes and Ministery by Him: And in Processe of Time, after He Had Been from His Meanes Eleven Years, He Was Lately Againe Restored. As Also, How Hee Was Cast in Prison, What Miseries He There Sustained, and His Deliverance from All. By Giles Gulter, Batchelour in Arts* (1641). After the debacle at Stisted, Newstead was given a chapel at Maidenhead where he was continually harassed by the authorities. By 1660, he seems again to have been unemployed – *Notes & Queries* vol 153 No 26, p. 454 (24 Dec 1927); *CSPD* 1655, No. 8 (7 Feb); *CSPD* 1657-8, No 38/6 (18 Aug 1657); *HMC 5th Rept,* Appx. p. 18.

[48] Griffith was accused, as Roode had been, of 'the stirring up and fomenting of seditious divisions'. He would have a distinguished war record on the royalist side, being seriously wounded and having one of his daughters killed at the siege of Basing House. At the Restoration he was made vicar of St Helen's in Abingdon, but resigned almost immediately. A.G. Matthews, *Walker Revised* (1948), p. 49; Tai Liu, 'Griffith, Matthew ', *DNB;* Preston, *St Nicholas,* p. 226.

[49] *Walker Revised* p. 49; *CJ,* iii, pp 263-5 (5 Oct 1643).

[50] Montagu Burrows (ed), *Register of the Visitors of the University of Oxford,* (Camden Soc o.s. 135, 1881), p. 525; *CSPD* 1654 p. 358 (Sept 2 1654); Cal of Letters Patent 1654-56 (19 July 1655) in *Reports of the Deputy Keeper of Public Records,* 4th Rept, (1843), Appx p. 192; *CSPD* 1655 (10 May 1655).

[51] Agnes Baker, *Historic Abingdon, 56 articles* (1963), pp 8-10. There were (at least) two prominent men named John Mayott at the time, and I am not convinced the mayor was Alice Dayrell's brother.

[52] Anthea Jones, *Tewkesbury* (2nd edn, 2003), p. 67. The Tewksbury charter of 1610 cost the town £427, which was raised by taxation.

[53] Challenor, *Selections,* pp. 42-55.

[54] This phraseology seems to have been common in borough charters of the time; cf Barnstaple, also 1610, 'a borough and parish of peace and quiet, to the terror and dread of evil offenders, and in reward of the good' – J.B. Gribble, *Memorials of Barnstaple* (1830) ii p. 393.

[55] ATCA, Mayors' Book, p. 39.

[56] Challenor, *Selections,* pp. 56-68.

[57] J. H. Baker, 'Williams, Sir David (1550–1613)', *OND.*

[58] L.M. Hill, 'County Government in Caroline England 1625-1640' in Conrad Russell (ed), *The Origins of the English Civil War* (1973), pp. 66-90 at pp 80-82; Brian Quintrell, 'Williams, John (1582–1650)', *DNB.*

[59] Challenor, *Selections,* pp. 69-74. In fact, the bridges should have been the Hospital's responsibility.

[60] Cox, *Peace and War,* pp. 75-7, 83.

[61] Christ Church (Oxford), Letter, Fell to Laud, (13 August 1628), Ms Estates 141 fols 247v-248v.

[62] Preston, *St Nicholas,* p. 87.

[63] BRO, Preston Papers, D/EP 7/53.

[64] ATCA, Corp mins i 148, 149v.

[65] The current bishop was John Davenant, a moderate Calvinist, opposed to Laud.

[66] Baker, *Historic Abingdon,* p. 8-9; Berks RO, D/EP 7 61 Bundle 2 ff.175-6; *CSPD* 1628-9 No 26 (9 Nov 1628); TNA, SP16, v.120 f.26.

[67] *APC*, July 1628–April 29, pp.226, 230.

[68] Tesdale would die the same year. Whitelocke would complain bitterly of the trouble that the Abingdon factions gave him, which on one occasion led to a summons to explain a decision to the Privy Council, Berks RO, D/EP 7/71; ATCA Corp. Minutes i 155; Ruth Spalding, *The Diary of Bulstrode Whitelocke 1605-1675* (1990), pp. 62, 92, 116.

[69] The classical account is the one of Dorchester given by David Underdown, *Fire from Heaven; life in an English town in the seventeenth century* (1992), esp. Chap 5.

[70] ATCA, Corp. Minutes i 156v; Abingdon Chamberlains a/cs 1633-4 (A.E. Preston transcript in BRO, D/EP 7 118). It should be noted that the setting up of Houses of Correction was enjoined by the government's Book of Orders of 1631, and was not purely a Puritan initiative – Hill, in Russell (ed), *Origins*, at p. 79.

[71] Berks RO, Citations relating to churchwardens, D/A2 C.165 f.6.

[72] The screen would finally be pulled down, by five carpenters working for three days, after the entry of parliamentary troops in 1644 – ATCA, St Helen's Churchwardens accounts, Vol 3, p. 389.

6. *In honour of Abingdon*

It has long been customary to ascribe the outbreak of the Civil War to some arbitrary point in 1642, perhaps the sparsely attended ceremony at Nottingham in August when the king formally raised his standard, or the first pitched battle, that of Edgehill in October, after which there could be no going back. More recently, scholars have become aware that the descent into the abyss was a long process: a gradual fragmentation of the body politic that seemed at first manageable, but which eventually accelerated out of control. Throughout the 1630s, the policies − the religious policies, mainly − of the king and his archbishop, William Laud, had pulled the body politic in a direction it did not want to go. In 1640, those policies involved that body in an unpopular, ineptly conducted, and in the end disastrous war against its Scottish neighbour, and many Englishmen found to their surprise that they did not wish for a royal victory. From its opening in November of that year, the Long Parliament provided an alternative pole of attraction, deliberately setting its own influence and authority in opposition to that of the king. Like some physical object caught between two powerful fields, the body of the nation tore apart.

The breakdown of harmony between the nation and its rulers, and within the nation itself, can be followed by various strands of evidence, but perhaps especially in the almost vertical rise in the rate of publication of printed pamphlets that began during 1640, even before the royal government had lost its nominal control of the printing industry.[1] 'Paper bullets' were flying well before the more directly lethal sort. One effect of religious enthusiasm had been an intensification of literacy even at relatively low levels of society, and authors now might be, like their readers, of a class that would not previously have been considered part of the political nation. The bulk of such plebeian scribbles originated in London, since it was there that religious and political debate was perhaps most heated, and presses certainly most numerous. But Abingdon, as we have seen, had its differences and debates; and there was a university press at Oxford. Abingdon's main contribution to the literary strife came from the unlikely pen of its serjeant-at-mace, John Richardson, who produced an account, in endearingly naïve rhyming couplets, of a civic celebration held at the instigation of Parliament on Tuesday, 7 September 1641.[2] Richardson's poetical talents were slim, but his work can nonetheless be read at different levels, and gives an excellent indication of local preoccupations in Abingdon as the national crisis deepened.

Richardson's status in the town was never quite as humble as his position might suggest. He first comes to notice in 1625 as a witness to John Blacknall's will.[3] His employment as serjeant-at-mace dates from 1628, in the mayoralty of John Mayott.[4] He seems to have spoken somewhat out of turn to Mayor Benjamin Tesdale, who had him dismissed in December 1637 as 'having opposed the maior, bailiffs and principall burgesses in matters concerning this corporation'. The minute in the corporation records was signed by nine members. But he was reinstated without any particular comment in the following March.[5] Plainly, he was of the Mayott faction.[6] It can only have been as a contribution to the local factional conflict that his 'weake and illiterate' verses could have justified the expense of being set in print. What might at first sight appear to be a straight description of an enjoyable civic occasion was actually tendentious and provocative, and must have been so understood.

The significance of the publication was more than purely local. The king was in Scotland, where he had gone ostensibly to make peace with his rebellious northern subjects after twice being ignominiously defeated by them in the so-called Bishops' Wars. It was fully understood that his real intention was to rally what political support he could in Scotland against the Puritan-led English parliament that had been steadily stripping him of his traditional kingly powers. He was comprehensively out-manoeuvred. A peace treaty between Edinburgh and Westminster had been long in the making, but this was now quickly ratified in both places. The two armies that faced each other across the Tyne, both of them paid by the English parliament at the cost of the English taxpayer, could be disbanded. A small, tightly-knit Puritan faction effectively managed the Westminster parliament, and it was well understood that the Scottish army had been kept in being only because they might have a use for it. The English army, or at least its officer corps, was loyal to the king, and there was wild talk of marching it down to London and dealing with the parliamentary leaders in a radical manner. A civil war might well have started in the hot summer of 1641, but the treaty removed the immediate fear and brought about a palpable release of tension. It was this that, at Parliament's behest, was being celebrated.[7] Richardson dedicates his work 'to the worshipfull the Major, Bayliffs and Burgesses of the Burough of Abingdon, in the County of Berks' but celebrates in the introduction 'the unexpected making up of great Brittaines dangerous Breaches'. 'The mercy,' he declares, 'was great, and the miracle wonderfull.'

The day was to consist of 'prayers, reading, and preaching the word, in all churches and chapels of this realm'. The parliamentary order was made on 27 August, but was not published until the 30th, giving very little time for preparation. It is unclear why Abingdon decided to make a civic rather than a purely religious occasion of it, but a sermon and feast was due about that time anyway to celebrate the new-made mayor, and it may have been felt convenient for the two occasions to be merged. [8]

In Richardson's description, the festival started much as Parliament had intended. The bells of both churches began ringing at dawn, and by 7 a.m. the population had flocked in great numbers to St Helen's.[9] Two sermons, preached by different but unnamed divines, held (one hopes) the attention of the congregation until midday. After a two-hour lunch break, a third sermon must have completed the satisfaction of even the most zealous. Richardson says nothing of the content of the sermons, but if they followed the model being set the same day in London they will have used a discourse of Puritan triumphalism and called confidently for renewed purification and a return to the principles of the Protestant Reformation after the disgraceful backsliding of the Laudian years.[10] It was at four o'clock that the celebrations took a more popular turn. The author, with a newly gilded mace, preceded the mayor and burgesses in solemn procession to the steps of the market cross, where the clerk led a crowd of two thousand people in a spirited rendering of the 106th Psalm. The local trained bands marched with 'drums and fifes and colours flying' and gave a display of musketry. There were bonfires, and drinks paid for by the council; there were shouts of 'God save the king'; and after the formal celebrations had come to an end with the dignitaries escorted by the musketeers to their homes, street parties continued until late. Richardson emphasizes that there was no drunkenness, and that the charity collection realised the satisfactory sum of £13 or £14.

It is hard to avoid the suspicion of a point of irony in Richardson's dead-pan description of seven hours of sermonising as the Puritan idea of a delightful party. But the account as a whole carries an ideological freight that will not have been lost either on the local Puritans, if they could ever have brought themselves to read it, or on their conservative opponents. Richardson's description of the day holds up a conservative ideal of urban life, an ideal that would have had the approbation of Francis Little and his colleagues of a generation earlier. The citizens come together harmoniously in a celebration commanded from above. They do so under the benevolent oversight of the mayor and his brethren; they pay their due respects both to God (at extreme length) and the king, and at the end of the day return home to an evening of traditional sociability. It was exactly those traditions of reciprocal respect within the social hierarchy and of conviviality among neighbours that the Puritans were accused, with some justice, of subverting.

In comparing Richardson's idealised account with the reality they had experienced, his readers will have had to confront the extent to which their world had already changed. The old ideals still resonated, but by this time harmony had given way to dissonance. Magisterial authority throughout the country was being questioned, contested, even ignored. Neighbourly friendship was to be replaced by a joyless fellowship in Christ.[11]

The poem is not overtly polemical, but Richardson makes his position on current controversies clear. The main concern is a carefully calibrated attack on Puritan opposition to sacred music, church bells, and market crosses. All of these were in jeopardy. The recent treaty agreed to bring England into 'nearer conformity' to the Presbyterian Scottish church. On the eighth and ninth of September, as Richardson was pondering his poem, the House of Commons discussed and agreed a declaration against 'images'. Its legal status was unclear, and its promulgation haphazard. Yet it provoked in London and elsewhere a wave of iconoclasm and destruction that in turn produced an anti-Puritan backlash.[12] It is this that will have provided the context for his literary effort.

Thus,

> '...th'unparall'd, harmlesse, threaten'd Crosse
> (Yet lately blest from Babylonish drosse)
> Where *Aarons* bels in *Helens* Church doe ring
> Peales, that doe blesse us from the poyson'd sting
> of death eternall...'.

The allusion is to Exodus Chapter 28, on the accoutrements of the high priest when he enters the sanctuary and ministers at the altar, 'that he die not'. Richardson is quoting scripture against people who were claiming a monopoly of biblical interpretation, and using verses that they would have difficulty in explaining away. Puritans rejected priesthood as an unholy attempt at magic; their ideal clergyman was a minister who would teach and exhort, but had no esoteric powers. The idea of ringing bells to ward off supernatural dangers would have seemed to the Tesdales and their party as obscene superstition. But yet, could they really maintain that that was the function of Abingdon's church bells? In fact, the Abingdon bells would survive the Civil War and its aftermath.[13]

But the poet also shows his concern for the 'threaten'd cross'. There was an intense campaign against market crosses, seen, however unreasonably, as relics of popery and as standing invitations to popish idol-worship. Abingdon conservatives were proud of their cross, a noble construction that brought in visitors and had been rebuilt by the care of Francis Little as recently as 1605.[14] It was admired or, in some quarters, abominated, as second only to the Cheapside Cross in London, which had to be guarded round the clock against attempts by zealous iconoclasts to deface, dilapidate, or destroy it.[15]

Again,

> 'Over my head, I saw King *David* stand,
> Listning toth' Musick, with his Harp in hand,
> Sure when the Psalmist liv'd, with's sacred Lire,
> He seldom play'd, or sung to such a Quire.
> If either King could speake, hee'd sweare by's Crown
> No Haire-braind Separatist would pull him downe:
> For why, this heavenly joy, we had so late,
> Did seeme, in part, the Crosse to consecrate.'

The section is rich in biblical references that would have been familiar to contemporaries, whether Puritans or not. The Puritans, it suggests, consider themselves more holy than King David, who exercised his musical skills with divine approbation. The nearest approach to sacred music allowed by the Puritans was the lining-out technique which Richardson describes, where the clerk sings a line of a psalm and the congregation repeats it.[16] But the main key to the passage is the apparently rather strained trope that the cross was somehow being consecrated. This points to 1 Chronicles, chapter 16. The cross becomes a figure for the ark of the covenant, which David himself brought into Jerusalem and consecrated with instrumental music, singing, and dancing. His wife Michal was cursed with sterility for her disapproval. The Puritans, who wanted the cross demolished, were implicitly warned of the fate of Uzza, who touched the ark with impious hands and was instantly struck dead.[17] The threat in fact did not save the cross, which would, less than three years later, become a casualty of the war.

A further allusion allows Richardson himself a brief moment at centre stage. This is to Ezra 3:5,10-13 and Nehemiah 12:27-47, describing the elaborate musical celebrations at the re-consecration of the Jerusalem temple

79

by the exiles returning from Babylon. Their intent was 'to praise the Lord, after the ordinance of David king of Israel'.[18] The ordinance in question was the one delivered at the consecration of the ark; it was to worship 'in the beauty of holiness', a concept now considered Laudian and utterly rejected by the Puritans.[19] The poet is able to present himself in the guise of the biblical writer. Nehemiah was cup-bearer to the king, as Richardson is serjeant to the mayor. Both of them, by virtue of their functions, stand somewhat apart from the celebrants as well as being recorders of the events. 'So stood the two companies of them that gave thanks in the house of God, and I, and half of the rulers with me', says Nehemiah, while the serjeant takes his position on the steps of the market cross with the rulers of the town, although he is not one of them.[20] Richardson has a privileged insight into local political affairs, while his fellow-townsmen can only respond to them.

Abingdon in the early 1640s was thus a divided town. Among the élite, it was conservatives who held the smaller of the town churches, St Nicholas, and the grammar school; they formed an admittedly unstable majority in the borough council and among the governors of Christ's Hospital, and had seen their candidate returned to Parliament. Yet the larger church of St Helen's was a battleground, and overall it was the Puritan faction that held the initiative. It is not necessary to accept Richardson's description of a 'quire' of 2000 – though there is nothing inherently unlikely about such a figure – to recognise the hold that Puritan ideology had gained among the ordinary townsfolk. If church bells could start ringing at dawn on a holiday, if St Helen's could be filled 'as full as it could thwack' for seven hours of sermons and the worshippers in their lunch break could still be imagined as singing 'sweet anthems to Jehova's name', if the market place could fill with townsfolk communally belting out psalms and evidently enjoying it, if even Richardson himself could refer to the churches as 'Nicholas' and 'Helen's' without putting 'Saint' before the appellations, then it is plain that Puritan ways of thought and of behaviour had become a norm against which the conservatism of the Mayotts and the Bostocks, of Newstead and Stone, could be billed as innovative and unacceptable.

---

[1] David Cressy, *England on Edge: Crisis and revolution 1640-1642* (2006), pp. 292-3.

[2] John Richardson, *In honour of Abingdon, or on the seaventh day of Septembers solemnization* (Oxford, 1641). See Appx 2.

[3] TNA, PROB 11/147

---

[4] ATCA, Corp Minutes i fo. 148v

[5] ATCA, Corp Minutes i fos. 161, 162.

[6] He was a witness to the will of John Mayott 'the elder', in 1644, Berks RO D/ER T 154/2. He would continue as serjeant until his death in August 1663, when the St Nicholas registers record him as buried 'in the vestry'. The Corporation would then grant his estate 50s in exchange for his gown and cloak and any arrears of wages. – ATCA, Corp Minutes i fo. 194v.

[7] John Adamson, *The Noble Revolt: the overthrow of Charles I* (2007), Chaps. 11 and 12.

[8] *CJ,* ii, pp. 273-4 (27 August 1641); *LJ,* iv, p. 383 (30 August 1641).

[9] 7 a.m was not unreasonably early; people would normally be up and about by 5 a.m. – D.M. Palliser, 'Civic mentality and the environment in Tudor York', in Jonathan Barry (ed), *The Tudor and Stuart Town* (1990), pp. 206-243 at p. 215.

[10] Adamson, *The Noble Revolt*, pp. 353-4.

[11] The social fragmentation that preceded the Civil War is well described by Cressy, *England on Edge.*

[12] BL, Thomason Tracts, 669 f.3[14], and see also Anon, *The orders from the House of Commons for the Abolishing of Superstition and Innovation* (1 September 1641); Adamson, *The Noble Revolt*, pp. 355-361, 384-390; Conrad Russell, *The Fall of the British Monarchies 1637-1642* (1991), p. 371; A. Fletcher, *The Outbreak of the English Civil War* (1981), pp. 119-120.

[13] Unlike, for instance, those of the strongly puritanical village of Longworth, a few miles from Abingdon – Bodleian, 'Collections for illustrating the history of Berkshire', Ms Top Berks c.57, p. 108.

[14] For a description of the cross, said to be the finest in the country outside London, see M.J.H. Liversidge, 'Abingdon's 'Right Goodly Cross of Stone' in W.J.H. and M.J.H. Liversidge, *Abingdon Essays: Studies in Local History* (Abingdon, 1989), pp. 42-57. Richardson shows his polemical intent by describing his opponents as separatists, thus identifying the majority of the Puritans, who wished to reform the established church rather than separating from it, with an extremist minority.

[15] David Cressy, 'The Downfall of Cheapside Cross: Vandalism, Ridicule and Iconoclasm' in idem, *Agnes Bowker's Cat: Travesties and Transgressions in Tudor and Stuart England* (2000), pp. 234-250. The Cheapside Cross would be demolished in an elaborate civic ritual in 1643.

[16] Horton Davies, *Worship and Theology in England* (Princeton, 1962-70), II p. 279.

[17] 1 Chr 16:9-10; 2 Samuel 6:6-23.

[18] Ezra 3:10.

[19] 1 Chr 16:29.

[20] Nehemiah 13:40. Nehemiah was cup-bearer to King Artaxerxes, who had authorised the return to Zion.

7. Civil War

If in the 1630s there were any portents of the catastrophes to come that were visible to Abingdon people, no record has survived. Divisions and factionalism in the corporation and in the town's religious life were in no way abnormal. The town militia probably trained harder and more frequently than usual, but will have worried more about rebel Scots and, perhaps, malevolent papists than a full-scale civil war.

With hindsight, people may later have considered the levying of a ship money tax as ominous. There had been no parliament since 1629, and the government's arbitrary extension of this tax, hitherto imposed only on coastal regions, was highly controversial. The official line was that the tax was for the fitting out of a fleet, hence for national defence, and as such was within the king's prerogative. A legal challenge by John Hampden was narrowly rejected by the courts in 1638. The county sheriff who was responsible for its collection in 1637-8 was Sir George Stonehouse of Radley, brother of the former Abingdon MP, and there seems to have been little trouble. In the next year, the sheriff was Humphrey Hyde, probably of Sutton Wick and so also a local man, and in February 1639 he was informed that 'The mayor, bailiffs, burgesses and the rest of the inhabitants of Abingdon' had sent in a petition to the Privy Council.[1] He was instructed to consider the case, and 'give them such relief as you find just and agreeable to H.M.'s writ'.[2] We know nothing of the outcome, but if Abingdon paid little or nothing in that and the following year it will have been in good company.

The long crisis started early in 1640. The tax strike was national and now almost total. The first of the Bishops' Wars against the Scots had ended inconclusively at Berwick in June 1639. The Scots were fighting to prevent the imposition on them of Laudian religious practices, and there was much sympathy in England for their cause. The king, nonetheless, was desperate for money with which to reopen hostilities.[3] He had no choice but to summon a new parliament. At first, it seemed that there would not need to be a poll in Abingdon. Sir George Stonehouse would succeed naturally to his late brother's seat. An enquiry was received from Robert Knollys, a kinsman of the late Earl of Banbury who had been Abingdon's high steward until 1630. This may have been one of the men of that name who had sat for Abingdon before Sir John Stonehouse, or may have been another, since the Knollys family was a large one. He was sent a letter of courteous discouragement, and the current high steward, the Earl of Holland, who was of the same family, made no objection.

But not everyone was happy. Joshua Tesdale, on behalf of a section of the corporation, invited the recorder, Bulstrode Whitelocke, to stand against Stonehouse. He warned that success was not certain. Whitelocke, writing much later in exculpatory vein, claimed that he had been reluctant to stand and did so only in view of the seriousness of the times. Tesdale had hoped to restrict voting rights to corporation members, but the mayor, John Mayott, had opened the poll to a wider electorate. This favoured Stonehouse, who spent money freely with the Abingdon tradesmen and treated his supporters, in Whitelocke's words, to 'beef, bacon, and bag pudding' with unlimited amounts of strong drink. There was some suggestion of an appeal to the House's Committee of Elections and Privileges, but the parliament, refusing to do what the king hoped of it, was dissolved after only a few weeks and the opportunity was lost. The extent of the parliamentary electorate in Abingdon, as in many other towns, would remain an open question and a source of trouble and confusion for many years to come.[4]

Tensions developed in the spring and summer. The dissolution of the Short Parliament in May eliminated any last hope the king's government may have had of war finance being granted. At the July assizes in Abingdon a judge gave the assembled notabilities a pep talk about their duties to the king, but complained of the recalcitrance of the deputy lieutenants and JPs in giving evidence against men who had refused to be enlisted.[5] The grand jury sent a remonstrance to London against 'illegal', meaning unparliamentary, taxes, including 'the new taxe of coat and conduct mony, with the undue meanes used to inforce the payment of it, by messengers from the councell table', and against 'the compelling of some freemen by imprisonment and threatnings to take presse mony'.[6]

In spite of Judge Jones, there was a very general belief that both the tax and the conscription were unconstitutional. A large section of the Berkshire gentry withheld their cooperation, refusing to collect the coat and conduct money that would equip the recruits and pay them on their march out of the county. These were all in the north-west of Berkshire, where the major landowner was the father of Henry Marten, the future republican and regicide. Nearer to Abingdon, the ex-MP George Stonehouse, as a deputy lieutenant, reported he had been able to secure only 120 recruits, all from his own division, but these levies had simply dissolved within a hundred miles of home. Those deserters who had returned had been put into jail, and would remain there 'until further direction'. He asked to be excused from further such duties for the present, since he was about to leave for Hurley where his wife (a Lovelace) was expecting to lie in.[7]

It is not clear how many of Stonehouse's recruits had been from Abingdon itself, but it is revealing that country-wide it was men from the lower ranks of society into whose reluctant hands the king's shilling was forced. A militia manned by more substantial citizens existed and will have had at least a cursory training, but its role was seen as defence of the county, not the nation. Anyone conscripted who could afford it would pay a poorer man to replace him. Pro-Scottish preachers worked to convince the recruits that the war to which they were being sent was, somehow, a papist conspiracy.[8] At Faringdon, very much in Marten country, recruits coming from Dorset mutinied, lynched one of their officers in the belief that he was a Catholic, drove the others away, and ran riot in the town. The situation was serious enough for the sheriff, George Purefoy of nearby Wadley, to call out the Abingdon trained bands. They marched through the night, but were deemed too few in number to quell the disorders, which petered out.[9] Eventually, three of the ringleaders were arrested at Woodstock, and two of them were sentenced and executed at Abingdon.[10] The Privy Council decided that Berkshire and Oxfordshire should be put under martial law and all the imprisoned deserters executed, but Purefoy blandly informed them, contradicting Stonehouse, that 'they came not into Berkshire, but, as their commander assures me, they were lately seen travelling towards Somerset'.[11] The local leaders would not countenance usurpation of their rule by a provost-marshal, and could only be horrified at the prospect of mass executions. The central government had reached the limits of its authority. As far as Berkshire was concerned, this was probably the effective start of 'the revolt of the provinces'.[12] The war would end in the disaster of Newburn, leaving much of northern England under Scottish military occupation.

There were new elections in October for what would be the Long Parliament, which would sit, with interruptions, for almost twenty years. Stonehouse was returned unopposed for Abingdon. Whitelocke would stand for Marlow where, paradoxically, it was a broader electorate that secured his return.[13]

Oblivious of the wrath to come, the corporation continued its traditional squabbling and its routine appeals to the Privy Council. On 27 October 1640, the Council (which must have had more pressing matters on its agenda) wrote to the assize judges for the Oxford circuit about an Abingdon petition 'concerning the differences arising between the principal and the secondary Burgesses (as they call them) touching the leasing and granting of the lands and revenues belonging to the Corporation.'[14] Control of corporation leases, very profitable to those who could manipulate them, was a perennial problem, and it is unsurprising that the junior members of the corporation might think they were not getting their full share of the proceeds. Back in 1626, the borough's common seal had been kept in a chest with five locks and with keys held by senior corporation members, each one of whom could exercise an effective right of veto by leaving his key at home. It had been decided to withhold a key from Christopher Tesdale for doing exactly that.[15] The chest they were now using had 'a great lock' and seven small ones. Also on 27 October, and obviously after long discussion, it was decided that four keys would in future be held by the mayor, the immediate past mayor, and the two bailiffs for the time being, and the other four by two named principal burgesses and two named secondaries who would be permanent custodians. All keys would have to be produced following a majority vote on the corporation.[16] A later clarification would provide that no lease could be sealed without majority approval both among primary and among secondary burgesses.[17]

There seems no way of correlating the factions that had formed over the division of the spoils of magistracy with those that were primarily driven by religious and political antagonisms. Richardson's poem, with which we have already dealt, shows the significance that the latter must have assumed by September 1641. By the summer of 1642 it was national politics that were all-important. Relations within the corporation were breaking down or had already done so. On 12 July, William Castell, a past mayor of Abingdon, took himself to Westminster and informed the House that the king's commission of array had been proclaimed in the town, and that copies were posted and watched at night so that they would not be torn down. The commission of array was in direct contradiction to Parliament's militia ordinance; both king and parliament were claiming the sole right to levy a national army. Castell named John Richardson, the serjeant-at-arms, but loyally insisted that the mayor – Edmund Franklyn – had been absent at the time. The House angrily summoned both Franklyn and Richardson who on 26 September were forced to kneel at the bar and beg for forgiveness.[18] Similar humiliation was imposed on the aged Alderman Thomas Turnor of Reading and on other 'delinquents', as they were now called, from elsewhere in the county. This was part of a campaign led by two men who, as parliamentary agents, were now all-powerful in Berkshire, in towns and in the countryside indifferently. They were the current high sheriff, Tanfield Vachell of Coley, who was of the Knollys family, and the younger Henry Marten, now one of the county MPs.[19]

At the end of October 1642, following the indecisive battle of Edgehill, the Royalists garrisoned the town. Joshua Tesdale, the incoming mayor, even before his inauguration had taken the town's defences in hand and managed some rudimentary measures against invading cavalry, but they proved of no value.[20] Most of the soldiers were quartered in a hutted fortified camp on Culham Hill.[21] Parliamentarian propagandists attempted to drum up atrocity stories, but with little of substance beyond the looting, theft and extortion that are always inseparable from military occupation.[22] At least five townsmen were prevailed upon to lend substantial sums to the king's war treasury, against the personal signatures of Royalist grandees. Among them was James Curten, a future mayor and hospital master, whose contribution was £366.[23] It must be an open question whether these men were simply naïve, or whether their arms were twisted in some way. St Nicholas was taken over and used as a barracks, although services somehow continued.[24] The more perceptive of the townsfolk might have foreseen, from the disorder in the camp, the likely outcome of the struggle. One unit was in dispute with another over accommodation and victuals, and its officer was threatening to hang his prisoners. He considered that holding his quarters 'will bee a harder task to perform then to defend the towne against the enemy' and held it 'a greate misfortune, to be tyed to this place'.[25] The mingling of townsfolk with soldiers from many different places meant an upsurge of sickness and infection. Between 1 April and 25 August 1643 when records become deficient, the 186 burials at St Helens represented a sevenfold increase over the same period of 1641.[26] Even if we eliminate identifiable soldiers and their dependants, the increase is still almost threefold. At the Royalist military hospital at Sunningwell, the young Thomas Clarges, a former apothecary's apprentice, seems to have understood the role of lice in spreading typhus, which would be unknown to mainstream medical science until the twentieth century. He put out an appeal for spare shirts that his patients could wear while their own were cleansed.[27]

William Castell seems not to have returned to his place in the Council, and was formally dismissed by order of the Royalist authorities in November 1643.[28] Some corporation members died in the epidemics of that year; others were probably told informally to keep away. By the end of 1643, nine new men had been elected to the corporation, of whom seven duly took their oaths. The mayoral election in September proved difficult. Joshua Tesdale had served out his term, which must have been difficult for him. John Mayott was chosen his successor but refused to take the office. This may have been because of failing health, but if so his colleagues were not sympathetic. He was fined and imprisoned, but finally accepted to take the oath and then promptly died. Edward Franklyn was coerced into serving out Mayott's term. In the following year, 1644, by which time the Parliamentarians had taken over, the whole charade was repeated. Richard Barton, like John Mayott, took the oath only after being fined and imprisoned, but died in or before March 1645. The military authorities then ordered the reinstatement of William Castell, who was immediately elected mayor. He also died in office, and finally Thomas Steede officiated from July to September.[29]

A new era started for Abingdon on 26 May 1644, when the Parliamentarian general William Waller took advantage of a communications failure in the Royalist army to occupy the town.[30] Later historians have followed contemporary propaganda to present Waller's destruction of the market cross and of the remaining stained glass windows at St Helen's as the work of a philistine outsider, but he must have been applauded, and perhaps assisted, by local Saints.[31] Royalist writers did not conceal their disgust for the action:

> While *Essex*'s Forces were fighting at *Gosworth, Waller's* were not idle at *Abingdon*, who this Day plundred that Town, and sawed down the Cross (standing upon Pillars in the Market place) being the greatest Ornament of that place, and a goodly Piece for Beauty and Antiquity. An Act so barbarous, no People that ever served a God (but such a one as they had fancied to themselves) would ever have done, who while they pretend to avoid Idolatry, commit all the Sacrilege, Murther and Impiety that can be imagined.[32]

It is plain from John Richardson's work that the more provocative of religious images had long been absent from the cross, and the parliamentary ordinance that justified iconoclasm specified that non-religious items were to be saved and damage made good.[33] But the puritan dislike of market crosses, if hard for moderns to understand, went too deep to be assuaged by cosmetic measures. Abingdon's cross had indeed been a remarkable one for a small provincial town, and had been reckoned second in splendour only to the Cheapside Cross in London.[34] That had been taken down a year previously in a solemn civic ceremony, with the Lord Mayor and dignitaries in attendance, after almost a century of ceaseless campaigning and organised vandalism.[35] Waller's men would later repeat their exploit against another market cross at Burford. The royalist press taunted them as brave only against targets that could not shoot back.[36]

The Parliamentary authorities threw into Abingdon every fighting unit and every ounce of equipment they could scrape together.[37] They knew that the royalists would be desperate to retrieve their error and retake the town, which had been an important part of the defensive screen around their capital at Oxford and was now a serious threat to it. Nonetheless, its condition was not good. The military governor, Major-General Richard Browne, was at odds with Waller, who commanded the field army operating in the district, and Waller was the darling of the London Puritans who effectively held the parliamentary purse strings.[38] As time passed, money and munitions became increasingly short. Penniless soldiers mutinied and deserted.[39] Disaffection was rife; a night-time cavalry patrol, realising that a large Royalist force was getting into position to attack at dawn, simply rode away without giving the alarm.[40] With the parliamentary support of Bulstrode Whitelocke, who maintained his interest in Abingdon, repeated decisions were made to send money and supplies, but little arrived.[41] There was now no perceived need to man the fortifications at Culham Hill, and the garrison, which may well have outnumbered the townsfolk, was billeted in their houses and living largely at their expense. Government, both civil and military, was by terror. Browne enforced an oath of allegiance, the Solemn League and Covenant, and imprisoned those who refused to take it.[42] He hanged deserters, prisoners of war if they were Irish, and anyone accused of spying for the Royalists, including a child of eleven.[43] Lord Digby, for the Royalists, initiated a lengthy correspondence with Browne, playing with considerable skill on his frustrations and hoping to persuade him that his services would be more highly valued by the king than by Parliament. Browne strung him along, carefully keeping his own side aware of the negotiations.[44] Royalist attacks were repeatedly beaten off, and aggressive sorties made into Royalist territory.[45] In June 1646, after the fighting had ended, Parliament authorised charitable appeals to be made in the churches of London and Westminster 'for and towards the Relief of the visited, and other poor distressed People of the Town of *Abingdon*'.[46] The garrison was disbanded only in January 1647, after which a relieved Corporation made up an account of moneys spent on its behalf.[47] Unpaid for months or years, the soldiers were still petitioning for their arrears in 1652.[48] Browne finally did change sides in 1647 when Cromwell's army faction seized the person of the king. He was imprisoned in Wallingford

Castle, but would benefit at the Restoration, becoming a baronet and Lord Mayor of London in 1660.[49]

Under the Parliamentarians, the corporation was once more purged. There were no formal dismissals, but in 1645 eight new secondary burgesses were named; three in 1646, two in 1647, and three again in 1648. During this period, at least four new principals were appointed who may never have been secondaries (although given the limitations of the corporation minutes, this cannot be certain). Two men, Richard Cheyney and a John Mayott of a new generation, who had entered the corporation under the Royalists, were required to resign and be re-admitted.[50] There was again difficulty in getting people to serve as mayor. In 1647, Edmund Franklyn, still smarting, no doubt, from his experience of five years earlier, refused the position, and the standard fine of £40 was reduced for him to 5s. Richard Cheyney reluctantly took his place. In the following year, Andrew Blanchard withdrew in favour of John Tesdale.[51] James Curten, one of those who had lent money to the king, refused and also paid a 5s fine in 1649.[52] Francis Paine refused in 1650, but was assessed for the full £40, and changed his mind.[53] But with power over Abingdon now wielded by a hyper-active parliament, it was its parliamentary representation that began to be of unprecedented importance, and this moved out of local control.

The man who sat for Abingdon following both of the elections of 1640 and who would do so again in 1660 was Sir George Stonehouse of Radley, some three or four miles from the town. It does not seem that Sir George was in any way an enthusiastic Parliamentarian; his only appearances in the Commons Journal are as a member of large committees where his absence might go unremarked. Membership of Parliament for him was part of a public persona for mainly local display, along with his baronetcy, his position as deputy-lieutenant, and his year in the limelight as high sheriff of the county.[54]

Stonehouse's lack of interest in the major political struggle of his time comes out clearly in his record. When, with other members, he was asked to specify what personal contribution he would make to the parliamentarian cause, his offer of four horses was probably the least he could get away with.[55] But it was impossible not to take sides. Faced in June 1643 with the particularly obnoxious loyalty oath that was the Solemn League and Covenant, he seems to have ceased attending the House, and in January 1644 he was formally disqualified from membership.[56] The date and manner of his dismissal from the House of Commons suggests that he may have chosen to attend the counter-parliament that the king called in Oxford.

Meanwhile, the town came into the sphere of influence of Henry Marten, whose father, a very successful lawyer, had amassed a portfolio of estates in north-west Berkshire. Marten was a republican, one of that minority of 'fiery spirits' on the parliamentary side who had understood from the start that the struggle was not a casual spat between two rival sets of royal advisors but over the principle of monarchy itself, and that it might not end while the king lived. This view, cogently expressed before his parliamentary colleagues were psychologically ready for it, had earned him exclusion from the House and brief imprisonment.[57] But on his release he had returned to Berkshire and become an important member of the county committee which Parliament had set up as its prime agent of local government, supreme over both town and country.[58] By 1645, opinions had evolved. Marten was elected burgess for Abingdon in Stonehouse's place, but before he could take his seat his friends had managed to overturn his previous exclusion and he could once more appear as a knight of the shire.[59] His replacement in Abingdon was a protégé, William Ball, a London lawyer and fellow-member of the county committee.[60] Ball died two years later, and was followed by another friend of Marten's, Henry Neville from Billingbear in the south-east of the county, also a republican and a writer of political, satirical, and mildly pornographic tracts.[61] So far as is known, all these candidates were returned by no wider electorate than the Corporation itself and were unopposed.

The war had been a period of trauma for Abingdon. It had been in the front line for almost four years without a break; its death rate had been unprecedentedly high both from direct military action and from epidemics spread by the soldiery; it had experienced the reign of terror that was a deliberate policy of military governors; there had been destruction of property and general impoverishment. The town remained notionally self-governing under its charter, but in William Castell it had had at least one mayor forced on it. Its corporation had been subject to purges and would be so again. The representative it had elected to parliament twice in 1640 had been disabled from sitting, and arbitrarily replaced with individuals it had had no real part in selecting. The town badly needed a period of tranquillity in which to recover its equilibrium. But this would be denied it.

---

[1] He is noted as 'of Weeke' – *The High Sheriffs of Berkshire* (Berks Record Office, 1997), p. 51.

[2] *Privy Council Registers* V p. 95 (13 Feb 1638/9).

[3] M.C. Fissel, *The Bishops' Wars; Charles I's campaigns against Scotland, 1638-1640* (Cambridge, 1994), pp. 3-39.

[4] John K. Gruenfelder, The Spring 1640 Parliamentary Election at Abingdon' *Berks Arch J.* 65 (1970) 41-7; BL, Whitelocke's memoirs, Addl Ms 37343 fols 197v-198v.

[5] Anthony Fletcher, *Reform in the provinces : the government of Stuart England* (1986), p. 49; TNA, Letter from William Jones, 25 July 1640, SP 16/461/13. Judge Jones was a great supporter of the king's prerogative in matters connected with defence.

[6] TNA, Petition of the Berkshire Grand Jury, (July 1640), SP 16/466/42 (reprinted in John Morrill, *The Revolt of the Provinces: conservatives and radicals in the English Civil War1630-1650* (2nd edn, 1980), p.148).

[7] TNA, Letters from Privy Council to Judges of Assize for Co of Berks, (7 July 1640), and to Earl of Holland, Lord Lieutenant of Berks, (8 July 1640), PC 2 52, p. 622; Letter G. Stonehouse to Earl of Holland, (14 July 1640), SP 16/460/4; Lord Northampton to Lord Conway, (21 July 1640), SP 16/460/56; *CSPD* 1640, Nos 103 (13 July), 4, 5 (14 July), 38, 40 (18 July), 56 (21 July).

[8] *CSPD* 1640, no. 43(2) (19 July 1640).

[9] *CSPD* 1640, (18 and 20 June 1640); Fissel, *Bishops' Wars,* pp. 279-80.

[10] Marjorie Marlen (ed), *Woodstock Chamberlains' Accounts 1609-1650,* (Oxfordshire Record Society 58, 1998), pp. 185-8; James F. Larkin (ed), *Stuart Royal Proclamations* ii (1983), pp. 718-20 (1 July 1640); TNA, Northampton to Conway, (21 July 1640), SP 16/460/56.

[11] *CSPD* 1640, no. 43(2) (19 July), no. 83 (23 July).

[12] Morrill, *Revolt*, p. 29.

[13] D. Hirst, *The Representative of the People? Voters and Voting in England under the Early Stuart* (Cambridge, 1975), pp. 62, 65, 80.

[14] *Privy Council Registers* XII p. 41 (28 Oct 1640).

[15] ATCA, Corp mins i fo 142v

[16] ATCA, Corp mins i fo. 165.

[17] ATCA, Corp mins i fo 167.

[18] *CJ,* ii (12 July 1642, 26 Sept 1642).

[19] Sarah Barber, *A Revolutionary Rogue: Henry Marten and the English Republic* (2000), p. 6; Manfred Brod, *The Case of Reading: Urban governance in troubled times* (2006), p. 22.

[20] A. Coe, (publisher), *Speciall Passages and Certain Informations from Severall Places Colle&Ed [sic] for the Use of All That Desire to Be Truly Informed* (1642), p. 5.

[21] I.G. Philip (ed), *The Journal of Sir Samuel Luke* (1947), pp. 79, 81; John Barratt, *Cavaliers: the Royalist army at war1642-1646* (2000), p. 114.

[22] G. H., *Abingtons and Alisbyries Present Miseries Both Which Townes Being Lately Lamentably Plundered by Prince Robert and His Cavaliers* (1642).

[23] *CCAM* ii 999. This was under the scheme known as the Oxford Engagement.

[24] A.E. Preston, *St Nicholas and other papers* (1929), p. 92.

[25] Bodl., Letter (copy) from Lewis Dyve to Prince Rupert, (21 January 1642/3), Ms Top Berks d.43.

[26] ATCA, St Helens registers; J. Dils, 'Epidemics, Mortality and the Civil War in Berkshire 1642-6', *Southern History* 11 (1989), pp. 40-52.

[27] BL, letter Clarges to Sir Edward Walker, (13 July 1643), Harleian Ms 6804 fos. 122-3. Clarges would be an important political figure later in the century - see *DNB*.

[28] ATCA, Corp. Mins i fo. 166v (struck through), 168 (when he was re-instated).

[29] ATCA, Corp. Mins i fos. 166, 167v, 168.

[30] Clarendon, *History of the Rebellion,*(various editions) viii pp. 38-9.

[31] e.g., Mieneke Cox, *Peace and War* (Abingdon, 1993)*,* pp. 100-101; Preston, *St Nicholas,* pp. 96-97. The basic source is *Mercurius Aulicus,* under 31 May 1644, pp.1002-3.

[32] Sir Edward Walker, *Historical discourses, upon several occasions* (1705), p. 17. Walker had been the king's secretary at war.

[33] *A&O* i p. 426

[34] M.J.H. Liversidge, 'Abingdon's "Right Goodly Cross of Stone"' in W.J.H. and M.J.H. Liversidge, *Abingdon Essays: Studies in Local History* (Abingdon, 1989), pp. 42-57.

[35] David Cressy, 'The Downfall of Cheapside Cross: Vandalism, Ridicule and Iconoclasm' in idem, *Agnes Bowker's Cat: Travesties and Transgressions in Tudor and Stuart England* (2000), pp. 234-2

[36] *Mercurius Aulicus,* under 31 May 1644, pp.1002-3.

[37] *CSPD* 1644, p. 387 (1 Aug), p. 393 (3 Aug), p. 454 (27 Aug), p. 458 (28 Aug).

[38] *CSPD* 1644 pp. 466-546 (September) passim.

[39] *CSPD* 1644 p. 471 (3 Sept), pp. 526-8 (22 Sept); *CSPD* 1644-5 p. 205 (31 Dec 44).

[40] Bodl., Col. George Payne to Speaker Lenthall (2 March 1645/6), Ms. Tanner 60 fo. 501.

[41] R. Spalding (ed), *The Diary of Bulstrode Whitelocke 1605-1675* (1990), pp. 153-5, 167, 184-5; *CJ* iv 28 June 1645 and 12 Nov 45; *LJ* vii 12 Nov 1645. Whitelocke remained recorder of Abingdon.

[42] Sir R. Browne, *The Lord Digbies Designe to Betray Abingdon, Carryed on for Divers Vveeks by an Intercourse of Letters. Which Are Here Published for the Satisfaction of All Men, by Sergeant Major Generall Brown. Together with the Cipher Which the Lord Digby Sent Him for That Purpose* (1645), p. 22

[43] Cox, *Peace and War,* p. 107, 111; *Mercurius Academicus,* 2-7 March 1646, p. 111.

[44] Browne, *Lord Digbie's designe.* Browne was never allowed to forget his former rather plebeian occupation of timber merchant or 'wood-monger'. In a time when soldiering was considered honourable and trade was not, such reminders could be painful. Digby tried similar tactics in a number of towns; they were never successful.

[45] Bodl., Ms Tanner 60 fo. 77.

[46] *CJ* iv 580-581 (18 June 1646).

[47] ATCA, Corp. mins, fo. 171v. Unfortunately, the account itself has not survived.

[48] Bodl., Ms Tanner 56, fos. 178, 255. Their mistake was letting themselves be disbanded. Priority for arrears of pay was always given to units still in being − since they were in a better position to make nuisances of themselves.

[49] Keith Lindley, 'Browne, Sir Richard, first baronet (c.1602–1669)', *DNB*.

[50] ATCA, Corp. mins , i fo. 172. Cheyneys and Mayotts were related by marriage.

[51] ATCA. Corp. mins,i fos. 173v, 174.

[52] ATCA. Corp. mins, i fo. 175.

[53] ATCA. Corp. mins, i fo. 176v.

[54] He was high sheriff in 1637-8 − J.R.T.E, *The High Sheriffs of Berkshire* (Berks Record Office, 1997), p. 51.

[55] *CJ* ii 772 (19 Sept 1642)

[56] *CJ* iii 117-8 (6 June 1643), 256 (28 Sept 1643), 374 (22 Jan 1644); iv 288 (26 Sept 1645), 397 (6 Jan 1646). His name does not appear among those who took the Covenant − *An Ordinance.... 5. Feb. 1643 (*1644) (BL, Thomason Tracts, E.33[8]).

[57] *CJ* iii 206 (16 Aug 1643, footnote); C.M. Williams, 'The Political Career of Henry Marten' unpubl. DPhil thesis (Oxford, 1954). pp. 102-3.

[58] Brod, *The Case of Reading,* p. 31.

[59] ATCA, Corp. mins, i fo. 169; Williams, 'Marten', p. 333.

[60] ATCA, Corp. mins, i fo. 169v; H.E. Bannard, 'The Berkshire, Buckinghamshire and Oxfordshire Committees of 1642-1646', *Berks, Bucks and Oxon Archaeological Journal* 31 no 2 (1927), pp. 173-192; Berks RO, D/EP 7/81 bdl. 22. Ball should not be confused (as he sometimes is) with the republican writer of the same name from Barkham, who was publishing new work long after the MP's death.

[61] ATCA, Corp. mins, i fo. 175; Nicholas von Maltzahn, 'Neville, Henry (1620–1694)', *DNB*; Gaby Mahlberg, 'Henry Neville and English Republicanism in the Seventeenth Century', unpubl. PhD thesis (University of East Anglia , 2005).

8. After the war

The English civil war was not the first European revolution: it was the last of the Wars of Religion.

John Morrill [1]

When one of the factions is extinguished, the remaining subdivideth.

Francis Bacon, *Essay LI*

The first civil war, which came to an end in the summer of 1646, had been fought without any clear definition of war aims. Distrust between king and parliament was of long standing. The king saw his prerogative as a God-given right which he dare not renounce. This included a free choice of counsellors both clerical and lay. Parliament objected to the choices he made, and feared that they would drive him, and the country, into a nightmare state of Catholicism in religion and despotism in government. Those who took the Solemn League and Covenant swore that they had 'no thoughts or intentions to diminish His Majesty's just power and greatness'.[2] This limitation, by 1646, with the king defeated and a prisoner, might be thought to be obsolete. Similarly, they would 'endeavour the extirpation of Popery, prelacy ...' where prelacy meant the traditional apparatus of the English church, with its hierarchy of bishops and disciplinary jurisdictions. What the framers of the oath had had in mind was the institution of an alternative hierarchy following the Presbyterianism that already existed in Scotland. But Scotland was another country with different social structures, and even if England was ready to abolish episcopacy, there was limited enthusiasm to replace a discredited system of ecclesiastical governance with one that was foreign and untested. The victors of 1646 found that their side had split into a muddle of factions, as hostile to each other as they all had been to the king. On the right (to use a later system of classification) were the Presbyterians, only loosely identified with that religion, but standing for a careful conservatism in policy, a monarchy under their ultimate control, and a minimum of social upheaval. On the left were the Independents, a congeries of groups united mainly by hostility to the Stuarts and a rejection of any imposed religious discipline. The Presbyterians included the gentry and the solid citizens, the parliamentary majority, some of the senior army officers. But the army rank and file were not solid citizens, and they held the muskets. They also had legitimate complaint against the majority in the House for neglecting their pay and conditions in favour of lower taxes for the well-to-do. The big tent of Independency sheltered the parliamentary minority, the army after it had purged itself of Presbyterians, social conservatives who would have been Presbyterians but for some religious scruple or other, Levellers who wanted social reform on the basis that all men were created equal, republicans like Marten and Neville, Fifth Monarchists preparing to welcome the thousand-year reign of King Jesus, and every conceivable sort of mystic and radical and minority of one. Abingdon had its share of every one of these tendencies.

After Roode's death in October 1643, a replacement, William Jekyll, was instituted by Bishop Duppa of Salisbury and inducted by his archdeacon John Ryves. He would be the last clergyman to be locally inducted under the old dispensation. Unfortunately, he died before the end of the year, perhaps another victim of the typhus epidemic.[3] He was not replaced. John Stone's service at St Nicholas had also ended. He died in August 1643. Anthony Huish, the headmaster of Roysse's School, took on the duties of reader at St Nicholas; but St Helen's would seem to have become the domain of occasional visiting preachers.

The army regiments that garrisoned Abingdon in 1644 came from London, where new and sophisticated religious ideas were furthest developed.[4] The mixture of such troops with townsfolk already sensitised to religious conflict proved heady. The Independent Colonel Pickering did his own preaching, and caused riots, of whom and against whom is unknown; questions were asked in the House, and he was reprimanded, but died shortly afterwards.[5] Pickering's chaplain – one wonders why he needed one – was Henry Pinnell, an antinomian and visionary. Antinomians took to its limit the Calvinist theory of double predestination; if you were doomed to hell, no good deeds could save you, but correspondingly no crime was black enough to damn a pre-elected saint. It was a heady but troubling doctrine.[6]

At some time after the parliamentarian take-over, John Pendarves appeared and took over the vicarage of St Helen's.[7] A Cornishman, born in 1622, he had taken his bachelor's degree at Oxford shortly before the war but had then left and had no doubt marched with one or another of the parliamentary armies.[8] He held somewhat advanced religious ideas, and may well have been the soldier, mentioned with horror by the Presbyterian heresiographer Thomas Edwards, who at Wantage had preached in favour of the baptism of adult believers and, what was worse, had offered to debate the matter with his hearers.[9] To a Presbyterian, doctrine was to be accepted, not contested. Once he had been confirmed in possession by the allocation of a stipend from the oddly-named Committee for Plundered Ministers, Pendarves married Thomasine Newcomen, from a wealthy and godly Dartmouth family, some years his senior, and with opinions even more radical than his own. He seems to have been a charismatic individual. In 1648, Richard Wrigglesworth, a Marcham man who had made his fortune in London, endowed a series of 'lectures', which were to be held weekly in St Helen's in the winter and in Marcham in summer, and for which Pendarves was to be the preferred preacher so long as he wished.[10]

The end of the war did not mean the end of military occupation for Abingdon. Colonel Thomas Rainsborough had first brought his regiment there in January 1646.[11] The spate of mutinies and disorders of the summer of 1647 saw Rainsborough sitting in parliament while his men were at Southampton, under orders to clear the Royalists out of the Channel Islands. They refused to embark, and began their march to join the main centre of the rising which was at Oxford. Rainsborough caught up with them at Abingdon and they reached a pragmatic agreement by which the soldiers would not continue to Oxford but could stay indefinitely where they were. They were charging the inhabitants 2s 6d per day per man for their maintenance.[12]

Rainsborough was one of the few senior officers to support the Levellers. The Levellers, led by John Lilburne, were an early version of an oppositional political party.[13] They had a newspaper, published pamphlets, and organised popular demonstrations. Their constitutional ideal was a commonwealth of small tradesmen organised as local democracies and with only a minimum of national administration. They appealed to a number of constituencies which had not previously been the concern of national politicians – small tradesmen anxious over the uncertainties of business, the 'sea-green battalions' of women who turned out in the Leveller colours to demand the return of their men from the army and an end to shortages and high taxes, religious independents and sectaries who wanted freedom from persecution, and especially the army rank and file that needed their arrears paid and the certainty that their jobs would be open to them when they returned home.[14] Rainsborough was a spokesman for the common man. It was he who famously declared at the Putney debates in 1647, 'I doe think that the poorest man in England is not at all bound in a strict sense to that Government that he hath nott had a voice to putt himself under'.[15] Pendarves, in addition to his other duties, was Rainsborough's regimental chaplain.[16]

An enthusiastic young man, Pendarves seems to have found it difficult to cater for the less enthusiastic among his parishioners, and at some time decided to make a separation between the more godly of his flock and the others. The legacy of Roode at St Helen's was a strongly Puritan group among whom were several lay preachers. From October 1647, Pendarves was also minister at Wantage, twelve miles away, and found, or nurtured, a similar group there. He trained a young man, Robert Keate, as its leader.[17] By 1649 or earlier, he was in contact with William Kiffin, a wealthy London merchant who was one of the founders of a new sect, the Particular or Calvinistic Baptists, and during 1650 he led his own following into that denomination. His duties at St Helen's were amicably transferred to a younger Oxford graduate, also a west-countryman, John Tickell.[18]

There were by now several sects that held that the only valid baptism was that of adult believers. In the controversial literature they were always referred to as 'anabaptists', alluding to the horrors that had been perpetrated in the short-lived anabaptist republic of John of Leyden in Muenster in 1535. Propagandists asserted, improbably, that men like Kiffin and Pendarves were dangerous anarchists, hatching their plans and awaiting their opportunities.[19] In fact, the Particular Baptists were the most respectable among the sects that pullulated now that the bishops and their courts were no more. Presbyterians insisted on infant baptism as a matter of form, but few found adult re-baptism in itself objectionable. The only serious difference in worship was in the frequency with which the Baptists took communion – perhaps once a month, versus at most three times a year for the Presbyterians.[20]

The main reason why Pendarves's followers separated was not because of scruples over baptism but out of religious snobbishness. Even while their principles seemed to be becoming dominant in the state, they insisted on defining themselves as an embattled minority. In this, they were following a venerable Protestant tradition.[21] Accordingly, the organisation they adopted was rigid and disciplined. Something of the atmosphere can be gained from a pamphlet by a disgruntled ex-member of Pendarves's conventicle, John Atherton, who, for his questioning, had been formally excommunicated and 'delivered to Satan'.[22] The account is certainly biased, but rings true in its picture of a rigid authoritarian organisation, dominated by Pendarves and a few subordinate preachers, where doubt was seen as disloyalty and sanctioned by consignment to supernatural punishment. The Baptists, of course, justified their autocracy on the basis that believers' baptism implied an enduring dedication to the only true church, that doubters should not be tarried for, and that those left behind were in any case among those predestined for damnation.[23] What they certainly did not wish to do was to share the Lord's Supper with the profane multitude.

Pendarves's main administrative achievement was the Abingdon Association of Particular Baptist Churches, which made Abingdon an important regional centre of the sect. By the time of his death the association would have twelve member-churches and cover an area stretching from Andover in the south-west into Buckinghamshire and Bedfordshire in the north-east. Further evidence of the fanaticism described by Atherton can perhaps be deduced from an incident that took place at an administrative meeting of the association in 1655. One of the participants so far forgot himself as to say something funny ('a speech ... which savoured of some lightnes'), at which a few others smiled ('not to be commended'). The meeting broke down into a flurry of 'heart opening' and 'soule melting confessions' and finished with the drafting of a letter to be sent to all affiliated churches warning them against 'lightnes and vanitie' and citing Ephesians 5:4 against 'jesting'.[24] Recent authors have tended to insist that the Puritans were not the sour-faced killjoys of contemporary satire, but it is a charge of which Pendarves's followers at Abingdon must stand condemned.

As the wartime effervescence settled, Abingdon found its public life transformed. New corporation members had appeared in large numbers. Since the charter allowed only twelve principal burgesses, there must have been a corresponding number of resignations or dismissals. The corporation minutes make no mention of these, except for the case of Thomas Orpwood who had allegedly absented himself for all of twelve years past, and for William Castell, whose dismissal had been expressly ordered by the Royalist lord chief justice and who was now reinstated.[25] Seventeen men attended the council meeting of 11 June 1650 which was to discuss a weighty financial matter. The Commonwealth government, as usual, was in dire straits for ready cash, and was encouraging corporations to redeem their fee farms. Abingdon was to pay £925 9s 3d, exactly nine years' purchase. As was normal practice after important decisions, all the participants signed the minute book. Only John Mayott was present from the men who had been recruited during the royalist occupation, and there were five who had survived from the ante-bellum period.[26] Eight of the seventeen would appear in the post-Restoration records as religious non-conformists, all of them, with two ambiguous cases, Presbyterians.[27] There was still, as always, a Mayott, but the Tesdales were represented only by a son-in-law, Francis Payne, and his brother Robert. At least some of the new men were not of the classes that normally aspired to such positions. One, the glover Bedford Stacey, made his mark instead of signing. Some had broader experience than their predecessors. Thomas Trapham had had a successful career as an army surgeon, was head of a military hospital in London, and personal surgeon to Cromwell.[28] John Hanson, whose election as churchwarden had provoked a complaint to the archdeaconry, was (almost certainly) a grandson of William Lee who had been several times mayor about the turn of the century, but his paternal family was of prospering London merchants.[29] These burgesses were also expected to act on a wider stage than their own town, and served on various commissions. The mayor was *ex officio* a member of the county committee, which was supposed to administer the county on behalf of its new masters, but this found its attributions much reduced after 1650. Nonetheless, John Hanson from 1650, William Stevenson from 1652, James Hearne and William Bostock from 1656, and Thomas Trapham after 1657 helped to distribute the county's tax assessments. John Mayott was a militia commissioner in 1659.[30]

There seems to have been little direct interference from the commonwealth and the later protectorate authorities in the working of the corporation. Such interference becomes visible only once, in 1655. After the Royalist rising led by John Penruddock in Wiltshire, the government decided to divide the country into districts, each of which would come under one of a new breed of military governors, the Major-Generals. With a certain lack of geographical logic, Berkshire was united to Hampshire and Sussex, and put under William Goffe, better known for religious ardour than for administrative efficiency. On 5 December, he held a first meeting in Reading with what was to be his Berkshire advisory committee. The twenty-seven members were mostly either army men or minor county gentry acceptable to the soldiers; only two were from Abingdon: Major Francis Allen, a JP but not a member of the Corporation, and Thomas Trapham, the surgeon. A week later, Richard Cheyney, a former mayor, resigned 'voluntarily' from the Abingdon corporation. He had been promoted to principal burgess during the Royalist occupation. At the same time, four secondary burgesses who had entered the Corporation in that period and who seem no longer to have been active were dismissed as 'illegally elected'.[31]

High on the corporation's agenda was, inevitably, recovery from the destruction and general dislocation of the war. There was plainly a housing shortage which must have become acute as soldiers returned or came to settle in the town. On 21 April 1646, John Reason was granted a tenement and backside late in the occupation of Edward Chandler on condition of 'building two space of howsing and slatting the same' and, apparently, let off the usual entry fine. Similarly, on 1 April 1647, Thomas Steede got a lease on the 'piece of ground in Ock Street where (Robert) Cornishe his house did stand' at 10s rent and without a fine. Steede's son and heir John still held the plot in 1687, presumably rebuilt, and had to pay £2 5s for the renewal.[32] Other tenements were subdivided. On 3 September 1646, John Prince, scivier (sievemaker), renewed the lease on 'the messuage wherein he dwelleth' for 10s rent and a fine of £3, except for the part of it now occupied by William Collins, mason, who would pay 5s rent and a 10s fine for his own new lease. On 28 August 1649, Nicholas Butler agreed a similar division with his sub-tenant Robert Evans; they would divide the £1 rent in the proportion of two to one.[33]

Poor harvests in the late 1640s exacerbated the problem. Food prices went up by almost half between 1646 and 1650, and the result was further impoverishment and a slow-down in trade.[34] In October 1649, the corporation updated and reissued its old provisions that tradesmen were to be organised in companies or guilds, and had the proclamation countersigned by the circuit judges. There were to be three such companies, nominally of grocers, butchers and skinners, and each was to group sixteen or seventeen individual trades which might or might not be interconnected in some way and which included callings of different degrees of social prestige. The grocers' guild united mercers with schoolmasters and barbers, the butchers had both vintners and slatters, the skinners included cordwainers and sawyers. No one could exercise a trade unless he had served a seven year apprenticeship in the town, nor could any operate more than a single stall or shop. Each company would have a master and two wardens, elected annually, with extensive powers that included the levying of fines. The aim was obviously to restrict entry to the various trades.[35] There is little evidence that these companies, any more than their predecessors, ever came to play a significant role in the town. Certainly the quarter sessions records, which are sketchily available after 1660, show men accused of illegal exercise of their trades, but there is no mention of the companies as initiating the prosecutions.[36] The bailiffs' accounts do show that a tailors' company maintained a somewhat tenuous existence from the restoration period until the nineteenth century, but this guild is absent from the 1649 list and may already have been in existence.[37] The Berkshire antiquary John Richards, writing in the 1830s, states that the skinners' company was still in operation in his day.[38]

In the period between its occupation by the parliamentary armies and the Restoration, religious pluralism flourished in Abingdon. Diversity seems to have been institutionalised *de facto* if not *de jure*. The Presbyterians did not, and probably could not, abuse their political dominance, and religious Presbyterianism, with its paraphernalia of elders and classes, never appears.[39] John Atherton, the ex-Baptist, makes no special comment on the fact that, when already minister of the local Baptists, Pendarves could deliver the weekly 'lecture' in St Helen's in 1653 or 4 before the presumably Presbyterian mayor, Henry Langley, and the principal burgesses.[40]

There was, however, vicious squabbling among the different sects. The separation of the Baptists from St Helen's was by no means as sharp and tidy as later writers have assumed. Pendarves kept some sort of position at the church, and its bells rang a knell for one of his children who died in 1654.[41] Baptists' life events continued to be noted in St Helen's registers, with their children marked as 'born' rather than 'baptised'. The total number of Baptists must have been in the hundreds, and there is nowhere other than St Helen's where they could have worshipped. There would be no Baptist burial ground until 1656. The situation seems to have been similar to that of the 1630s, with two contending factions under their own leaderships. Pendarves's nominal successor, John Tickell, had a hard time of it. He was an able young man; on graduation in 1649 he had immediately been made a fellow of New College.[42] A publication of 1656 speaks of his despair.[43] He had, it seems, been ready to give up and had made his preparations to leave Abingdon.[44] Representations by some members of the congregation had led him to reconsider, but the reconsideration, when it became known, caused further ructions. Finally, following the example of John Calvin in Geneva a hundred years earlier, he proposed a set of church rules which, if the congregation agreed to accept them, would encourage him to stay.[45] Tickell kept clerical company with Presbyterians, but his main concern was to counter all forms of religious radicalism that went beyond his own relatively moderate position.[46] Whether for principled or propagandist reasons, his pamphlet has nothing in it of elders or classes. What the rules seek to define is an Independent congregation practising a more or less open communion. Joining it would be an act of deliberation; the neophyte would have to be approved, first by the minister, and then by 'the whole body, or the major number of the men at least'. But rejection would only be through 'real, known, or strongly presumed Scandals', and anyone making a solemn profession of repentance and faith would be given the benefit of the doubt.[47] This congregational vision is supported by lengthy quotations from contemporary divines, all of them Independents or non-conformists, both in England and New England.[48] Infant baptism gets only an ambiguous mention, with confirmation in adulthood given equal importance. Tickell continues with an essay criticising 'the Anabaptists' who 'superstitiously preferre the Supper before all other ordinances'. He claims to be victimised by them, and describes himself to his readership as their 'suffering, bleeding, abused Minister'.[49] The closing section is a vituperative personal attack on Pendarves.[50] Tickell may have stayed in Abingdon a little longer, but by the end of November 1657 had been replaced by John Biscoe, known as an Independent.[51]

The general picture at St Helen's, thus, was a confused one, and denominational labels derived from a later reality are not particularly helpful. Puritans of various sorts were dominant, but divided among themselves. The main division was not on baptism but on who should partake of the Lord's Supper. Pendarves's Baptists, and possibly others among the congregation, wanted the sacrament limited to those who they could accept as being predestined for salvation. Tickell was less exigent, but still required a formal act of adhesion. The two groups, under their respective leaders, competed for godly members. It was the difficulty experienced by those of more moderate piety in getting their religious needs satisfied that ensured the survival through the interregnum of the unfashionably – and illegally – conservative church of St Nicholas.

St Nicholas was vulnerable. It was out of touch with the prevailing attitudes of the time, and found it hard to dissemble. After Cromwell's victory over the Scots at Dunbar in September 1650, Parliament decreed that 8 October would be a day of national thanksgiving. St Nicholas did not participate. Parliament then let it be known that it was collecting the names of recalcitrant clergy and that action would be taken against them. Discretion was the better part of valour, and St Nicholas had its own thanksgiving day on 24 October, publicising the fact with 5s-worth of bell-ringing.[52]

It was in the nature of its congregation that weekday services would not be well attended, but Anthony Huish, who had succeeded to the readership after the death of John Stone, had to be encouraged to continue with them, for fear of giving an opening to its opponents: 'I know it must needs be some *discouragement* to you to read to Walls, or to pray in publick with so thin a *company,* as will hardly amount to a Congregation' wrote his main supporter, the Laudian publicist Peter Heylyn, who had taken up residence in Abingdon after ejection from his clerical livings.[53] But the alternative was to be accused of misuse of the Blacknall charity money that paid the Reader. In 1650 and again in 1655, parliamentary commissioners enquired into the charity, involving the churchwardens in considerable trouble and expense, but without finding anything untoward. On the second occasion, the wardens confirmed that:

> ...there is noe Minister in this towne of Abingdon from whom generally and publiquely the people of this towne have for many years past received or can now obtaine the administracon of ye Sacrament of the Lord's Supper for themselves, and of Baptism for their children besides Mr. Huish.[54]

The commissioners will not have needed to be told, for they included the mayor and four other current burgesses of Abingdon.[55] That the sacraments were 'generally and publiquely' available was exactly what the more zealous of the brethren found objectionable: 'it was thronged with *Malignants*, who seduced others from their godly way'.[56] In 1657 there was a proposal to the government committee that dealt with such matters, the Committee for Augmentations, that the St Nicholas parish be merged with St Helen's and the church demolished.[57] There was a series of hearings both official and unofficial, with the advantage swinging from one side to the other. The intolerant Thomas Trapham was strongly for merger, but other burgesses disgreed. St Helen's 'cannot receive' all who wished to worship, and it would be better to enlarge St Nicholas rather than pulling it down.[58] One of the churchwardens, Robert Mayott, went to London, and Heylyn ran an intensive lobbying campaign apparently at his own expense.[59] Some members of the new élite, plainly, were open to persuasion. One was Sir John Lenthall, son of the speaker of the Long Parliament, who was now resident at Besselsleigh. He would represent Abingdon in the 1659 parliament, and seems already to have been working to attain local prominence. The final outcome, in June 1658, was that the Trustees for Preaching Ministers would add £20 a year to the £40 that the St Nicholas parishioners now promised to raise for a regular vicar.[60] Once all danger was past, in 1661, the churchwardens would return to their old rate of payment, of £3 per annum.[61]

If the conflict in the religious establishment was echoed in the council chamber, this has left no trace in the records. There is no sign until the end of the Protectorate of the sort of faction fighting that had prevailed before 1642, and political changes appear to have proceeded smoothly. In September 1649, the recorder, Bulstrode Whitelocke, resigned. He had become not only a leading lawyer but also an important national politician. With an increasing workload as member of parliament and as Keeper of the Great Seal, and recently widowed with ten young children, he was divesting himself of all duties that would take him away from his normal path between London and his home at Henley.[62] An old legal friend, Bartholomew Hall, took over, apparently without discussion, his recorderships at Abingdon, Oxford, and Wallingford and his position as attorney-general of the Duchy of Lancaster.[63] At Reading and Oxford, Whitelocke became high steward. Abingdon did not care to fill that position, perhaps remembering that its last high steward, the Earl of Holland, had been executed only in the previous March in exasperation at his constant trimming between Royalist and Parliamentarian parties; nonetheless, Whitelocke would remain open to requests for help and advice from the town.[64]

A young cousin of Whitelocke's, Richard Croke, was put on the Abingdon Commission of the Peace in 1649 along with Hall, presumably to act as his deputy. In July 1653, he was joined, and in practice probably replaced, by Thomas Holt, who had local connections – his wife was from Chawley, near Cumnor.[65]

In the meantime, more dramatic developments had been taking place in national politics. The House of Commons had been purged by the Army in December 1648, and the removal of its Presbyterian majority had permitted the execution of the king. The House of Lords had followed the bishops into extinction. But the now unicameral parliament, irreverently known as the Rump, still refused to do what the Army wanted of it, and after years of rising frustration was dissolved by Cromwell in the coup of 20 April 1653. The remaining history of the Interregnum is the unending and futile search of the Army for a parliament that would lend legitimacy to its rule. The new assembly that met in the following June – the 'Barebones Parliament', so-called after one of its pious members – was hand-picked by Army officers on the model of the biblical Sanhedrin, and had no formal representation of specific towns or counties.[66] This collapsed in December, and Oliver Cromwell became Lord Protector. New elections took place in June 1654 for what would be the first Protectorate Parliament. There were new electoral rules, under which Abingdon would no longer differ from other towns, since those that had previously had two seats in the Commons would now have only one. There is no record of a contest in Abingdon, but sixty-nine electors sent Thomas Holt, the deputy recorder, to Westminster.[67] He proved a tolerably active MP, participating in committees to examine the new constitution, the Instrument of Government, under which the parliament had been called, and, with Whitelocke among others, to consider abuses in the legal system which there was public pressure to reform. During the life of the parliament, members were asked to sign a 'recognition' of the state as it now was, ruled by 'a single person and a parliament'.[68] Over a hundred members, republicans, refused to sign and were expelled. Holt was not among them.

Nonetheless, he was no political cipher. In 1555, Holt, by now a justice of the peace for the county as well as the town, was prominent by his absence from Major-General Goffe's advisory committee.[69] In the hard-fought election campaign of the summer of 1656, when the Army was trying by all means to exclude its opponents, Goffe wrote to the Secretary of State, John Thurloe,

> I was all ye last weeke in Barksheere, and was at ye Assizes where things were caryed very well by ye Judges: I found too many Differences amongst ye Godly people there: and did what I could to reconcile them, & exhorted them to agree & unite against wickednesse wch I am sure is ye comon enemie: they seemed very desiring to unite in choosing mee for their parliament man at Abbington. But all ye rabble of ye Towne were last yeare for one Holt, who is an ill man & noe friend to ye protectorate.[70]

Cromwell and the army wanted at all costs a tractable parliament that would accept the principle of the Protectorate and vote funding for the disastrous war against Spain in the Caribbean. There is no evidence that Goffe risked standing for Abingdon − he took one of the Hampshire county seats − and Holt was again elected.[71] But he was one of the fifty-eight signatories to a letter of complaint to the speaker that, although duly returned, they were being wrongfully prevented by decision of the Protector's Privy Council from taking their seats. [72] It would seem that he missed most of the parliament, being allowed in only when it reconvened for what would be a short second session in January 1658 after a seven-month adjournment. He was immediately, and no doubt appropriately, named to the committee of privileges, but will hardly have had time to make his mark when the dissolution came on 4 February.[73] Abingdon, meanwhile, had re-affirmed its faith in him; Bartholomew Hall, permanently absent at his court in Lancashire, was dismissed as recorder in October 1656, and Holt chosen to replace him.

Interestingly, there is another, and much longer, list of excluded members where Holt's name does not appear, but where there is a mention of a John Hanson, who may well have been the current mayor of Abingdon. Conceivably, he had stood against Holt and, as often happened at that time, both candidates initially claimed to have won. If this was actually the case,

Hanson must have withdrawn, since there is no record of a Commons decision on his candidature.[74]

The early autumn of 1656 was a time of more than the average degree of political and religious turmoil in Cromwell's England. Over the years the regime had lost the support of its main constituencies. The republicans had been alienated by the coup of April 1653 that had dismissed the Rump parliament, the religious radicals by the engineered collapse of its Barebones successor in the following December. The Spanish war, begun in early 1655, was hurting the merchant class; the major-generals, installed in September, were infuriating the rural gentry whose local authority they compromised. The Levellers, leaderless with John Lilburne converted to Quakerism, were beginning to work towards a rapprochement with the Royalists. The parliamentary election campaign had been bad-tempered and divisive.[75] In early September, John Pendarves died in London of a 'griping of the guts' – what we would call dysentery.

His death at thirty-four, while at the height of his powers, caused a great stir among the religious. His body was sealed into a sugar chest supplied by the Baptist grocer Philip Lockton and brought slowly up the river to Abingdon, while arrangements were made for the funeral. It so happened that the Baptists had opened a new graveyard in Ock Street all of their own, and Pendarves would be the first apart from some infants to be buried there. The funeral, fixed for 30 September, would prove a traumatic event for Abingdon, and perhaps determine the course of its local politics over the next few years.[76]

As the date of the funeral approached, the town filled with radicals of every stripe from all parts of the kingdom. It became the scene of a great anti-government jamboree. Some local Baptists may have been mourning their minister, but most of the visitors had other purposes in view. For many, the funeral provided an opportunity for mass demonstrations against the regime; for some – the Fifth Monarchists – a cover for planning insurrection and recruiting collaborators. Providentialists and mystics wondered whether Pendarves's death might not be part of God's preparations for the second coming of Christ. The government's security services were there in force, listening, raiding the inns, searching baggage for incriminating papers. Every spare room, every open space, was filled with crowds listening to inflammatory and seditious sermons. Townsfolk were harassed as they went about their daily business. Pendarves was duly buried, but the jamboree went on. The mayor sent to the county militia headquarters at Wallingford, and 2 October saw the arrival of Major-General Bridge with fifty cavalry troopers.[77]

There was a tense stand-off in which one demonstrator was slightly wounded when he shook his fist too close to the edge of a cavalry sword, but the crowd was dispersed. Five individuals were taken to Windsor Castle for questioning, but only one of them, a known Fifth Monarchist from Norfolk, was detained for more than a few days.

The Fifth Monarchists did attempt to rise in London in the following April under the cooper Thomas Venner, but were arrested as they gathered. At least five of the would-be insurgents had been at Pendarves's funeral.[78] One of their planning papers captured by the security men named Philip Lockton, a Tesdale son-in-law, as a contact in Abingdon, although it is not clear how deeply he was involved in the plot. He does not seem to have been troubled by the authorities.[79]

The disorders at Pendarves's funeral probably served to inoculate Abingdon people against further excesses in religious polemic. With the relaxation of the discipline he had imposed, ideas previously suppressed surfaced among his flock. The brazier Edward Stennett convinced some of his friends that Saturday, not Sunday, was the true Sabbath, and some tradesmen began to close their shops on that day.[80] John Hanson debated with them, and there was an exchange of tracts. Both of these amateur theologians provide a massive superstructure of biblical citations, combined with impressive feats of logic-chopping to demonstrate their relevance to the argument at hand. But the controversy was conducted in tones of perfect courtesy on both sides. The opponents are 'eminent Christians', albeit perhaps deluded, and there is a noteworthy absence of the vituperation that was customary when professional clergy clashed in print.[81] It was about the same time, as we have seen, that the campaign to demolish the church of St Nicholas was abandoned. There was no repetition of Tickell's personal attack on the 'Anabaptists', and it may not be coincidental that Tickell's replacement at St Helens, John Biscoe, seems to have been an inoffensive individual, whose only known publications were long, scholarly, and quite unreadable.[82]

Thus Abingdon, by the end of the 1650s, had regained a degree of stability. Differences and tensions must have persisted, but the furious name-calling across unbridgeable religious divides had ceased. Royalists like Peter Heylyn no longer needed to keep their heads down; traditional Anglican worship at St Nicholas was tolerated. There must have been anxiety after Oliver Cromwell's death in September 1658, and even more after the resignation of his son and successor Richard in the following May when the regime was visibly collapsing; but there is no record of unrest. Further down the river, at Reading, republicans and army supporters clashed violently in the council chamber, but no such events were reported in Abingdon.[83] The restoration of the monarchy, when it came, would be welcomed by some, but there were no obvious outstanding problems which it would solve.

---

[1] *Royal Historical Society Transactions,* (5th Ser, Vol 34, 1984), p. 178.

[2] S.R. Gardiner, *Constitutional Documents of the Puritan Revolution, 1625-1660,* (3rd edn, 1906), pp. 267-71.

[3] Berks RO, Induction mandates D/A2 d.4 fo. 10; Rev. John Reynolds, personal communication (2000).

[4] *CSPD* 1645-7 p. 244 (1 December 1645).

[5] BL, D'Ewes Diary, Harleian Mss 166, fols 204v, 205; BL, Whiteacre's Diary, Add Mss 31116, fo. 207; Bodl. Ms Tanner 60, fo.77; Ian Gentles, *The New Model Army* (1992), p. 100.

[6] Henry Pinnell, (Untitled Pamphlet) (1648); William Sedgewick, *A Second view of the Army Remonstrance* (1648), last page (unpag); Nigel Smith, 'George Herbert in defence of Antinomianism', *Notes and Queries,* n.s.31 (1984), pp. 334-5.

[7] Ernest Payne states that he was already preaching in Wantage and Abingdon in 1642 and 3 – *The Baptists of Berkshire* (1951), pp. 24, 32 – but gives no authority for this.

[8] For at least a short period, he was a naval chaplain – Larry Kreitzer, personal communication.

[9] Thomas Edwards, *Gangræna, or, A catalogue and discovery of many of the errours, heresies, blasphemies and pernicious practices of the sectaries of this time, vented and acted in England in these four last years* (1646) III p. 174

[10] A.E. Preston, *St Nicholas Abingdon and other* papers (1929), pp. 116-7; Griffith-Boscawen, *Endowed Charities of the County of Berks* (HMSO, 1912) I pt 1, p. 37; I pt 2, pp. 1095-1112; TNA, C 93/24 No 2.

[11] Letter Maj-Gen Browne to Committee of Both Kingdoms, (19 Jan 1645/6), HMC *Portland Mss* XIII Part 1 Vol 1, p 340. The regiment, under different command, had been there earlier – Larry Kreitzer, 'The fifth monarchist John Pendarves', *Baptist Quarterly* 43 (April 2009), pp. 112-120

[12] H. Cary, *Memorials of the Great Civil War in England* (London, 1842) I 221-2; *CSPD* 1645-6 pp. 262-3 (15 Dec 45), p. 270 (18 Dec); S.R. Gardiner, *History of the Great Civil War 1642-1649* (1894) III p. 264. The standard rate of pay for a foot soldier was 8d per day – C. Firth, *Cromwell's Army* (1902), p. 184, ..

[13] According to Ernest Payne, *The Baptists of Berkshire* (1951), pp. 24-5, Lilburne himself was in Abingdon in April 1645 and it was there that he resigned from the Army rather than take the Solemn League and Covenant. Payne does not give the basis for this statement which seems unlikely. Lilburne's own account of his resignation is in his *Innocency and Truth Justified* (1646), p. 46.

[14] See, for example, Brian Manning, *The English People and the English Revolution* (1976, 1991), esp. Chaps 9 and 10.

[15] C.H. Firth (ed), *The Clarke Papers* (1891), I, p.301

[16] Ann Lawrence, *Parliamentary Army Chaplains, 1642-1651* (1990), p. 58

[17] A.G. Matthews, *Walker Revised* (1948), p. 71. It is not totally clear whether or not he resigned from the Abingdon living to take up that in Wantage. The Committee for Plundered Ministers mentions him as vicar of Wantage on 31 January 1650 but of St Helen's in Abingdon on 9 February – Bodleian, Ms Bodl 327, fos 17-19. Pluralism would be frowned on, but there *was* a shortage of ideologically approved ministers.

[18] Lambeth Palace Library, Augmentation of livings, COMM VIa/1 (11 Oct 1650).

[19] eg, William Hughes, *Munster and Abingdon, or, the open rebellion there and the unhappy tumult here* (Oxford, 1657).

[20] J. Tickell, *Church-Rules, Proposed to the Church in Abingdon and Approved by Them; an Essay Towards the Removing of Some Stumbling Blocks Laid by Anab. Spirits; a Few Antiquaeries to Mr Pendarves......* (1656), pp. 15-17.

[21] Patrick Collinson, *The Birthpangs of Protestant England* (1988), pp. 127-132.

[22] John Atherton, *The Pastor turn'd pope* (1654).

[23] John Pendarves, 'To the Reader', in Anon, *The Prophets Malachi and Isaiah prophecying* (1656), p. 28.

[24] White (ed), *Association Records*, pp. 141-2, (18 October 1655). The verse reads: 'Neither filthiness, neither foolish talking, neither jesting, which are things not comely, but rather giving of thanks' (Geneva version).

[25] ATCA, Corp mins i fos. 166v, 168. If Thomas Orpwood was the man who had been mayor in 1604-5, his absence may well have been due to old age.

[26] ATCA, Corp mins i f. 176 and compare ff 158 and 161.

[27] Robert Payne and William Stevenson seem later to have been persecuted among Baptists: see A.E. Preston, *St Nicholas and other papers* (1928), p. 124.

[28] Eric Gruber von Arni, *Justice for the maimed soldier* (Aldershot, 2001), pp. 250-251; Anthony Wood, *Fasti,* I col 469, II col 146; *CSPD* 1644-5, p. 25 (9 Oct 1644)

[29] Isabel Lee married a John Hanson of Basildon at St Helen's in 1594, and the later mayor may reasonably be presumed to be their son. Another son, Robert, baptised at St Helen's in 1608, would be Lord Mayor of London and stand unsuccessfully for election as Abingdon's MP in 1676. The *Dictionary of National Biography* is almost certainly wrong in confusing John Hanson of Abingdon with a Pembroke College contemporary of Henry Langley.

[30] W.N. Clarke, *Parochial Topography of the Hundred of Wanting* (Oxford, 1824), p. 17; *A&O,* passim.

[31] Bodl., Ms Rawlinson A33 fo. 73; *ThSP* IV pp. 284-5; ATCA, Corporation Minutes, i fo. 181v.

[32] ATCA, Corporation Minutes, i fo. 172; ii fo. 38.

[33] ATCA, Corp Minutes, i, fos 170v, 174.

[34] Phelps Brown and Hopkins, 'Seven Centuries of the prices of consumables' in E.M. Carus Wilson (ed) , *Essays in Economic History,* Vol 2, (1962), pp 193-6.

[35] BL, Richards Collection, Addl. Ms 39989 fos. 14-18.

[36] BRO, Quarter sessions records, A/JQs 1.

[37] ATCA, Bailiffs' accounts. They rented premises from the corporation at a modest 3s 4d per annum, but it would seem that the rent was scarcely ever paid before about 1750.

[38] BL, Richards Collection, Addl. Ms 39989 folios 2-8.

[39] A Presbyterian congregation was supposed to be governed by its minister, aided by lay elders. It would send representatives to a regional 'classis', which in turn was represented in a 'synod'. The system remained notional in most areas of the country.

[40] John Atherton, *The Pastor turn'd Pope* (1654), p.10 and *passim*. The weekly lecture was on a Tuesday (p. 13), to which it had been moved from Thursday in 1609. The Wrigglesworth lecture, which Pendarves was entitled to give in St Helen's during the winter season, was on Saturday evenings. (Preston, *St Nicholas,* p.116n). Henry Langley will have been a kinsman of his academic younger namesake, who was certainly a Presbyterian. In 1627, as a churchwarden of St Helens, he was to receive the fines of the Puritans who had tried to demolish the chancel screen.

[41] Berks RO D/EP 7 61 Bdle 2 p. 193.

[42] J. Foster, *Alumni Oxonienses 1500-1714* (1891-1901) I p. 1486

[43] John Tickell, *Church-Rules Proposed to the Church in Abingdon* (Oxford, 1656).

[44] Tickell had been named by the Lord Protector in February 1655/6 to the rectory of Ashbury, Berks – Lambeth Palace Library, Augmentation Records, Mss 996 fo.545.

[45] Tickell, *Church-Rules,* sig A2.

[46] John Tickell, *The Bottomless Pit smoaking in Familisme* (1651).

[47] Tickell, *Church-Rules,* pp. 2, 4.

[48] Tickell, *Church-Rules,* pp. 8-14.

[49] Tickell, *Church-Rules,* pp. 15-17.

[50] Tickell, *Church-Rules,* pp. 17-18.

[51] Lambeth Palace Library, Mss 968, COMM III/1, pp 124-5; George Yule, *The Independents in the English Civil War* (Cambridge, 1958), p. 134. Tickell moved back to Devon about this time – A.G. Matthews, *Calamy Revised* (1934), p. 485; Shaw, *History of the English Church* (1900) II, pp. 446-8.

[52] *CJ* VI (17 Sept, 17 October 1650); Berks RO, St Nicholas Transcripts, D/EP 7/66 (unfol). The parliamentary threats were probably directed at pro-Scottish Presbyterian clergy rather than Royalists, but with a possibly hostile enquiry into the finances of the church actually in progress, it will have been better to take no risks – Preston, *St. Nicholas,* pp. 102-3

[53] John Barnard, *The Life of Peter Heylyn, D.D.* (1683), pp. 230-232.

[54] Christ's Hospital Abingdon, St Nicholas Old Church Book, fo. 103, Book of Decrees and Presentments, 1655, passim; Preston, *St. Nicholas,* p. 107.

[55] Lambeth Palace Library, Augmentations, COMM XIIC/1 (Ms 1000), pp 4-5.

[56] Christ's Hospital Abingdon, St Nicholas Book of Decrees and Presentments, (unpag), Statement signed by Jo Thorogood and others, (29 April 1658); Barnard, *Peter Heylyn,* pp. 230-232.

[57] Lambeth Palace Library, Augmentations, COMM XIIC/2 (Ms 991), fo.399

[58] Lambeth Palace Library, Augmentations, COMM IV/10 (Ms 985), fo.36; TNA, Jurors' Presentment, (17 Feb 1657/8), C 94/4/3a.

[59] Barnard, *Peter Heylyn,* pp. 230-232.

[60] Lambeth Palace Library, Augmentations, COMM IV/10 (Ms 985), f.90; COMM XIIC/2 (Ms 991), f.435, St Nicholas Old Church Book f. 20; Preston, *St Nicholas,* pp. 101-111, 225

[61] Christ's Hospital Abingdon, St Nicholas Old Church Book, ff. 133d, 134; Preston, *St Nicholas,* p. 226.

[62] Ruth Spalding, 'Whitelocke, Bulstrode, appointed Lord Whitelocke under the protectorate (1605-1675)', *DNB.*

[63] TNA, Crown Office Docquet Book, C 231/6, p. 169; M.G. Hobson and H.E. Salter, *Oxford Council Acts 1625-1665* (1933) p. 165; Berks RO, Wallingford Records, MF 321, fo 136.

[64] Berks RO, R/HMC/LXI.

[65] Crown Office Docquet Book, C 231/6, p. 169, 263. Richard Croke became deputy-recorder of Oxford, and was later recorder and MP for that city - see Vivienne Larminie, 'Croke, Unton (1594/5-1670/71)', *DNB.* For Holt, see DNB article on his son: Paul D. Halliday, 'Holt, Sir John (1642-1710)', *DNB.*

[66] There was one member *from* − but not *for* − North Berkshire. This was Samuel Dunch, a godly Presbyterian of Pusey, related by marriage to Cromwell − Austin Woolrych, *Commonwealth to Protectorate* (1982), p. 416.

[67] BRO, A/A Ep 1 No 4.

[68] Ivan Roots, *The Great Rebellion 1642-1660* (1966), p. 186.

[69] TNA, Crown Office Docquet Book, C 231/6, p. 268.

[70] *ThSP* V p. 215. For an example the Army's electoral maneuverings in Berkshire, see Anon, *A True and perfect Relation* (1656).

[71] ATCA, Corp Minutes, i fo. 182.

[72] Bodl., Ms Tanner 52, fos 156-7. It seems that admission was by ticket only, and members regarded as of the opposition were simply not given tickets - *CJ* vii 423 (17 Sept 1656). The government's explanation was that the members being excluded were not 'Persons of Integrity to the Government, fearing God, and of good Conversation' − *CJ* vii 426 (22 Sept 1656).

[73] *CJ* vii 579-80 (21 Jan 1658).

[74] Anon., *To All the Worthy Gentlemen Who Are Duely Chosen for the Parliament, ... The Humble Remonstrance, Protection, and Appeale of Severall Knights and Gentlemen Duly Chosen to Serve Their Countrey in Parliament; Who Attended at Westminster for That Purpose, but Were Violently Kept out of the Parliament-House by Armed Men Hired by the Lord Protector* (1656). The name John Hanson does not appear elsewhere in the parliamentary records.

[75] Roots, *The Great Rebellion,* pp. 197-8.

[76] G.F. Nuttall, 'Abingdon Revisited 1656-1675', *Baptist Quarterly,* 36 (1996), 96-103: Hughes, *Munster and Abingdon,* passim.

[77] Hughes, *Munster and Abingdon,* pp. 85-94; Anon, *A witness to the Saints* (1657), p. 5; John Canne, *Time of the End* (1657), p. 80; Anon, *The Complaining Testimony of some of Sion's Children* (1656). Bridge was well outside his area, which was Lancashire, Cheshire and Staffordshire. Goffe was sitting in Parliament (*CJ* vii (1 Oct 1656) p. 431); it is not clear why Bridge was not.

[78] Manfred Brod, 'Dissent and Dissenters in Early Modern Berkshire', unpubl. DPhil thesis (Oxford, 2002), p. 127; Champlin Burrage, 'The Fifth Monarchy Insurrections' *English Historical Review* 25 (1910), pp. 722-747 at p. 735

[79] *ThSP* VI p. 185-6.

[80] Stennett may have learned of the idea, perhaps indirectly, from Peter Heylyn. Heylyn had written much on the Sabbath, and was about to publish again on the subject – *Respondet Petrus* (1658).

[81] J. Hanson, *A Short Treatise Showing the Sabbatharians Confuted by the New Covenant* (1658); E. Stennett, *The Royal Law Contended for, or, Some Brief Grounds Serving to Prove That the Ten Commandments Are yet in Full Force, and Shall So Remain Till Heaven and Earth Pass Away* (1658).

[82] On Biscoe, see Matthews, *Calamy Revised*, p.59, but there are discrepancies in the dating of his career. His publications: J. Bisco, *The Glorious Mystery of Gods Mercy, or, a Precious Cordiall for Fainting* (1647); J. Bisco, *The Grand Triall of True Conversion. Or, Sanctifying Grace Appearing .... Together with Precious Preservatives against Evill Thoughts* (1655).

[83] Manfred Brod, *The Case of Reading: Urban governance in troubled times, 1640-1690* (2006), Chap. 9.

9. The end of the Protectorate

That many headed beast, the Rout,
Who did turn the Father out
When they saw they were undon,
Were for bringing in the Son.
                    Alexander Brome, *Song XLII*.

Oliver Cromwell died on 3 September 1658, his mission unaccomplished. His regime had never achieved legitimacy in the eyes of a large section of his countrymen. The war had left deep wounds which he had undertaken to heal, but which remained open. Parliamentarians had never forgiven him for his assumption of a power which they believed rightfully theirs, and in obstinately refusing his offers to share it they had ensured their continuing impotence. The Army remained united, but only by dint of loyalty oaths and purges. The reformation of manners, long desired by the godly, had stalled, and social reform was no longer on anyone's agenda. The 'good old cause' had become an oppositional slogan, but it was essentially an appeal to the past, meaningless when applied to the greater complexities of the present. Political conflicts cross-cut with religious ones, and the result was confusion. Republicans were flirting with Royalists; so even were Presbyterians. Cromwell had kept to the end his ascendancy over his senior officers and the prestige of his office. It was obvious to many that the protectorate could not long survive him.

The mayor whose term of office started at the end of September 1658 was Francis Payne, a Tesdale by marriage. It will have fallen to him to arrange the election of a burgess to represent Abingdon in the parliament that Richard Cromwell called for early 1659. If Thomas Holt stood again and was defeated in a poll, the fact remained unrecorded. The new member for Abingdon was Sir John Lenthall, son and heir of the speaker of the Long Parliament, and resident at his father's property at Besselsleigh, a few miles from Abingdon.

John Lenthall was already an experienced parliamentarian. His father had been recorder of Gloucester, and the younger man had sat for that town in the Rump Parliament from 1645 until its forcible dissolution by Cromwell in 1653.[1] Thereafter, he had been building himself a local interest in Abingdon. As we have seen, the local godly party had worked hard to secure the demolition of the small church of St Nicholas. It was a haven for traditionalists, where Cranmer's prayer book, although nominally illegal, was still used. Perhaps somewhat unexpectedly given his record, Lenthall had joined the defenders of the church. They were led by the Royalist ideologue Peter Heylyn, who after losing his clerical livings had settled in Abingdon as convenient for the bookshops and libraries of Oxford.[2] Heylyn was a native of Burford where the Lenthalls had an estate, and it may have been their common links with that town that brought the two men together. William Lenthall, as Master of the Rolls, was one of the committee that made the decision, and by 1658 the church was saved.[3] No doubt this was one of the factors that disposed the electors of Abingdon – whoever they were at the time – to select John Lenthall as their representative. He presented the corporation with a silver tankard to commemorate the fact.[4]

The national political situation now became seriously unstable, as the Army, deprived of Oliver's restraining influence, split into factions and these sought the support of other groups. Richard Cromwell had been the only possible successor to his father precisely because he had no power base of his own.[5] His parliament lasted barely three months; it was dissolved on 22 April, and two weeks later the remains of the old Rump returned in triumph to continue where they had been interrupted more than six years before. William Lenthall, with great reluctance, left the 'other house' to which he had been elevated to re-assume the Commons speakership; Henry Marten was brought from the debtors' prison where he was confined in order to make up a quorum. John Lenthall found himself once more member for Gloucester, and Henry Neville for Abingdon. Richard's position was now untenable; he resigned on 25 May 1659 and his brother Henry, Lord Deputy of Ireland, a few weeks later. The Cromwellian era was effectively at an end.

Republicans and the godly were elated, and immediately set about the dubious task of reforming the army and the militia. Ingoldsby's regiment, that had once been John Hampden's and was largely drawn from the Abingdon area, was given to Colonel Sydenham who had shown signs of sympathy for republican ideas. His second in command was Lieutenant-Colonel Francis Allen, a former Leveller and a strong supporter of the Puritan sects. [6] Other officers included Captain Consolation Fox, also a Leveller and himself a sectary.[7] Both men would then or later be Abingdon residents. On 26 July, a new militia commission for Berkshire was named, with most of the members having a similar allegiance. They included Marten, Neville, Lt-Col Allen and Captain Fox.[8] On 15 August, three more Abingdon men were added: Robert Payne, Mayor Francis Payne, and the past mayor and religious controversialist John Hanson.[9]

But elsewhere the pendulum was swinging, and unnatural alliances were being forged. In the summer of 1659, Royalists and Presbyterians planned a series of risings. In fact only one took place, that of Sir George Booth in Cheshire, and General Lambert, one of the army leaders, marched north to suppress it.[10] John Lenthall wisely did not declare himself, but kept abreast of events and was in the confidence of the plotters.[11]

In October, the Rump was once again dissolved by the military, but was recalled on 26 December under conditions that were fundamentally changed. The Army was hopelessly split and correspondingly weakened. So, therefore, were its friends in parliament. London had turned against it, as had the fleet; and General Monck was marching south with troops from his occupation forces in Scotland sworn to uphold parliamentary government. Lenthall profited. He was made constable of Windsor Castle, and promised command of a regiment.[12] It proved to be that of Colonel Sydenham, who was suspected of collusion with Lambert.[13] Lambert was the only Army man who was seen as being capable of mounting a coup and proclaiming himself the new protector.[14] Sydenham's officers were purged. Allen and Fox, among many others, were dismissed, and the regiment, after a brief mutiny, moved out of London to be replaced by Monck's men.[15] On 21 February, Monck forced the return of the 'secluded members', the survivors of those, mostly Presbyterians, who had been excluded in Pride's Purge of 6 December 1648. The Long Parliament now had little to do but to prepare the ground for its successor. On 10 March, there was a new Militia Act, voiding the one of the previous July. The Berkshire militia commission was totally renewed; the republicans and assorted radicals were removed. Its Abingdon members were now Lenthall himself and John and Robert Mayott.[16] John Mayott was currently mayor of Abingdon, and the Robert Mayott was most probably the former churchwarden of St Nicholas who had joined in the defence of that church against the godly. Parliament was dissolved on 16 March, and new elections were planned for early April.

There were to be two candidates for the single Abingdon seat, and the election would be, in many respects, a re-run of that of twenty years earlier, at the start of the troubles that might now be coming to an end. Sir George Stonehouse, ejected from parliament by the rebels in 1644, naturally wanted his seat back. John Lenthall hadn't worked at building up his local interest to give up without a contest.

Lenthall, like Bulstrode Whitelocke twenty years earlier, was a relative outsider, a new man to the district. The elder Lenthall's successful legal career had enabled him in the 1630s to purchase the former Tanfield properties at Burford and the Fettiplace estates of Appleton and Besselsleigh near to Abingdon. William Lenthall had become enormously rich; his enemies, of whom there were many, accused him of peculation shameless even by the standards of the time.[17] Sir John was reasonably well provided on his own account. From 1643 to 1654, he had held the lucrative position of one of the Six Clerks of Chancery, a post so intensively sought after that it could rarely be achieved without accusations of gross corruption in the process, and certainly was not in his case.[18]

This was, of course, before the age of organised parties, but it is not difficult to distinguish the various political forces that were engaged. There were the Royalists, successors of the men who had been ejected from Parliament during the Civil War. They had been in eclipse for more than a decade, but now it was impossible to prevent their return to influence. There were the 'new Royalists' – the Presbyterians who had favoured continued negotiations with the king after the Independents and their Army allies had given that up as unprofitable, and who had been victims of the Army's purge of Parliament in December 1648. They were now rebranding themselves as ever loyal to the monarchy, and drawing the thickest of veils over their part in the Civil War. There were the commonwealthmen and republicans, successors of the Independents who had survived Pride's Purge and had sat until Cromwell's coup in April 1653; and finally there were the Cromwellians, supporters of the Army and devotees of de facto power, who had lorded it during the Protectorate.[19] Stonehouse fitted with the Royalists, though he had ridden out the storms more comfortably than many. Lenthall's position is harder to gauge; his support for Richard Cromwell had been ambivalent: 'I am for a single person to govern this nation. … I would have his Highness made as great as ever king was in England, that he may defend the Protestant religion.'[20] The speech was directed against the republicans active in Richard's parliament, and might easily be read as supporting a kingly rather than a protectoral outcome. But again, as late as early January 1660, as London dealt with the implications of Monck's arrival, he was reported as speaking against a restoration. Lenthall might be classified as a pure politician, taking whatever line was expedient at the moment; but he was the son of his father and he had been knighted by Oliver in March 1658. The electors of Abingdon warned him that he would have to position himself as a Royalist if he wanted to be re-elected.

Ther is great briguing all over ye kingdome about elections for ye next Parlement. Young Lenthall sent lately to Abington, for which place (as I take it) he now semes

to haue theire promise, to choose him one of theire burgesses. I heare they returned
this answer, that that towne and county were resolued not to choose any but such as
(they had good assurance off) would not act against ye interest and settlement of ye
nation according to ye known lawes of ye land, soe that he must comport himselfe
to that rule or bee noe member for that place; and I am told hee hath much changed
his note (if not his principles) since his envenomed speech (about 2 months agoe)
against the K. to the Commissioners of the citty.[21]

The electors of Abingdon were in a quandary. If, as now it seemed,
Stonehouse's ejection from the Commons in 1645 had been an illegal act, it
would be appropriate to re-elect him. In 1649, Stonehouse had proved himself
a local benefactor, helping to finance the new pound lock on the Swift Ditch.[22]
But Lenthall's service had been more recent, and some, at least, of the people
of Abingdon may have felt an obligation on them for his action in favour of St
Nicholas. The mayor, John Mayott, made his choice. He arranged a poll. We
know nothing of the electioneering there must have been, nor the votes for the
two candidates, but the numbers, whatever they were, gave Lenthall the
victory. Mayott sent in the indenture accordingly. Some other corporation
members, including the two bailiffs, disagreed, and petitioned in favour of
Stonehouse. Abingdon was no different from other towns and counties; some
fifteen percent of all returns were disputed, and time would be needed for the
House's committee to consider them all.[23] Lenthall was allowed to sit pending
a decision.[24] Before that decision could come, however, there was an
unfortunate incident that must have prejudiced any chances he might have had.

Lenthall had found himself in a most uncomfortable position. The decision
to recall the king, which was generally understood to be the prime purpose of
the Parliament, was soon taken, and members then addressed themselves to the
pleasurable business of repaying scores and pronouncing doom on their
enemies. The king had asked for an Act of Oblivion with a minimum of
exceptions. This was not to the taste of the aggressive Presbyterian group, who
were in vindictive mood. Anyone who had had anything to do with the late
king's trial and execution was in their sights, and prominent among these was
Lenthall's father, William.

William Lenthall was not technically a regicide, but this would have
seemed an inappropriate nicety to contemporaries, as indeed it did to himself.
Skilled lawyer that he was, he had known better than to sit in the High Court
of Justice that had condemned the king, but unlike many of his colleagues he
had not dissociated himself from it by leaving London at the operative time.
He had certainly presided over the debates that set it up, and was reasonably

suspected of having advised on its composition.[25] Thereafter, he had acquiesced in every Army decision, however repugnant to common notions of legality. In recent months, he had turned his coat most adroitly, working closely with General Monck in the dissolution of his own parliament.[26] But not all the recommendations that Monck could provide were enough to persuade the electors of Oxford to make him their representative, and it fell to his son to defend him in a largely hostile House.

On 12 May 1660 John Lenthall made an impassioned speech to the effect that all who had fought against the king were as guilty of treason towards him as those who cut off his head. The Presbyterians were outraged. Their self-righteousness was being questioned, and their alliance of convenience with the old Royalists put under strain. Lenthall was made to kneel at the bar of the House; the speaker, a Presbyterian himself, delivered a formal rebuke which was copied into the Journal, and Lenthall narrowly escaped being taken into custody by the serjeant-at-arms.[27]

The verdict of the Committee for Elections and Privileges was now easily predictable. The committee's chairman, Edward Turnor, had been educated at Roysse's in Abingdon, and may still have had contacts in the town.[28] He was routinely using his position to favour Royalist/Anglican candidates, and a decision in Lenthall's favour would have given gratuitous offence to the Presbyterians. But the forms had to be observed, and it was possible to find perfectly substantial reasons for his rejection.

Municipal charters were rarely specific on how a town's Parliamentary representative was to be chosen. They belonged to a time when selections were made in private and were usually uncontroversial. The word 'burgess', often used in this connection, might have been clear enough in the time of Phillip and Mary, but was now ambiguous. Did it cover all residents, or taxpayers, or only members of the corporation? Were almsmen included or excluded? The question had come up in Abingdon twenty years earlier in the contest between Stonehouse and Whitelocke, but it had not been settled at that time. Turnor's committee, no doubt having heard representations, had now come to a conclusion: 'It was resolved, that the word burgenses extends to the inhabitants at large within the borough'.[29] But who the 'inhabitants at large' were needed further elucidation.

It is not the case that John Mayott had restricted access to the poll. On the contrary: the indenture survives, and has 202 names; the nearest earlier surviving indenture, that of 1654, has only seventy. But it is a remarkable fact that only 91 of the names can be found among the 316 on the hearth tax list of 1664, and of these, 32 are exempted from the tax because of poverty.

Furthermore, many names that would have been expected to appear on the list were absent, including those of the two bailiffs, Edward Bond and Thomas Castell, who had submitted the alternative indenture.[30] Turnor's committee removed from the list two names as strangers, and fifty-four as paupers, after which Stonehouse emerged the winner. Plainly, the committee did not consider it a requirement for voters to be householders, but men were considered to be disqualified if they were in receipt of alms. It was often believed that paupers either did not have the independence necessary to cast a valid vote, or else that they would be tempted to sell their votes for cash or a meal. Mayott was supposed to be present when the House announced its decision and personally amend the indenture he had sent in, but for some reason was not. The indenture was altered by the clerk of the House, and Mayott was committed to the serjeant's custody for a couple of days.[31]

Sir George Stonehouse would represent Abingdon in the Commons until his death in 1676, and would be succeeded by his son Sir John, whose career would be similar in many respects to that of his father.

As for John Lenthall, his connection with Abingdon ceased after the events of 1660. Before the end of that year, he would be in the Tower accused of complicity in a plot against the new regime.[32] His second and third wives would be from noted Royalist families, and he would eventually achieve the dubious distinction of having being knighted both by Oliver Cromwell and Charles II. But by then he was no longer resident at Besselsleigh.[33]

The Interregnum, in the words of J.H. Plumb, had been 'a long political education'.[34] One thing men had learned was that Parliament might be an institution of greater importance to them than they may previously have believed. High politics might be a minority interest, but the tax system now affected more people than it previously had; everybody had to pay the excise. It was thus perfectly understandable for the town's electors to fix on John Lenthall in 1658. Stonehouse was still disqualified, but Lenthall resembled him in being local, wealthy, and involved in matters of local importance; and he had the advantage over Stonehouse of access to the centres of political power. One way of explaining the revival of the Stonehouse interest in 1660 is that power had shifted and Lenthall's future access was now in doubt.

Yet, it seems that the relatively poor still tended to support Lenthall. In 1640, Whitelocke complained that Stonehouse had 'bought' the election by treating his supporters. He was, of course, being disingenuous; treating was already a common feature of parliamentary elections. By 1660, it was the norm.[35] We know nothing of the Abingdon campaign, but Lenthall would not have scrupled to spend what was necessary; we do know that he canvassed in Oxford and entertained his father's supporters there to roast beef and ale at the Mitre.[36] The line between treating and bribery was narrow; there were certainly cases where a candidate offered a borough corporation help with its provision for the poor, and possibly where votes were bought and sold directly.[37] The winter of 1659 had been a hard one; food prices were high, and a free meal or a few shillings in the pocket could seem very tempting. But when two rich candidates clashed, there was probably no great advantage to be gained on either side. Men would dine according to how they intended to vote, and not the other way about.

Stonehouse's political creed, as would be shown in the ensuing years, was simple and authoritarian; Lenthall could point to his parliamentary record in 1659, when he had stood for equal justice to Parliamentarian and Royalist victims of the protectoral regime.[38] But in the final analysis the records of the candidates were of little effect. The year 1660 marked a tectonic shift in the political landscape of the sort that occurs only once in a generation: the revolution was seen to have failed; its personnel were discredited. In Abingdon, as throughout the country, it was the solid citizens who wanted a return to traditional politics, symbolised by once more sending a Stonehouse to Westminster. If it was the case that the poorer sorts still felt that a Lenthall might better serve their interests, they were destined to disappointment.

---

[1] A. Annesley, *England's Confusion* (1659), p. 10.

[2] John Barnard, *Theologo-historicus, or the true life of the most reverend divine and excellent historian Peter Heylyn D.D.* (1683), p. clvi.

[3] A. E. Preston, *St Nicholas, Abingdon, and other papers* (1928), pp. 101-3, 108-10, 224-5; Christ's Hospital, Abingdon, St Nicholas Old Church Book, fo. 103; Christ's Hospital, Abingdon, Book of Decrees and Presentments (unpag: 29 April 1658); Lambeth Palace, Augmentations COMM XIIC/2, fo. 399 and COMM IV/10, fo. 36; TNA, C 94/4/3a.

[4] Mieneke Cox, *Peace and War* (Abingdon, 1993), p. 137; Berks R.O., Preston Papers, D/EP 7/81 p. 26.

[5] J. Fitzgibbon, "Not in Any Doubtful Dispute'? Reassessing the Nomination of Richard Cromwell', *Historical Research,* 83 (2010), pp. 281-300.

[6] *CJ* VII (13 June 1659).

[7] *CJ* VII (17 June 1659).

[8] *A&O* (26 July 1659).

[9] *CJ* VII (15 August 1659).

[10] Godfrey Davis, *The Restoration of Charles II* (1955), pp. 139-40.

[11] *Cal. Clarendon SP,* Vol IV, pp 235-6, 386-7, 390. The important relationship was probably with Lord Falkland, who planned an Oxfordshire rising at Campsfield but was arrested before it could take place.

[12] *CJ* VII (18 Jan 1660).

[13] *CJ* VII (17 Jan 1660).

[14] Davis, *Restoration,* Chap IX.

[15] *CJ* VII (1,2 and 7 Feb 1660). For details of the mutiny, see Davis, *Restoration*, p. 274 and R. L'Estrange, *L'estrange His Apology* (1660), p. 63. At this point Francis Allen disappears from the records. He probably felt it safer to go underground. Anthony Wood says, unreliably, that he died in poverty - *Fasti* ii 111.

[16] A&O, (12 March 1660).

[17] J. N., *An Account of the Gaines of the Late Speaker William Lenthall, in Answer to a Letter,* (1660); Anon, *A More Exact and Necessary Catalogue of Pensioners in the Long Parliament* (1660). Lenthall's Mastership of the Rolls was said to be worth £3000 p.a., but the perks included a prestigious London residence in the Rolls Chapel – Anon, *The Mystery of the Good Old Cause* (1660), p. 17; J. Collins(?). 'Mysteria Revelata', (1674), in HMC 51, *Leyborne-Popham Mss*, pp. 204-239.

[18] Clement Walker, *History of Independency* (1661), p. 169, gives the value as £2000 per annum.

[19] Davies, *Restoration*, Chaps 15, 16.

[20] J.T. Rutt (ed), *Diary of Thomas Burton esq,* (1828), III (8 February 1658-9).

[21] Letter Col Robert Whitley to Sir Edward Nicholas, 9 March 1659/60, in G. F. Warner (ed), *Nicholas Papers IV*, (Camden Soc. 3rd ser. Vol 31, 1920), pp. 201-2.

[22] Fred Thacker, *The Thames Highway* (1920) II pp. 154-5.

[23] The total has been variously assessed at 61 (H. Mukerjee, 'The Elections to the Convention and Cavalier Parliaments', *Notes and Queries,* 166 (1934), pp. 398-403, 417-421) and 64, (*HoP 1660-1690* III p. 614). There were 478 members altogether.

[24] *CJ* VIII (27 April 1660).

[25] Sir T. Herbert, *Memoirs of the two last years of the reign of Charles I* (1702), pp. 300-303.

[26] C. H. Firth (ed), *The Clarke Papers* IV (Camden Soc. 2nd ser. Vol 62, 1901), p.272; J. Collins(?). 'Mysteria Revelata', HMC 51, *Leyborne-Popham Mss,* pp. 204-239

[27] *CJ* VIII (12 May 1660); Francis Newport (London) to his uncle Sir Richard Leveson at Trentham, May 15 1660, HMC *5th Report* (1876) p. 149; Lucy Hutchinson, *Memoirs of the Life of Colonel Hutchinson* (Everyman Edition, 1965), p. 320.

[28] John Callow, 'Turnor, Sir Edward (1616/17–1676)', *DNB*. It is unclear why he should have been sent to school in Abingdon, but the Edward Turnor who was a member of the Abingdon Corporation before 1635 may have been a relative.

[29] *CJ* VIII (23 May 1660).

[30] Berks RO, A/A Ep 1 No. 8. The list does end with the words 'and others'. For the Hearth Tax list, see TNA, E 179/243/24, 25.

[31] *CJ* VIII (23 May 1660).

[32] Letters to Sir Richard Leveson at Trentham, HMC 5th Report (1876) pp. 158 (20 Nov 1660), 196 (24 Nov 1660), 201 (24 Nov 1660); *CSP Venetian*, 1659-1661, p. 224; Richard L. Greaves, *Deliver us from Evil: the radical underground in Britain 1660-1663* (1986), p. 82; Lucy Hutchinson, *Colonel Hutchinson*, p. 320.

[33] His second wife would be the widow of Sir James Stonehouse, Sir George's indebted kinsman − see below, Chap. 14. The third was daughter to the Royalist martyr Eusebius Andrewes, executed in 1650 after entrapment by the Commonwealth security services − F. Buckley, *A true relation of the proceedings, examinations, tryal & horrid murder of Colonel Eusebius Andrewe* (1660).

[34] J. H. Plumb, 'The Growth of the Electorate in England from 1600 to 1715', *P&P* 45 (1969), pp. 90-116, at p. 107

[35] For a contemporary comment, letter Dr Betts to Marquis of Ormonde, 4 May 1660, quoted in F. Guizot, *Le Protectorat de Richard Cromwell et le rétablissement des Stuart 1658-1660* (Paris, 1859) II 216.

[36] A. Clark (ed), *Wood's Life and Times* (Oxford, 1891) I p. 312

[37] The Earl of Salisbury donated £10 for the poor of Hertford in 1640 − Lawrence Stone, 'The electoral influence of the second Earl of Salisbury 1614-68', *EHR* 71 (1956), pp. 384-400 at p. 393 − and a candidate at Hastings in the same year offered £20 plus £10 per year for life - J.K. Gruenberger, 'The Spring election at Hastings, 1640', *Sussex Archaeological Collections* 105 (1967), pp. 49-55. For a general discussion, see J.K. Gruenberger, *Influence in Early Stuart Elections 1604-1640* (Ohio, 1981), pp. 200-202

[38] Rutt, *Diary of Thomas Burton*, III (12 Feb 1658/9); IV (25 and 30 March 1659).

10. After the Restoration

> ... in so far as power is given, they ought to be both prevented from evil and
> compelled to good.
>
> St Augustine [1]

The restoration of the monarchy in the person of Charles II took place amid great public rejoicing and a good deal of private misgiving. It had something of the turn of fortune's wheel, so beloved of medieval moralists, and something of a palace revolution in a present-day third-world state. Its approach had long been visible to all but the most blinkered, and many had been manoeuvring for months to re-position themselves. Ingoldsby, whose old regiment John Lenthall had briefly taken over, had expiated his part in the regicide by arresting John Lambert.[2] William Lenthall worked with Monck and quietly sent £3000 to the king, which saved his life and property though neither his legal nor his parliamentary careers.[3] Others could not or would not recant. Henry Marten, proud and stoical, threw himself on the mercy of that House of Lords which he had once laughingly dismissed as 'useless and not dangerous', and had his death sentence commuted to life imprisonment.[4] His fellow-republican and sometime Abingdon MP Henry Neville plotted, was arrested, and eventually exiled himself to Tuscany where he had travelled before the war and still had friends.[5] Bulstrode Whitelocke narrowly avoided punishment for his part in the commonwealth and protectorate, but had made too many enemies to be completely rehabilitated.[6] His career was at an end, and he retired to a life of relative poverty and declining health.

In Abingdon, the corporation understood early what was expected of it. The king had entered London on 29 May 1660. On 13 June, it was decided that William Wickes had been 'unduly elected' principal burgess in 1647, as had John Hanson and Thomas Trapham in 1648, since there had already been a full complement of such burgesses at the time. Plainly the informal dismissals that had taken place after the end of the war were now seen as invalid. On the same day, it was accepted that the fee farm, which had been bought from the Commonwealth government in 1650, would have to be surrendered again, and an additional sum of £100 would be added as a gift.[7] The same was being done by numerous towns at the time, no doubt following broad hints as to what would be appreciated by the new monarch. In July, seven new secondary burgesses were named, although one of them refused to take the oaths.[8] One of the others, William Weston, was promoted to principal burgess in September 1661.[9] Weston, remarkably, would later be exposed as a Catholic. In November, another principal burgess, William Haynes, elected in 1646, was dismissed with no reason given, and a secondary, the brazier Richard Green, for alleged neglect of his duties.[10] The town preachers, Henry Langley and Henry Cornish, were now 'pretended lecturers' and their employment would cease at the end of the year.[11] Langley was the Abingdon man who had been intruded as master of Pembroke College in 1647, and Cornish one of his Oxford friends.[12]

The dismissed councillors seem to have a sought a legal remedy, and in December Edmund Franklyn and William Weston were given a set of documents that they could take with them to the Maidenhead assizes.[13] The corporation must have won its case, and in the following September its representatives had their expenses paid.[14] Immediately after, two further principal burgesses, Bedford Stacey and Henry Meales, and four secondaries were declared to have been illegally elected and were dismissed.[15] Stacey, the illiterate glover, was better advised than his colleagues. During the interregnum, faced with a spate of purges in all sorts of institution, the lawyers had devised a remedy, the writ of mandamus or of restitution. Office was to be deemed a freehold unless otherwise specified. The defendants would have to prove that there was some sort of explicit contract by which the complainant could be sacked, otherwise the assumption would be that his position was inviolate. Stacey presumably applied to the court of King's Bench, which had developed this technique, rather than to the judges of assize. In January 1662, he returned triumphant.[16]

But the current of events was moving fast, and would bear Stacey with it. There were new parliamentary elections in April 1661, which marked the end of the temporary alliance between Presbyterians and Royalists that had made the restoration possible. The Royalists enjoyed a landslide victory. Sir George Stonehouse was re-elected for Abingdon, and became a locally dominant figure, helped by the fact that his brother-in-law Lord Lovelace of Hurley was lord lieutenant of the county. The new assembly would become known as the Cavalier Parliament and would remain in being for seventeen years.

The new parliament met in May, concerned above all that the catastrophes of the past twenty years should never recur. Town corporations were high on its agenda. There was a degree of paranoia about them. It was the jumped-up urban tradesmen, men imagined, who had assumed liberties for which they were unfit and had been largely responsible for the great disaster. They would have to be brought to heel by the landowning gentry, the natural rulers of the country, or stability could never be guaranteed. The first drafts of the new legislation were extreme. The king and the Lords wanted all town charters to be cancelled and renewed, with the initial fill of councillors hand-picked by the crown; the crown would continue to appoint recorders and town clerks and to select mayors from a shortlist. County JPs, who, unlike urban ones, were always crown nominees, would sit on town benches. The parliamentary electorate would be restricted to the corporation itself. The Commons saw the danger of this as a way of packing future parliaments with crown placemen, and the Corporation Act, which became law in December 1661, was a compromise. It was limited to an immediate purge of corporations. The crown would name a commission for each county, which would have until March 1663 to visit all towns and cities and require all civic officers to take two oaths. One was that of Supremacy and Allegiance, and the other that it was not lawful to take up arms against the king on any pretext whatsoever. They were also to make a declaration that they did not consider themselves bound by the Solemn League and Covenant, which many of them would have subscribed on Parliament's instructions in 1643; and they must have taken the sacrament according to Anglican rites in the past year. Furthermore, the commissioners, or any five of them, had the right to remove and replace council members at their own discretion whether or not they were willing to take the oaths.[17]

The commission for Berkshire would be headed by Lord Lovelace. It is not clear whether or not they visited Abingdon on 26 May 1662, but on that day they produced a formal document citing their powers under the Corporation Act to 'displace and remove Bedford Stacie of the Borough of Abingdon aforesaid glover from his Offices or pretended Offices of principall Burgesse and secondary Burgesse within the said Borough'.[18] This, obviously, would trump the mandamus. The signatures were of Lovelace; Stonehouse; Humphrey Hyde sen and jun of Kingston Lisle, who were respectively son and grandson of Lovelace's stepbrother George; George Purefoy of Wadley; and Francis Pigott of Marcham.

Abingdon was plainly not giving the commissioners any great anxiety, and their definitive verdict did not come until 23 January 1663 when the deadline was already close. It was of doubtful legality, since there were only four signatures, those of Lovelace, Stonehouse, the younger Hyde, and Pigott.[19] They declared that Francis Payne had refused to take the oaths or subscribe the declaration against the Covenant, and that John Mayott had merely refused the declaration. Both would be disabled from membership of the corporation. On the same day, and for the same reason, they were dismissed from being governors of the Hospital.[20] The commission then produced a list of sixteen men who were now to be dismissed irrespective of oaths and declarations. This was not as drastic as it may appear, since eight of them had already been ejected and one had been named to the corporation in 1660 but never actually joined. Of the remaining seven, four are known from later court proceedings as members of dissenting sects.[21] Francis Payne in the following October changed his mind, took the oaths, and was reinstated.[22]

The process of bringing towns safely under government control continued. Royal policy for municipal charters was the subject of a declaration of June 1663.[23] Oaths of allegiance would be imposed as they already were, but in addition all recorders and town clerks would have to be individually approved by the crown before they could assume their offices. These were the men who ran the borough courts and enrolled local juries, and it was they who would ultimately decide whether central policy would be applied in their localities or not. The purged and, presumably, now totally loyal corporation was agreeable to a revision of the town's charter on these terms. Abingdon was one of sixty-five municipalities that had their charters renewed during the decade, receiving its new document on 3 December 1663.[24] The immediate purpose was no doubt to ensure that the laws now being developed against religious dissenters would actually be enforced.

A further cause for concern was the constitution of a town's magistracy. The normal practice, in Abingdon as in other English chartered towns, had until then been that the bench was limited to the current mayor and his immediate predecessor, the recorder and any deputies he might have had, and perhaps a few outsiders who would regard the appointment as honorary. Already in 1662, this was under threat. The authority by which warrants were sent out in connection with the town sessions was usually described as 'The Justices of the Peace within the said borough'. Now, Mayor Edward Bond used the formula 'me or some other of his Majesties Justices assigned to keep the peace within the said borough'.[25] In August 1664, a commission of association was issued for Abingdon.[26] This was a novel device, which had been pioneered by a group of Berkshire gentry led by Sir Thomas Dolman of Shaw, and was already being used in Newbury and Reading.[27] The effect was to negate the tradition whereby county justices had no power within urban boundaries. The corporation received a writ of dedimus potestatem directing that the oaths of supremacy and of magistrature, copies of which were helpfully attached, were to be administered to Sir George Stonehouse, his second son John, Humfrey Hyde, George Purefoy and Francis Piggott.[28] Court records do not show these men crowding the bench, although one or other of them attended most of the local sessions until 1671.[29] The important point was that they could be called in in controversial cases, and the regular town magistrates could, in case of need, be overwhelmed and outvoted by reliable gentlemen from outside.

The early 1660s, thus, were years in which Abingdon, in common with other English towns, lost the most important of the privileges that it had acquired over a century earlier with its charter. The crown would henceforth have to approve its choice of the main civic officials, and, having carried out one purge of the corporation, would obviously be able to carry out others. Effective oversight would be exercised by local gentry under the lord lieutenant, and their right to sit on the local bench could give them the same control over towns as they had traditionally had in the countryside. Ironically, it would seem that these powers were not needed in Abingdon. Even before the purge and the commissions of association, the Abingdon corporation was well able to act in the way the government and the royalist gentry will have wanted.

In parallel with restrictions on municipal freedom, measures were being taken to limit freedom of religion. In a well-governed community, only one sort of religious practice could be permitted. In the restored English monarchy with its hierarchy of nobility and gentry, this could only be the Anglican church with its archbishops and bishops. People who thought for themselves in religion might want to do so in politics as well, and the dangers had been amply demonstrated in the 1640s. Those dangers still existed, as shown by Venner's second attempt at a Fifth Monarchy rising of 6 January 1661, after which a royal proclamation forbade all meetings of 'Anabaptists, Quakers, and Fifth Monarchy men, or some such like appellation ... under pretence of worshipping God'.[30] On the following Sunday, the Abingdon Baptist meeting was raided by the militia, and some worshippers arrested.[31] Older laws originally designed to counter Catholicism could be pressed into service. In August and September 1662, Edmund Franklyn ended his mayoral term in spectacular fashion, fining twenty-three individuals 12d each for not having attended an approved church or chapel on a Sunday; five of them finished in prison, having neither money to pay the fine nor any goods that might be taken and sold in lieu.[32] He was acting in exact conformity with an Elizabethan act of 1559.[33]

From then on, Abingdon Dissenters were subjected to a degree of repression that varied with current political concerns both local and national, and with the development of anti-dissenter legislation. The sequence of laws known as the Clarendon Code (unfairly to the eponymous chancellor, who, like the king, was not in favour of them) attempted to make dissenting associations, practices and worship illegal and entrench an Anglican monopoly in municipal offices. Not the least of the services that A.E. Preston rendered to Abingdon history is in the preservation and analysis of the relevant legal documents recording indictments, fines and distraints. But what must have been as galling to Dissenters as legal prosecution will have been the constant threat of harassment, vandalism, and mob violence.[34]

The campaign instituted by Franklyn continued unabated after his time in office, and was encouraged by the Conventicle Act of 1664, by which attendance at unapproved religious services became an indictable offence. The number of individuals prosecuted runs to approximately a hundred and fifty, and many of the names appear with great regularity.[35] This act lapsed after three years and prosecutions declined. The church authorities filled the gap, using the medieval device of excommunication. The current vicar of St Helen's, James Eglesfield, was losing money, since the Dissenters would not pay his fees for baptisms, marriages and funerals, and probably made difficulties over his tithes. In 1669, he listed sixty people in St Helen's 'that come not to the Church nor receive the sacrament'.[36]

Excommunication was supposed to be a spiritual penalty, but its main force was that the subject was disabled from action in the church courts and thus, at least in principle, could not make or execute a valid will. This was a difficult situation for tradesmen and men of means, and many found themselves constrained in spite of themselves to seek absolution, for which church officials gathered generous fees. At least seven Abingdon Dissenters of the more prosperous classes, three of them corporation members, were caught in this manner. One poor curate, Richard Dolphin, who served parishes in the Longworth area, found that acting as an intermediary in such cases provided a useful supplement to his income.[37]

The campaign of repression had unintended consequences of many sorts. One was in the employment of the moneys left by Richard Wrigglesworth, the Marcham fishmonger, for regular 'lectures' – sermons – and other charitable purposes in Marcham and Abingdon. The trustees, who would administer the endowments and select the lecturer, were supposed to be the mayor for the time being and 'four of the godliest burgesses or masters and seven of the wisest and most discreet commoners'. The Act of Uniformity came into force on 24 August 1662, and thereafter no clergyman could officiate unless he was fully in communion with the established church. No such clergyman was acceptable to the existing trustees. In January 1664 a commission under Chancery had the delicate task of remedying the situation. The commission consisted of Thomas Holt, the Abingdon recorder, and four local gentlemen: George Purefoy of Wadley, Francis Piggott of Marcham and his brother Alban of Oxford, and Paul Calton of Milton. George Stonehouse was presumably too busy sitting in Parliament. They accused the trustees of mismanagement and mis-employment, dismissed them, and named a new set of men. The 'godliest burgesses or masters' were now a scratch lot of principal burgesses under James Curtaine, the current mayor, and only one of the commoners had been on the old committee. The future that Wrigglesworth had foreseen was one in which laymen could choose preachers to their liking, but in post-restoration England this was no longer acceptable. There would be no more Wrigglesworth lecturers.[38]

A second Conventicle Act was passed in 1670, even more restrictive than the first. Premises could be broken into if there was a suspicion they were being used for illegal services, and their owners fined the large sum of £20 – perhaps half of a yeoman's annual income, or the value of a good horse. The whole congregation would be liable for the fines of each one, and the wealthier members would have property distrained once the poorer had become destitute. Religious meetings of more than three people were legally defined as riots, and there are lists of highly respectable families – husbands, wives, and their children – improbably rioting through the streets of Abingdon.[39] One innovation introduced a totally new, and totally parasitic, industry into the national economy. Men who informed on a conventicle were now entitled to one third of the fines levied on the attendees, the remainder being shared between the crown and local poor relief. This opened a new trade, and soon professional informers were weaving a network of corruption that extended to constables, court officials, clergy, and even to politicians and magistrates. Successful practitioners could run substantial businesses, with junior employees to do the spying.[40] Of course, it was never to their advantage that many cases would come to court, since fines would then have to be shared; the real profits were to be had from blackmail and hush money.[41]

Dissenters found their patience sorely tried, and there does seem to have been a particular vendetta that developed between the two Baptist old soldiers, Richard Greene and Consolation Fox, and a certain William Browne, gardener and constable. On several occasions, Browne complained of being insulted and assaulted, *'vi et armis',* by Fox, Greene and others, usually marked as 'unknown'.[42] In August 1671 Browne handed in a list of people he alleged had attended a large conventicle at Marcham, but six of these provided alibis and he finished as the one who was fined.[43]

But in March 1672, religious persecution had to give way to considerations of high politics. The king issued a Declaration of Indulgence, by which Dissenters could worship so long as they took out a licence for each meeting place and each minister. The Dutch state was in danger of dismemberment by Louis XIV, and his own foreign policy was resolutely pro-French. The measure was a sop to the more intensely Protestant, who might otherwise be driven by their accumulated frustrations into rebellion. It was noted with disquiet that Catholics would also be allowed to worship, albeit only in their own homes.[44] Nonetheless, three licences were taken out for nonconformist congregations in Abingdon, probably two of them for Baptists and one Presbyterian. Henry Langley, at Tubney, also opened a Presbyterian meeting. The Quakers refused on principle to apply to human authority for permission to worship. Extremist Anglicans were furious. An unnamed but zealous curate at St Helen's, on his own initiative, pronounced excommunication on eighty people, but this was not followed through, being done 'without order'.[45] Parliament was even more furious, seeing the threat inherent in such an application of the royal prerogative. In the next year, the Indulgence had to be rescinded, and a new Test Act reiterated the requirement for all officials, including town councillors, to take public oaths of allegiance and the Anglican sacraments. But once the existence of dissenting communities had been acknowledged, it was not easy to return to the pretence that there was no such thing, that nonconformists were simply deluded or malignant individuals who could and should be suppressed. Prosecutions in Abingdon do not seem to have recommenced after 1673, and the local Baptists were sufficiently confident to engage a new minister, Henry Forty, in 1675.[46] When the Presbyterian Henry Langley died in 1679, his mantle fell on Thomas Danson, like him a respected academic, who did not feel the need to reside away from the town.[47] And in spite of the Test Acts, both Robert Sellwood and Robert Blackaller, who had earlier been in trouble as Dissenters, were mayors during the 1670s.

Present day historians, with the benefit of hindsight, can trace the beginnings of a modern two-party system back to almost any arbitrarily selected period, but by the 1670s contemporaries could have no doubt that such a system existed. There was a court party, loudly royalist and intensely Anglican, spiritual descendants of the cavaliers; and there was a country party, more concerned with constitutional balance, and not entirely happy with the persecution of Dissenters. By the early 1680s, they would have taken on the more familiar names of Tories and Whigs.

Sir George Stonehouse, Abingdon's MP, died on 31 March 1675. Within the next month, three candidates for his seat were admitted as freemen by the Abingdon corporation. They were Sir John Stonehouse, Sir George's second son and, since he had quarrelled with the first, his heir; Sir Robert Hanson, alderman of London; and John Wickham esquire of Garsington, Oxfordshire.[48] All had local connections. Hanson's mother had been Isobel Lee, whose father had several times been mayor of Abingdon, and he had been educated in Abingdon.[49] Hanson had been one of the London sheriffs in the difficult year of 1665-6, coping with plague and fire, and had been lord mayor in 1672-3. He was described as 'a person (who) heartilie loves the King's interest'.[50] John Wickham was brother-in-law to the John Mayott who had been mayor of Abingdon in 1659-60. He seems to have been persuaded to stand by Lord Wharton, a pillar of the country party.[51] Sir John's politics were less clear. The parliamentary managers for Danby, currently the king's chief minister, considered him one of their own, but so did, or soon would, those of Lord Shaftesbury, Danby's main opponent.[52] The young Lord Lovelace, Stonehouse's cousin, was leader of the country party in Berkshire and Oxfordshire. No details of the election have come down to us, and it is now unknowable whether the electorate was swayed more by ideological or by personal factors. Stonehouse sat; Hanson appealed, and the case seems to have dragged on without a decision by the House to end almost three years later only because Hanson grew tired and gave up.[53] Wickham had presumably come in third and admitted defeat.

It may have seemed to Abingdon people that by the mid 1670s they had recovered from the traumas of war and usurped government, and that an acceptable degree of stability had been regained. But a further period of febrile volatility was ahead. If indeed the 1675 election had been fought purely on the personal merits of the candidates, it would be the last time for many years that that would be the case.

---

[1] Letter (No. 173) to Donatus, AD 416. http://www.newadvent.org/fathers/1102173.htm

[2] Godfrey Davies, *The Restoration of Charles II, 1658-1660* (1955), pp. 335-7, 339.

[3] J. Collins(?). 'Mysteria Revelata', (1674), in HMC 51, *Leyborne-Popham Mss*, pp. 204-239. Stephen K. Roberts, 'Lenthall, William, appointed Lord Lenthall under the protectorate (1591–1662)', *OND*.

[4] A.L. Rowse, 'Henry Marten, republican and regicide' in ibid., *Four Caroline Portraits* (1993), p. 88.

[5] Gaby Mahlberg, 'Henry Neville and English Republicanism in the Seventeenth Century', unpub PhD thesis (East Anglia, 2005), pp 117-123.

[6] R. Spalding (ed), *The Diary of Bulstrode Whitelocke 1605-1675* (1990), pp. 590-609.

[7] *CSPD* 1660/61 No. 12 (25 June 1660); ATCA, Corporation Minutes, I fos. 186v, 187. Wickes had been removed from the Corporation as 'unfit to continue' on 29 July 1659. In spite of his removal, it was he who headed the list of council members relinquishing the farm. He had been mayor when it was purchased.

[8] ATCA, Corp. mins I fos 187, 188.

[9] ATCA, Corp. mins I fo. 189.

[10] Greene was probably the former parliamentary soldier and religious dissenter who still liked to be known as 'Captain Green' - see A.E. Preston, *St Nicholas and other papers* (1929), pp. 123, 124 (footnotes).

[11] ATCA, Corp. mins I fo. 188. This Langley is not the former Corporation member since the ages don't match. The Corporation man had been churchwarden in 1627 and secondary burgess in 1629. The preacher and academic was born in 1610.

[12] Douglas Macleane, *History of Pembroke College* (1897), pp. 224-231; Montagu Burrowes: *Register of the Visitors of the University of Oxford from A.D. 1647 to A.D. 1658,* (Camden Soc, 1881), pp. 40, 176, 492, 493, 540, 568.

[13] ATCA, Corp. mins I fo. 188.

[14] ATCA, Corp. mins I fo 189.

[15] ATCA, Corp. mins I fo. 189.

[16] P.D. Halliday, *Dismembering the Body Politic: Partisan Politics in England's Towns 1650-1730* (Cambridge, 1998), p. 141 and passim.

[17] J.H. Sacret, 'The Restoration Government and the municipal corporations' *EHR* 45 (1930) pp. 230-252; ATCA, Corp. mins. i, fo. 190v.

[18] BRO, A/A Oz a. They, or some of them, would certainly be in Reading the next day, where they dismissed the greater part of the Corporation.

[19] BRO, A/A Oz b.

[20] In July, the Hospital would impose the oaths of allegiance on all its leaseholders – BRO D/Ex 144/1.

[21] The full list is as follows: **William Haynes**, **Henry Meales**, **William Wicks**, **John Hanson**, **Thomas Trapham**, Robert Payne, Arthur Hearne, Thos Parlles (Parkes), **Thomas Bettenton**, **Edmund Brookes**, William Stevenson, William Dyer, **Richard Greene**, **Samuel Pleydell**, Anthony Banister, Thomas Castle. Names in bold are of men already off the Corporation. Those underlined are known or believed to be Dissenters. The first three were allied with the Tesdales in 1647.

[22] A.E. Preston, *St Nicholas and Other Papers* (1929), p. 120; ATCA, Corp mins i fo. 195.

[23] *CSPD* 1663, p. 169 (13 June 1663)

[24] *CSPD* 1663, p. 358 No. 98 (Nov. 1663); Bromley Challenor, *Selections from the Records of Abingdon* (1898), Appx LVI. Challenor mistakenly dates this document to 1676.

[25] BRO, A/JQw 4

[26] TNA, Chancery docquet book, 1660-78, C 231/7 p. 237.

[27] Manfred Brod, *The Case of Reading; Urban governance in troubled times, 1640-1690* (2006), pp. 81-2; Paul D. Halliday, 'A Clashing of Jurisdictions: Commissions of Association in Restoration Corporations', *Historical Journal* 41 (1998), pp. 425-455.

[28] BRO, A/JQ c. John Stonehouse, born 1639, was to be Sir George's heir after a disagreement between the latter and his firstborn, George junior. His name had not been on the original commission. The dedimus was the normal form for swearing in a magistrate.

[29] BRO, A/JQs 1/1

[30] Anon: *Documents Relating to the Settlement of the Church of England by the Act of Uniformity of 1662* (1862), pp. 104-6

[31] Letter Dr Thos Lamplugh to Joseph Wilkinson, *CSPD* 1660-61 No. 56 (15 Jan 1661).

[32] Preston, *St Nicholas,* p. 119

[33] 1 Eliz c.2, *SR* IV 356-7

[34] Preston, *St Nicholas,* Chap 6. The references given by Preston as 'O.N.D.' are in the Berks Record Office under A/JQz 11

[35] This is based on Preston's transcripts and churchwardens' presentments for the period.

[36] BRO, D/A2 c.100 fo. 34; c.163 fo. 4

[37] BRO, D/A2 c.110 fo 12; c.188 fos 75-6; c.1 fos 2, 14-15, 30, 34-36, 41-2. Dolphin acted for Consolation Fox, Phillip Lockton, Simon Peck, Edward Tomkins, and William Stevenson. Other excommunicates were Robert Blackaller and Robert Sellwood.

[38] TNA, C 93/28/6. See also C 93/24/2 for earlier difficulty with the terms of the bequest.

[39] Tim Harris, *Restoration: Charles II and his kingdoms* (2005), p. 300; J.P. Kenyon, *The Stuart Constitution 1603-1688* (1966), pp. 383-386; BRO, A/JQz 11 nos 63-66.

[40] O. Sansom, *An Account of Many Remarkable Passages of the Life of Oliver Sansom* (1710), p. 293; for the notorious 'Parret the Parritor' active in and around Abingdon in the 1660s, see Wilts Record Office, Quorum Nomina citations 1664-5, D1/41/1/43. Parrett's game was to frighten people by claiming they were the object of accusations to the ecclesiastical court, and that for money he could smooth the matter over.

[41] M. Goldie, 'James II and the Dissenters' Revenge: The Commission of Enquiry of 1688', *Historical Research* 66 (1993), pp. 53-88, esp p. 56.

[42] Berks RO, Preston Papers, A/JQz 11, fos. 49, 64-68.

[43] ibid, fo. 71.

[44] Anon, *Tertullius Christianus, or Thanks for the King's Indulgence* (1672); Anon, *The judgement of a good subject upon his Majesties late Declaration* (1672).

[45] TNA, SP 29/306/166 (30 April 72)

[46] Walter Wilson, *The History and Antiquities of Dissenting Churches and Meeting Houses* (1808), p. 50

[47] William Lamont, 'Danson, Thomas (*bap.* 1629, *d.* 1694)', *DNB*; Preston, *St Nicholas*, p. 145 fn. 3; C. Webster, *The Great Instauration* (1975), p. 196

[48] ATCA, Corp mins i, fo. 229.

[49] J.R. Woodhead, *The Rulers of London 1660-1689* (1966), pp 81-95; Nigel Hammond, *A Record of Tesdale Ushers and Bennett Scholars 1609-1870* (Abingdon, 2004), p. 30. Hanson had been a Bennett Scholar, 1620-6.

[50] Alfred P. Beavan, *The Aldermen of the City of* London (1908), pp. 168-195.

[51] *HoP 1660-1690*, I, p. 129

[52] *HoP 1660-1690*, III, p. 493

[53] *CJ* ix 459 (21 March 1678).

11. The two Earls

It would be an exaggeration to consider the 1660s as a honeymoon period when the king, whatever he did, could do no wrong; but there is no doubt that the 1670s were a decade of disillusionment. The Civil War and its aftermath had failed to settle the great political question of whether the monarch's powers were absolute or co-ordinate, and had raised a new problem, that of institutionalised religious dissent. If your political ideal was an absolute monarch taking counsel from his magnates, you were likely also to accept the hegemonic position of the Anglican church with its hierarchical structure. Alternatively, a belief in the sovereignty of the people as expressed through their representatives in the House of Commons would tend to go together with the notion that individuals and groups, if otherwise law-abiding, had the right to worship God in their own way even if that was not the way of the Church of England. But a basically simple dichotomy was complicated by many factors: all agreed that Catholicism could not be tolerated; all agreed that the House of Commons should be independent and powerful, even if the extent of its independence might be contested. Questions of foreign policy needed to be considered in somewhat different terms, since notions of absolute monarchy coming in from France were necessarily tainted with Catholicism, while their logical opposite, republicanism, was associated with the Netherlands, England's traditional rival in trade and empire-building.

As we have seen, Abingdon seems not to have been unduly disturbed by questions of high politics in the middle years of the 1670s. Outside magistrates stopped sitting in the town sessions after 1671 and prosecutions of Dissenters ceased. In 1675, Danby's government, for reasons of its own, tried to stimulate them over the whole country, but there was only a brief flurry of cases in Abingdon.[1] With the passage of time, and in despite of the oaths legally imposed on members of town corporations, the uniformly loyalist composition of the corporation was diluted; men were admitted who in their time had been fined for dissenting activities. During this period, several events took place that would influence Abingdon's history in the decades to come.

One was the appointment of a new high steward. In Sir William Knollys, later Earl of Banbury, high steward from before 1610 to 1630, and his successor, the Earl of Holland, Abingdon had shared a patron with Reading. Holland had been executed in 1649; Bulstrode Whitelocke had taken on his function for Reading but not, or at least not officially, for Abingdon. After the Restoration, the two towns diverged, each choosing from among the great personalities of the time: Reading selected Lord Albermarle, the former General Monck, while Abingdon opted for the chancellor, the Earl of Clarendon.[2] Abingdon's choice proved a poor one; there is no record of any service rendered it by the earl, and in 1667 he fell from power and was forced into exile. However, when Albermarle died in 1670, Reading put into his place Clarendon's son and heir, Henry Hyde, Viscount Cornbury.[3] It could not have been an easy choice. Clarendon's disgrace meant that his son was financially embarrassed and not at the centre of political power; but on the other hand he was brother-in-law to the Duke of York, the king's brother and heir presumptive to the throne. After Clarendon's death in 1674, Abingdon followed Reading, electing the new earl to the position of high steward, though allowing him only half the honorarium that his father had received − £3 6s 8d per annum.[4]

In 1675, the Abingdon corporation decided on a new recorder to run its courts and give it legal advice. Thomas Holt had held the position both for Abingdon and Reading. He was replaced by Thomas Medlicott, a Londoner by origin but resident in Abingdon. The official complaint against Holt was that he lived in Reading and was not readily available to the Abingdon council when they needed counselling. There may have been more to it than that; as would become obvious, Holt tended to the court and Medlicott to the country parties. Holt objected to his dismissal and got a mandamus, but Medlicott was allowed to defend himself at a cost of £29 to the corporation, and apparently won his case.[5]

About the same time, a more significant occurrence than either of these was the resurgence of the Norris family, descendants of that Sir Henry Norris, Baron Norreys of Rycote, who had been powerful in Berkshire and Oxfordshire a hundred years earlier. It will be recalled that a grandson of Sir Henry, who had become Earl of Berkshire, had an unfortunate tendency to lose his temper and kill people, and had, perhaps sensibly, killed himself in 1624. In the absence of a male heir, the earldom became extinct; but the barony could descend through the female side, and his granddaughter Bridget married, as his second wife, Montague Bertie, second Earl of Lindsey.[6] Her son James Bertie, born in 1653, became the fifth Baron Norreys. It was his good fortune that his half-sister Bridget married Thomas Osborne, the future Earl of Danby, and that his half-brother, Charles Bertie, became one of Danby's leading aides and supporters.[7] Young James was ambitious and intelligent. In 1674, he was named lord lieutenant of Oxfordshire, and set about making a career for himself and a position for his family.[8]

The great political issue of the later 1670s was 'exclusion' – whether the Catholic Duke of York should be allowed to succeed to the crown if his brother happened to pre-decease him. But the main source of excitement was the fantastical revelations of Titus Oates, alleging a 'Popish Plot' to subvert English liberties in the Duke's interest by assassination and insurrection. Oates was a nonentity, with unstable opinions and very unsavoury friends. What gave his allegations the impact they had was the sensational and still unexplained murder, in October 1678, of Sir Edmund Berry Godfrey, the magistrate who had taken his initial deposition. It is unclear to what extent country politicians sincerely believed Oates's nonsense or how far they saw it as a politically useful windfall; but it was enthusiastically taken up by the leadership of what would, a few years later, become known as the Whig party. Within weeks, the Plot had built up into an enormous conspiracy theory. To voice doubts was to be suspected of involvement. 'Tis a grand *piaculum'* – a heresy – 'not to believe the worst of reports', declared the Oxford antiquary Anthony Wood; his rooms were repeatedly searched, and he had to put his historical notes into friends' safe-keeping for fear they would be considered as incriminating.[9] Other sceptics were arrested.[10] Abingdon was not exempt from the hysteria. In December 1678 the corporation declared a 'tyme of danger iminent' and instituted a special night watch. Eighteen men, householders, always led by a member of the corporation, were to guard the town each night from 9 pm to 5 am. Defaulters would be fined 3s 4d.[11]

The corporation by now was divided between loyalist – Tory – and oppositional – Whig – factions, with no clear majority. But this did not necessarily represent feelings in the town. The Cavalier Parliament was finally dissolved early in 1679. In the election of February, Sir John Stonehouse was returned for Abingdon, apparently unopposed. But the parliament that resulted insisted on the Duke of York's exclusion from the succession, and was rapidly terminated. There would be new elections in September 1679. Feelings ran high, no less in Abingdon than elsewhere. Sir John was challenged by Maijor Dunch, a young man of a well-known Presbyterian family from Pusey in the Vale of White Horse. The campaign was noisy, costly, and bad-tempered. The Stonehouse team, playing at home, was able to use threats of increased tax assessments, increased rents, and eviction from council and Hospital properties. Nonetheless, it was Dunch who won the poll with 297 votes versus 171. We need not take too seriously the story of Mayor Payne having to hide for two days in a thick nettle bed from irate Dunch supporters, but he does seem to have calculated that 171 was a bigger number than 297, and signed the indenture in favour of Stonehouse. Unfortunately Dunch at that point fell ill of a fever and died, and so the outcome was never challenged.[12] Mayor Payne presumably had a majority of the corporation behind him, but, if so, the population had different ideas.

The second Exclusion Parliament was as strongly anti-York as its predecessor and fared little better. Prorogued for much of its time, it was finally dissolved in January 1681. Meanwhile, the king had learned the lesson that had been beaten into his predecessors, including those of the Protectorate: it was the towns that returned the greater number of members of parliament, and it was the towns where the electorate was most likely to favour the opposition. It was probably by way of a warning shot that on 12 March 1680 all chartered towns were sent a letter requiring confirmation that their corporation members were all duly qualified under the Test Acts, and this was to be countersigned by the lord lieutenant of the county. For Abingdon, the reply seems not to have been a straightforward document, since Recorder Medlicott's charge for preparing it was 20s.[13]

A new turning point in national politics came in March 1681, when a parliament was held in Oxford and dissolved after a week by the king. It was, in fact, a well-prepared royal coup. It heralded a time that was to become known as the Tory reaction, when Whig activities were hampered by all possible means, including extreme distortion of electoral and legal procedures, dismissals from office, judicial murders, and harassment of all sorts.[14] It was also a great career opportunity for Lord Norreys, which that ambitious nobleman grasped with both hands.

As lord lieutenant of Oxfordshire it was his responsibility to ensure that all the arrangements for the parliament were in place and they were, indeed, satisfactory. But a greater responsibility came afterwards, when the start of the reaction was to be marked by a big and well-publicised show trial. The chosen victim was one Stephen Colledge, a Whig balladeer and satirist. Accused of plotting to seize the king, he was put on trial for treason in London where, as must have been expected, a Whig jury acquitted him. In defiant breach of the traditional bar on double jeopardy, the government then transferred him to Oxford for a new trial. This was where Norreys's contribution became vital.[15] He saw to the physical arrangements; although not a lawyer, he sat on the bench with the judges; he enlisted the infamous Edmund Warcup to recruit and rehearse the team of witnesses; and he made sure of the jury by packing it and putting his brother Henry on to it as foreman. As was usual in treason trials, Colledge was not allowed counsel. He defended himself as best he could, but stood no chance, and was duly sentenced on 18 August 1681.[16] That this was judicial murder no one on either side of the political divide doubted.[17] It put Norreys on the way to the earldom to which he was promoted in November 1682, and Warcup would eventually be knighted. On such foundations were successful careers based at this time.

Norreys was now able to expand his area of influence, and his taking the title of Earl of Abingdon was an indication of the direction of his ambitions. Although a close friend and collaborator of the Earl of Clarendon, he did not hesitate to encroach on that dignitary's prerogative as Abingdon's high steward, and there is no sign of resistance on Clarendon's part. Norreys had no official position in Abingdon, but his elevation, when it came, was the occasion of civic celebrations in the town, with bonfires, wine and tobacco provided at public expense.[18] The ground had been thoroughly prepared.

The king had published a declaration justifying his action in dissolving the Oxford Parliament, and corporations were expected to show their loyalty by formally thanking him for it.[19] Routine political activity at this time included the frequent preparation of declarations and petitions supporting or opposing government actions and policies. In July 1681 Norreys attended an Abingdon council meeting when the corporation flatly refused to draw up the required declaration of thanks.[20] Norreys was incensed; the current mayor, Robert Sellwood, a tenant of his, was amenable, or said he was, but he had no influence over the others. Chiding Clarendon for his inactivity, the younger man began to take charge. He chose as his tool Sellwood's successor in the mayoralty, George Winchurst.

Winchurst's father of the same name had entered the corporation in July 1660 and had survived Lovelace's purge, so must have had good royalist credentials.[21] He had died in 1680, and at some time his son had taken his place. Both men were maltsters and ironmongers, with business interests that extended from Henley in the south-east as far as Worcester to the north-west.[22] The records show the younger Winchurst making frequent visits to Rycote and to the royal court at Windsor at corporation expense.[23] To mix with the nobility and the great ones of the realm must have been a head-turning experience for a mere provincial townsman. It was probably Winchurst's doing that the corporation in August 1682 added its contribution to the current spate of declarations − known as 'abhorrences' − against the 'the association found in the earl of Shaftesburies house, as a treasonable design against his majestie'. As these abhorrences had been coming in since the previous

January, and Abingdon's was in the final trickle that made up the full total of 157, it may be supposed that there had been significant resistance.[24]

Much of the pressure on Abingdon was now coming from Oxford, where Norreys was developing alliances with the University in his struggle to bring the strongly Whig city council to heel. Abingdon was part of the see of Salisbury, but by the 1680s Bishop Ward's health was failing and John Fell, Bishop of Oxford and Dean of Christ Church, was not averse to expanding his empire. In 1681, he put a protégé, Peter Birch, into the vicarage of St Helen's. Birch had been a Presbyterian, and Fell had converted him; he in turn had 'reduced great numbers of Dissenters to the church'. But the income of the cure was not sufficient for him 'not amounting to above three score pounds per An, and that to be pickt up in little vicars dues, no house to put his head in', and by the middle of 1683 he was about to move on. To Fell, Abingdon was 'a town ... of considerable wealth, belonging both to the corporation and particular inhabitants; and of no less aversion to the Government.' A high class vicar was essential.

Fell looked for some 'ingenious and unobnoxious' means for augmenting the minister's stipend. He observed that Christ's Hospital had a regular income well in excess of its outgoings 'so that a great surplusage continually remains, emploied to the ease and benefit of the wealthy inhabitants', and proposed a Chancery commission that would re-order the Hospital finances 'not only to settle this affair of the Minister but the disposal of this very considerable revenue, according to right and equity'.[25] Whether or not the proposal was made known to the corporation, it was neatly side-stepped; the Earl of Clarendon, as high steward, was brought in, and enabled to apply to Bishop Fell with the promise of an extra £20 or £30 per year paid directly by the town to the minister. The man Fell recommended, Richard Knight, was an academic who would serve part time at St Helen's until his death three years later. It is perhaps unfortunate that Fell's commission was never set up; if it had been, the Hospital might have been spared its travails in the Chancery court some hundred and fifty years later.[26]

The persecution of Dissenters had now re-started, more merciless than ever. As mayor, Winchurst was hampered by the opposition of his fellow-councilmen and the recorder, Thomas Medlicott, who consistently outvoted him and mitigated the penalties prescribed by the laws. Medlicott had been removed from the county commission of the peace in 1681, but only the corporation could dismiss him from that of the town.[27] The Dissenters continued their nominally illegal meetings, sometimes in Abingdon and sometimes in the surrounding villages, and the most unpopular of them, the Quakers, came in from their local centre around Faringdon to run a recruiting campaign, preaching on occasion in the open street. There were disorders on midsummer night 1682, when a Whig procession some forty strong paraded through the town, 'in warlike array' and 'with swords and staves', according to the formal reports. The constables were mobbed when they tried to intervene.[28] Winchurst, no doubt at Norreys' urging, wrote to Sir Leoline Jenkins, secretary of state and MP for Oxford University, in London. 'We have in this town many factious fanatics. I have and shall endeavour to reduce them to their obedience by executing the laws on them'.[29] Norreys was showing himself to the high and mighty as an active governor of his region.[30]

The next mayor, William Foster, was a moderate, and in 1683 Winchurst wanted to be re-elected. The system was for the commonalty to gather and offer the names of two aldermen from whom the outgoing mayor would choose one. In fact, two lists were submitted, with Winchurst and Jonathan Hawe on one, William Cheyney and William Hawkins on the other, with the latter much more heavily supported than the former. In spite of being on the minority slate, Winchurst asked for a poll. He proposed to admit to the vote only men who took the oaths of allegiance, which all corporation members should already have done, but which were not compulsory for electors. One of the oaths, that of supremacy, could be read as a commitment to follow whatever religion was professed by the current sovereign, and with the likely prospect of a Catholic successor this would be unacceptable to many Whigs and Dissenters.[31] Medlicott ruled that Winchurst's plan would be illegal, and William Hawkins was chosen mayor.

Winchurst wrote again to Jenkins, explaining that in Abingdon the Whigs could always outvote the Tories, '... the Dissenters here, which procure the majority of voices and did by five to one, for many of the Dissenters are rich so that many beholden to them though not of their judgment dare give no votes'. Jenkins filed the letter, adding a note in his own handwriting to the effect that it should be placed before the king at the earliest opportunity, and that action would be justified.[32] Medlicott also wrote in, justifying his advice, but it would do him little good.[33]

The action followed. There was a writ of quo warranto against the Abingdon corporation. This was probably almost immediate, although the only surviving documentary mention is much later and does not give a date.[34] Quo warranto was a form of process in King's Bench where holders of a trust were accused of breaching it, and might be discharged. At this time, quo warrantos were being used regularly to force reluctant urban corporations to relinquish their charters for revision.[35] In law, corporations were regarded as trusts acting on behalf of the crown in administering their towns. It was always possible to find some point, perhaps trivial, in which they might be said to have acted improperly; for Abingdon, Winchurst's complaint about the mayoral election provided an obvious pretext. The normal response to a quo warranto was a rapid surrender to bring about a stay of process. The legal position was uncertain, but it was assumed that the town's charter would become void, the corporation would cease to exist and whatever property it held would return to its original owners or their heirs.[36] Since in Abingdon most of the corporation's extensive properties had been granted it from the spoils of the Abbey, these would be forfeit to the crown. A few towns, notably London and Oxford, had opted to fight their quo warrantos, but the king's judges had found against London in June 1683, and Oxford, under the Earl of Abingdon's urging, had caved in in August.[37] The Earl of Abingdon was not yet high steward of Oxford, but that town was definitely within his sphere of influence, and in view of his close cooperation both with Clarendon and with Winchurst, it seems likely that the letters to Jenkins had been expressly intended to bring about the result they did.

The decision in principle to surrender the charter seems to have been taken by June 1684 – it is not clear by whom. The corporation minute book limits itself to noting that selected members were being summoned to meet Lord Clarendon for important discussions.[38] The next several months will have been taken up with anxious negotiations between the corporation and the government over the terms of the new charter, and Clarendon, most probably, will have acted as intermediary. A strange lawsuit was started against the Whig Mayor Hawkins and some others. They appear to have been accused of the illegal acquisition of property by impersonation of its owner. The nature of the property is unclear in the otherwise very legible corporation minutes, and an unsuccessful attempt has been made to erase the owner's name, Waldron. The Corporation undertook to bear the legal costs.[39] While nothing can be said with certainty, it is hard to avoid the suspicion that the suit was deliberately vexatious and that arms were being twisted. By July 1685, Medlicott, although still nominally recorder, seems to have been suspended from his functions.[40] In October 1685, there was a most irregular transaction whereby John Saunders renewed his leases en bloc for a wide variety of corporation properties, paying the very considerable sum of £40 in entry fines, and immediately arranged to transfer the leases into the otherwise unknown name of Richard Ring, presumably a financier who would hold them as collateral.[41] John Saunders would become mayor, and in 1686 a hospital governor and treasurer. He had not previously been on the corporation, although his brother Thomas had. He was, however, a known Tory; at the time of the Rye House Plot, in the summer of 1683, he had reported someone for suggesting, with understandable cynicism, that it was a sham intended to encourage further harassment of Whigs.[42] John Saunders did not enjoy his new position long; he was dead by January 1687.[43] Thomas Saunders would be the next chamberlain or financial officer, and would run into trouble; his accounts are missing from the file, and his successor would have to call on the men who had stood as his securities to pay outstanding debts.[44] There is a hint of financial malpractice going in parallel with political chicanery. A corporation delegation accompanied Lord Clarendon to London on 9 November 1685 carrying the old charter and a formal instrument of surrender, summarising the terms which by then must have been agreed. The new town clerk, Richard Hart, took over almost immediately to oversee the preparation of the new document.[45] The corporation seems to have continued on a caretaker basis, with a loan of £200 obtained from Christ's Hospital against the signatures of five of the outgoing members.[46] Its very last recorded act was to pay £3 1s towards William Hawkins's legal costs.[47]

Clarendon was high steward of Reading as well as of Abingdon, and both towns surrendered their charters at the same time and received new ones on the same day, 9 March 1686. The differences are instructive. Reading's corporation was overwhelmingly royalist; the half dozen Whigs had long since been isolated and rarely attended meetings. Surrender was presented as a demonstration of their loyalty to, and trust in, the sovereign. There was no need for a quo warranto. The new charter was ceremonially brought home by the effective leader of the Reading corporation and one of the town's MPs, Thomas Coates. There were public celebrations, with bell-ringing, bonfires, and large amounts of wine and beer provided at public expense. The mayor continued in his function, and it was he who swore in the new corporation members.[48] In Abingdon, there were no recorded celebrations or public ceremony. The underlying assumption was that the corporation had ceased to exist. The charter was brought in by the MP, Sir John Stonehouse, and a group of other Berkshire and Oxfordshire gentry acting as commissioners, and it was they who tendered the oaths of allegiance and of office to the new councilmen.[49]

The new charter was a long and complex document, which contained much that was useful. There was some standardisation of terminology and structures: principal burgesses would in future be aldermen, and there would be twelve of these, and twelve ordinary burgesses instead of sixteen. Members of parliament would be elected by the mayor, aldermen and common council, removing an ambiguity of long standing. As was usual when charters were renewed, initial membership of the new corporation was specified. Thomas Medlicott was no longer recorder; that post went to William Finmore. Five of the twelve principal burgesses would not return as aldermen. Those ejected included the previous moderate or Whig mayors, Foster and Hawkins.[50] Even the new serjeants at mace were named, and it may be assumed that they were Tory supporters in good standing.

The document included a clause, now customary, that the crown could remove any corporation member at will. It did not say, as charters renewed somewhat later would, that it would be the crown rather than the corporation who would nominate their replacements, but in the following years the crown would assume such powers notwithstanding. But the major innovation in the new Abingdon charter was that henceforth the town's bench of justices would be reinforced by no fewer than nine county gentlemen from Berkshire and Oxfordshire, including those who had acted as commissioners.[51] They would easily be able to overrule the local men on the bench, and the frustrations suffered by Winchurst would not recur. The traditional principle that towns selected their own ruling body within the terms of their charters had been irreparably breached by Lovelace's commission in 1663. The no less sacrosanct one that county magistrates had no standing within town boundaries had also been set aside by the commissions of association of 1664, but that could be presented as a temporary measure to meet an extraordinary situation.[52] Now, the authority of outsiders was enshrined in the new charter, which specified that the named JPs should serve for life. The charter, as will be seen, would prove short-lived, but the supremacy of central policy-makers over town and city administrations would be permanent.

It is worth looking in more detail at the nine men who were to assume judicial powers. Six of them were from the immediate vicinity. They included Sir John Stonehouse of Radley, the M.P., and his brother James from Tubney, Edmund Wiseman jnr from Steventon who was currently high sheriff of Berkshire, Thomas Reade from Appleford, and Paul Calton from Milton. There was a Humphrey Hyde, no doubt of the family based at Northcourt, although this individual perhaps came from further away at Kingston Lisle.[53] If a slate of local gentry had to be selected to help Abingdon run its affairs, these men would be naturals for places on it. The other three were not local, although one of them had local connections. Charles Perrot, Doctor of Laws, was an Oxford man, and one of the MPs for the university.[54] Jenkins had died during the period of negotiation, but Perrot may be seen as his, or the university's, candidate.[55] Edmund Warcup of Northmoor was the specialist in suborning witnesses. He had been closely associated with Lord Norreys in the affair of Stephen Colledge in 1681, and would get his knighthood thereafter, as Norreys had got his earldom.[56] Warcup saw himself as a client of the earl, who might well wish to use him as an agent to develop his interests in Berkshire.[57] The man who did have local connections was Robert Mayott, an Abingdon man by birth who would return there to die, but who had been living since 1658 on an estate he had bought at Fawler in Oxfordshire.[58] This made him a neighbour of Lord Clarendon, whose home was close by at Cornbury, and in spite of the difference in status he had become a trusted personal friend.[59] The Mayott family had been prominent in Abingdon affairs through many generations, and it is not unexpected to find that the new mayor, John Saunders, and his brother Thomas were Mayotts through their mother.[60] So was William Finmore, the new recorder.[61] A John Mayott jnr appears in the new charter as a secondary burgess.[62] Clarendon's correspondence shows that he took his responsibilities as high steward seriously, and it is likely that Robert Mayott was on the list not merely as his agent but also to help protect the town's interests against potentially hostile manoeuvrings from outside. But even this degree of benevolence could not hide the fact that ultimate control of Abingdon was now in the hands of a single party, that of the crown, acting through its magnate supporters and their gentry nominees.

But the situation was less stable than it seemed. Although the new rulers of Abingdon cannot have known it, their charter was obsolescent even before it was granted. Quietly at first, the king was in process of changing his policy.

---

[1] BRO A/JQs 1/1 fo. 48.

[2] ATCA, Corp Mins, i, (31 July 1661), fo 183v. (He had been made Earl of Clarendon in April 1661.)

[3] Manfred Brod. *The Case of Reading: urban governance in troubled times* (2006), p. 81. The writ of mandamus was a challenge to the Corporation to show that the

dismissal of Holt was within its legal powers. The Hydes of Cornbury do not seem to have had any connection with the Hyde family that had long been active in Berkshire.

[4] ATCA, Corp Mins, i fo. 229.

[5] ATCA, Corp Mins, i fo. 230.

[6] Titles of viscount or above were bestowed by letters patent, which would specify the rules of inheritance and in most cases exclude females. A baron might be made simply by a royal summons to sit in the Lords at a parliament, and then normal rules of inheritance, as for property, would apply. If there was a single daughter as in this case, she would be baroness in her own right.

[7] Mark Knights, 'Osborne, Thomas, first duke of Leeds (1632–1712)', *DNB;* Stuart Handley, 'Bertie, Charles (1640/41–1711)', *DNB.*

[8] A. Clark (ed), *L&T* ii, p. 283.

[9] Clark, *L&T* ii p. 421

[10] John Miller, *Cities Divided: Politics and Religion in English Provincial Towns 1660-1722* (2007) pp. 211-2

[11] ATCA, Corporation Minutes i, fo 237. The terms 'Tory' and 'Whig' did not come into common use until the early 1680s. Their use here, if anachronistic, is convenient.

[12] A.B., *A letter from a friend in Abingdon, to a gentleman in London concerning the election of Burgesses for the ensuing Parliament* (1679); Mieneke Cox, *Peace and War* (Abingdon, 1993), pp. 160-1.

[13] ATCA, Corporation Minutes i, fo. 240, 27 April 1680. P. D. Halliday, *Dismembering the Body Politic: Partisan Politics in England's Towns 1650-1730* (Cambridge, 1998), p. 124.

[14] R. Pickavance. 'The English Boroughs and the King's Government: A Study of the Tory Reaction 1681-85.' Unpub DPhil thesis, Oxford University (1976).

[15] *CSPD* 1680-1, Letter Leoline Jenkins to Norreys, (11 July 1681).

[16] *Cobbett's State Trials,* VIII, cols. 566 et seq.

[17] Gilbert Burnet, *History of his own Time* (Oxford, 1823) I p. 283; Harold Weber, *Paper Bullets: Print and Kingship under Charles II* (Kentucky, 1996), pp. 178-208. G.W. Keeton, *Lord Chancellor Jeffreys and the Stuart cause* (1965), pp. 195-201, argues, no doubt correctly, that the trial was properly conducted by the standards of the time, but it does not follow that Colledge was guilty as charged. It does seem, to the earl's credit, that the case weighed on his conscience – Mark Goldie (ed), *The entring book of Roger Morrice, 1677-1691* (CD, Cambridge, 2007), R34.

[18] Agnes Baker, *Historic Abingdon - 56 Articles* (1963), pp. 58-61; ATCA, Chamberlains Accounts, 1682.

[19] (Charles II), *His Majesties Declaration to All His Loving Subjects, Touching the Causes & Reasons That Moved Him to Dissolve the Two Last Parliaments* (1681).

[20] Bodleian, Norreys to Clarendon, Ms Clarendon 155, fo 33. There is no record of the meeting in the Corporation minutes.

[21] ATCA, Corporation Minutes, i, fo 187 (25 Aug 1660).

[22] TNA, Winchurst vs Mundy, 19 June 1669, C5/581/22; Winchurst vs Mee, 3 Dec 1683, C 9/451/116.

[23] Baker, *56 Articles*, pp. 58-61; ATCA, Chamberlains' Accounts, 1682.

[24] N. Luttrell, *A Brief Historical Relation of State Affairs from September, 1678 to April 1714* (1857) I pp. 163, 213; Tim Harris, *Restoration: Charles II and his kingdoms* (2005), p. 277.

[25] It is certainly the case that the Hospital was accumulating funds at a significant rate; the accounts show that during the decade of the 1670s, it had added a total of £700 to its exchequer. But this money was not, of course, directly available to the governors.

[26] Bodl., Letters Fell to Sancroft , Ms Tanner 34, fo 55 (June 26 1683) and fo 117 (22 Aug 1683); Preston, *St Nicholas,* pp 142, 229; Letter Clarendon to Rochester, (24 Aug 1686), printed in Samuel Weller Singer (ed), *The Correspondence of Henry Hyde, Earl of Clarendon and .... Rochester* (1828), I pp. 554-6; Clark, *L&T* III, p. 194. According to Wood, there was a serious epidemic in Abingdon at the time of Knight's death.

[27] HMC, *Ms of the House of Lords* Vol 2 Appx ii p. 175 (9 July 1681).

[28] O. Sansom, *An Account of Many Remarkable Passages of the Life of Oliver Sansom* (1710), p. 274 ; Berks Record Office, Preston Papers, A/JQz 11 fos 79-87, 88a-c.

[29] *CSPD* 1682 p. 225 (1 June 82).

[30] Baker, *56 Articles*, pp. 58-61

[31] J.R. Tanner, *Tudor Constitutional Documents* (Cambridge, 1951), pp. 130-135.

[32] TNA, Winchurst to Jenkins, SP 431 fo. 111 (foliation as printed, which does not conform with that in the Calendar).

[33] *CSPD* July-Sept 1683 p. 419 (23 Sept.)

[34] ATCA, Corporation minutes i, fo 262 (9 March 1686)

[35] Halliday, *Dismembering,* Chap 6.

[36] Anon. *The Case of the Burgesses of Nottingham, in reference to the surrendering of their charters* (1682); Halliday, *Dismembering,* Chap 6; Blackstone, *Commentaries,* Vol 1 p. 484.

[37] M.G. Hobson, *Oxford Council Acts 1666-1701* (Oxford, 1939), pp. xxii, 157.

[38] *CSPD* May 1684- Apr 1685 p. 74 (21 June 1684); ATCA, Corporation Minutes i, fo. 255 (2 July 1684).

[39] ATCA, Corporation Minutes i, fo.254v (5 June 1684) and fo. 261 (2 March 1686).

[40] Sansom, *Life*, p. 347.

[41] ATCA, Corporation Minutes i, fo 259v (20 Oct 1685)

[42] BRO, D/EP 7/73 No 54.

[43] CH, Minute Book i, fos. 203v, 298 (5 Oct 1686, 10 Jan 1687).

[44] ATCA, Corporation Minutes ii, fo 46v (2 Dec 1687)

[45] ATCA, Corporation Minutes i, fo 260 (19 Nov 1685)

[46] CH, Minute Book i, fo. (25 Nov 1685). 290.

[47] ATCA, Corporation Minutes i, fo 261 (2 March 1686).

[48] Brod, *The Case of Reading*, p. 93; Berks Record Office, Reading Corporation records R/AC/1/1/16 and /17; Reading chamberlains' accounts, R/FA 3/48.

[49] ATCA, Corporation Minutes i, fo. 262 (9 March 1686).

[50] ATCA, Corporation Minutes i, fo. 262 (9 March 1686). The number five is not quite certain, since there is no complete list of principal burgesses before the change.

[51] Challenor, *Selections*, pp. 75-97.

[52] It should be pointed out that individuals of high status were commonly named both to county and town benches, but these appointments were honorary and they would not be expected to sit. The Abingdon charter of 1610 named the then high steward, William, Lord Knollys; Sir John Parry, Chancellor of the Duchy of Lancaster; and Sir David Williams, a judge of King's Bench resident nearby at Kingston Bagpuize – Challenor, *Selections,* p. 59 and *DNB* sub nom.

[53] According to Wood, in A. Clark, *L&T* ii, pp. 41, 365, a Humphry Hyde of Northcourt had died childless in 1676/7. The man named in the charter was presumably the Humphry Hyde JP who was one of Oliver Sansom's persecutors at the time and must have resided somewhere close to Faringdon – Sansom, *Life,* pp. 335, 371, *VCH Berks* IV 315.

[54] A drunkard, in the opinion of Anthony Wood – Clark, *L&T* ii 460. Note that this is *not* the Charles Perrot of Oriel College who was a Stonehouse by his mother – Clark, *L&T* ii 372.

[55] Several Oxford colleges held property in the vicinity of Abingdon, and the Abingdon archdeaconry was controlled, always by an Oxford man, from headquarters just south of Folly Bridge. No doubt Abingdon was seen as lying within the university's sphere of interest.

[56] 'Lord Norris made a freeman of Oxford, I with him' – Warcup's diary for 2 June 1681 – E. Warcup, K. Feiling and F. R. D. Needham, 'The Journals of Edmund Warcup, 1676-84', *The English Historical Review* 40 (1925), pp. 235-260. Stephen Colledge, who conducted his own defence with great skill, repeatedly got witnesses to admit they had been suborned by Warcup and, indeed, relied on him for their income – Anon, *The Arraignment, tryal and condemnation of Stephen Colledge* (1681).

[57] Bodleian, Warcup to Hugh Jones, Ms Rawlinson Letters 48, fos. 19 (24 July 1682), 41v (14 Sept 1685), 70 (22 Dec 1688); Clarendon to Abingdon, Ms Clarendon 155, fo. 85 (2 June 1685); Clarendon to Abingdon , Ms Clarendon 153, fo. 65 (9 July 1685). Warcup had been a commissioner when the Oxford charter was renewed in 1684, in which the Earl of Abingdon had played a decisive role – Hobson, *Oxford Council Acts,* p. 164.

[58] *VCH Oxon* X, p. 138; TNA, Will of Robert Mayott, (16 January 1713), PROB 11/531. He was probably the Robert Mayott who lobbied in defence of St Nicholas in the 1650s, but this is not certain. There were at least three men of that name active at the time.

[59] Samuel Weller Singer (ed), *The Correspondence of Henry Hyde, Earl of Clarendon and .... Rochester,* 2 vols (1828) II pp. 290, 291, 398; Bodleian, Ms Clarendon 153, fos 8, 14; BL, Addl Ms 18675 passim.

[60] Clark, *L&T* ii p. 52; St Nicholas, Abingdon, Parish registers (CD issued by Berks Family History Society).

[61] Finmore would die in 1687, and be replaced by Simon Harcourt.

[62] He was probably the apothecary son of the John Mayott who got into trouble with parliament in 1660; he died in October 1686 of the current epidemic. Clark, L&T iii p. 194; BRO, D/A1/98/170. William Cheyney, another council member related to the Mayotts, had died in August of that year – ATCA, Mayors' Book p. 92.

12. Revolution

> All, all of a piece throughout:
> Thy chase had a beast in view;
> Thy wars brought nothing about;
> Thy lovers were all untrue.
> Tis well an old age is out.
> And time to begin a new.
>   John Dryden, *The Secular Masque.*

It was on 6 February 1685, while Abingdon's new charter was still under negotiation, that the Whigs' worst fears were realised. Charles II died. The 'reaction' since 1681 had been devastating for the Whigs; their party was all but extinct, its leaders dead or in exile, local organisers in gaol or terrorised into inactivity. James II was proclaimed with all the customary ceremonial, and the Abingdon corporation was among those that sent congratulatory messages.[1] They could expect to draw benefit from Lord Clarendon's relationship with the new king; he was a brother of James's first wife, Anne Hyde, and uncle to his two daughters. Throughout the exclusion crisis, the support of the two Hyde brothers, Clarendon and the Earl of Rochester, for the Duke had been a constant. Immediately on his accession, James announced that the Anglican church would be safe in his hands, and the Tories felt vindicated. Their opposition to Exclusion would prove to have been justified. The parliament that met in May had a Tory majority so large as to be embarrassing.[2] Stonehouse was again returned for Abingdon, unopposed.

In June, the ill-starred landing in Dorset of the Duke of Monmouth provided a further occasion for the king's partisans to show their loyalty. The duke was the oldest of Charles's illegitimate sons, and his father's favourite. He was also the darling of the Whigs, whom he courted intensively. For if only the famous black box, that was supposed to contain proof that his parents had been secretly but legally married, were to be discovered, he would replace the Duke of York as heir apparent to the throne. And even if that unlikely event did not occur, there was every possibility of some unforeseen crisis that might have the same effect. But once York had become king, those hopes were dashed, and he determined to try a direct challenge. It was a serious misjudgement of the national mood; the Whig and Dissenting support he had relied on did not materialise, and the result was failure.

Nonetheless, there was anxiety. The files of letters that passed between the Earl of Abingdon, fulfilling the military functions of the lord lieutenant of his county, and Clarendon, as Lord Privy Seal at the heart of events in London, show the urgency with which the situation was viewed.[3] Anthony Wood describes the excitement in Oxford, with hastily-formed companies drilling and training, Lord Abingdon's brother Henry Bertie leading the county's mounted militia out to war, and agents of the king's footguards beating their drums for recruits. They accepted, says Wood, some thirty or forty sturdy fellows and rejected more; but when they came to Abingdon, 'being a most factious towne', the total number of volunteers was only four.[4] Monmouth's failure may have seemed only to strengthen the king's position, but it was not so. It was plain to all that the 'footguards' were in fact a standing royal army, against the spirit if not the exact letter of the 1661 and 1662 Militia Acts; it was impossible to overlook the fact that many of its officers were Catholic, and that the king was dispensing them from the oaths that the law required.[5] Parliament was uneasy; the courts found for the king only after six judges had been sacked and replaced.[6] The Tories' trust in absolute kingship was beginning to be less absolute than it had been.

Generations of historians in the Whig tradition have laid stress on James's shortcomings of intellect and character, and accepted uncritically the Whig propaganda of the time that presented him as aiming for a French-style absolute monarchy in an exclusively Catholic state. In fact, it was not unreasonable for him to wish to free the crown from its exclusive dependence on a single party, the Tories, and a deeply intolerant Anglican church. This might in itself have been achievable. But bundled with it was the establishment and official approval of Catholicism as a second state religion, and this would prove impossible to push down the throats of a nation that had been taught over the past century and a half to see anti-Catholicism as an essential part of its identity.

Even as Abingdon's new charter was being drawn up, there were the first rumours that the king was preparing the great reversal of alliances that would result in disaster for him and his progeny. His strategy was to exploit the persecution of Protestant Dissenters by the magistrates and the church. Ending this would gain him the gratitude of the Dissenters, and would lead ineluctably to the release of Catholicism from the legal restrictions under which it laboured. At the Berkshire sessions of 12 January 1686, Oliver Sansom, leader of the local Quakers, told the magistrates that 'the king is inclined to shew us some favour', and he and his Quaker co-defendants, imprisoned for refusing to take the oaths of allegiance, were allowed to go free.[7] Even the most hidebound among the justices must have understood the political dangers of appearing unwilling to do what the king could eventually compel, and letting a

Catholic monarch appear as the saviour of one set of Protestants from the contemptuous hostility of another. On 10 March, a royal proclamation exempted, or purported to exempt, Dissenters in general from punishment under the repressive laws.[8] The king's dispensing power was now at the centre of political controversy, and the courts were in confusion. At the July Berkshire assizes, the former Abingdon recorder, Thomas Medlicott, was defending a group of Dissenters, mostly Baptists and with eighteen of them from Abingdon. He handed the shocked judges a dispensation in the name of James's minister Sunderland and authenticated with the king's own signature, and rubbed salt in their wounds by pointing out that it was only by their own rhetoric of royal absolutism that such proceedings could be justified. For another group from Abingdon, there was a further such dispensation freshly signed.[9] James would eventually suspend the penal laws completely, giving rise to formal declarations of thanks from Abingdon and Berkshire Dissenters which, for once, might well have been sincere.[10]

The men who the charter of 1686 had seemed to confirm as the rulers of Abingdon must have found their triumph short-lived. There will have been anxiety when, as early as 29 January 1687, a commission of association was granted to the moderate ex-mayor William Foster.[11] The Tory/Anglicans would no longer have it all their own way on the magistrates' bench. What further changes might this presage?

The uncertainty may have been even greater in high places. The king was progressively abandoning his erstwhile supporters of the Tory and high Anglican party in favour of Whigs, Dissenters, and Catholics. His old ministers were subjected to a private interview, a technique that became known as closeting. Clarendon was spared this experience, but his brother Rochester underwent it in December 1686 and failed. Both brothers were removed from the centre of affairs. The Earl of Abingdon had his turn in November 1687. Unlike Rochester, he was not invited to embrace Catholicism, but was asked to support the king's efforts to end the Test Acts which kept non-Anglicans from official positions. He refused. In his account, he claims to have told the king 'though I did not doubt his Majesty's sincerity in what he professed, yet I did not know who might succeed him; and though we were told of a Protestant successor, yet how if it should prove otherwise?'.[12] He must have had remarkably early knowledge of the queen's pregnancy, or else was simply embellishing his story. He too fell from favour, and was replaced as lord lieutenant by the Catholic Earl of Lichfield, a very young man who had married an illegitimate daughter of Charles II.[13] The

Berkshire lord lieutenancy was already held by the Duke of Norfolk, whose Protestantism may have been more a matter of convenience than of conviction. The court interest and the Tory/Anglican were no longer congruent. Clarendon and Abingdon went into opposition taking somewhat different ideological positions. Clarendon became high steward of the Anglican and Tory Oxford University, which was reacting strongly against court-inspired Catholicisation, on 5 January 1687.[14] Abingdon had repositioned himself from the great persecutor of the strongly Whiggish city of Oxford to its defender against the opressive demands of the university. He became its high steward on 2 May, although here also James replaced him with Lichfield.[15]

In July 1686, James set up an ecclesiastical commission. Its immediate activity was to take action against Anglican clerics who angered the king, but the formal remit was to correct abuses in church, educational, and charitable institutions – in other words, to prepare them for possible take-over by Catholics. In December, the chancellor of the Salisbury diocese was obliged to report on the schools and hospitals of Berkshire. For Abingdon, he listed Roysse's and the new school recently set up under the will of Richard Mayott, Christ's Hospital, and the older Hospital of St John.[16] The commissioners were informed that for three of these the governors were the mayor and aldermen for the time being, and that the master and governors of Christ's Hospital were largely from the same group of people. The hospital was 'the king's foundation'. What a king had granted, a king could resume, and James had already started what appeared to be a programme of such resumptions.[17] No specific reactions have come down to us, but there must have been growing unease as leading citizens faced the possibility of the loss of prestigious functions, local control, and, on the evidence of Fell's letter to Sancroft already mentioned, a significant part of their income.[18]

The king and his minister, the Earl of Sunderland, instigated a determined campaign to 'regulate' commissions of the peace and municipal corporations throughout the country. The immediate aim was to ensure a compliant parliament in late 1688 to back the king in a wide-ranging reform of institutions that would allow full political rights to both Protestant Dissenters and Catholic recusants. Gentry, magistrates, town councillors were subjected to interviews and enquiries by royal agents, and appropriate measures were taken. On 3 and 26 December 1687, the Abingdon corporation considered successive royal letters. One version of the earlier of these, now in the Berkshire Record Office, is a remarkably informal document considering its content; there is no parchment, wax seal, or elaborate penmanship. On a half sheet of ordinary paper, apparently in his own handwriting, Sunderland ordered the dismissal of eight corporation members along with the recorder and town clerk, and their replacement with other named individuals. The later missive brought the number of removals to twenty-two, apparently the totality of survivors from the list of 1686.[19] The Abingdon Town Archives have more formal versions of both letters, written in the name of the king in council, and signed by Philip Musgrave, clerk to the Privy Council. These order the dismissals but say nothing about replacements, presumably because the king had no legal right to prescribe these.[20] The corresponding entries in the Privy Council minutes likewise make no mention of replacements. The designated newcomers included at least seven Baptists, two Presbyterians, and a Catholic.[21] It was, as Wood remarked, the Baptists who were readiest to accept the poisoned chalice of the king's dispensations; it was they who had borne the brunt of the Anglicans' persecution.[22] The Presbyterians were always seen as more respectable, and had less scruple about attending services at the parish church in addition to their own conventicles. It is probable that, as at Reading, some men originally approached had refused to let their names go forward, and indeed two of those finally selected declined to serve.[23] The individuals who had been removed in 1686 were back, and the then mayor, William Foster; the recorder, Medlicott; and the town clerk, Knapp, all resumed their functions. There was another letter of thanks, which showed that the new team understood exactly why they had been put into office: 'And when it shall be your royal pleasure to call a Parliament, we shall make it our business to elect such a member who shall as well answer Your Majesties expectations, as be to the Satisfaction of all good Subjects'.[24]

Of the nine justices who had been intruded in 1686, one had died and seven were now regarded as untrustworthy. Stonehouse had declared to the lord lieutenant that, if he were again an MP, he would not agree to the abolition of the Test Acts. The seven were dismissed in August 1688.[25] Only the egregious and unprincipled Warcup remained.

In September, the new corporation elected John Southby to the freemanship; he was the son of a former Whig MP for Berkshire, and was intended to be a candidate for the Abingdon seat.[26] The Whigs and Dissenters were enjoying the luxury of putting up rival candidates: Southby was preferred by the Presbyterians; a Mr Trinder by the Baptists; 'Mr Tomkins declines to stand'.[27] Mr Tomkins will have been one of the Baptist family of that name, possibly the wealthy maltster Benjamin. William Trinder was of a prominent partly Catholic family of Westwell, Oxon. The Baptists were repaying a debt of honour. Benjamin Tomkins and a Henry Tomkins, glover, had been among the Dissenters saved from punishment at the 1686 assizes. The dispensations had been obtained by Thomas Medlicott from the king's rather shadowy political agent Robert Brent, and the intermediary was probably Henry Trinder, a lawyer intruded by James as recorder of Oxford and who worked closely with Brent.[28] This was exactly the kind of unnatural alliance that the king's strategy was designed to promote.[29]

The new and inexperienced corporation had its difficulties. It doubted the word of its town clerk, Henry Knapp, when he told them the cost of the legal documents they would need, and challenged him to prove that other boroughs similarly situated were paying as much as £20. In the end, they had to give him £53, over a formal objection by six of them.[30] Having the new and expensive County Hall to fill, it made complaints about the assizes being at Reading, but these were referred to the judges themselves. A delegation had to be sent to meet the judges at Gloucester, which was on their circuit, and no doubt give them suitable entertainment.[31] The corporation ran short of money, since the men who had been displaced demanded payment for the services they claimed to have rendered, and had to borrow £20 from Benjamin Tomkins.[32]

But all would end in anti-climax. With the birth of a son to James, William of Orange was no longer in line to the English throne. He would follow the example of Monmouth, but at a more propitious time, with carefully prepared political support, and with infinitely greater resources. News of the invasion fleet threw James into a panic. He lost his nerve; the planned parliamentary election was cancelled at the last moment, and by a proclamation of 17 October 1688 all changes to town charters since 1679 were declared cancelled.[33] There seems to have been some posturing, but by the end of October, the old corporation was back in action. William Hawkins had been elected mayor, but this was now void. Under the proclamation, Robert Blackaller should have returned to the position he had held nine years previously but he did not, and Foster continued in office.[34] One thing he had to do in February 1689 was to pay out £6 7s to prevent a body of foot soldiers from quartering themselves overnight on the town.[35] They will have been a part of James's army that had been removed from London to avoid confrontation with William's Dutch regiments. There was a risk of disorder; these men had kept their Jacobite allegiance, and were liable to provoke clashes with William's partisans.[36] It would be some time before the corporation could return to its full complement of secondary burgesses, but there was no period, as in some other places, when the administration of the town was effectively in abeyance, or when rival corporations strove for mastery.[37]

The two earls reacted differently to the Williamite invasion. The Earl of Abingdon was the first important peer to make the pilgrimage to Exeter, and carried the allegiance of his paternal Lindsey clan with him.[38] No doubt this was the influence of Danby making itself felt.[39] Viscount Cornbury, Clarendon's son, defected at the same time, much to his father's distress. Clarendon himself eventually followed, torn between duty to the king who had treated him so shabbily and love for his young niece, the Princess Mary. Both earls were shocked when the Prince's minister, Bentinck, assured them too emphatically that his master had no intention of seizing the throne and they realised that that was exactly what he did intend.[40] When the Convention Parliament met for its decisive session, both voted that the throne was not vacant, and Clarendon argued strongly, but in vain, for a regency.[41] He wrote despairingly to his niece, arguing that she should not allow her husband to reign.[42] She ignored him. He finished in a sulky retirement, with occasional involuntary stays in the Tower. The Earl of Abingdon, by contrast, made his peace with the new regime and continued his career, with an occasional friendly gesture towards the older man.[43]

The moment when the nation, or most of it, united − Tory and Whig, Dissenter and Anglican − against a royal exponent of 'popery and arbitrary government' has been referred to as a 'short glimpse of a golden age between two iron ages'.[44] For the town of Abingdon, at least, the gold was as that of the fairies; it faded almost before the next dawn. William was firmly in control, and it was necessary to give him some legal recognition. The situation was remarkably similar to that of early 1660, and local events would follow a similar path. A convention was called. Southby, after some obscure manoeuvres against him, did not stand.[45] Trinder obviously could not. Stonehouse had the support of the restored corporation with its Tory majority. He was opposed by the recorder, Thomas Medlicott, Anglican, but a Whig, and able to glory in the fact that William himself had lodged a few hours at his house in East St Helen's Street before leaving for London when the news of James's flight reached him.[46] The campaign was stormy and violent. Medlicott's supporters had not forgiven Stonehouse for his part in the charter renewal of 1686; their cry was 'No Radley charter!'. A certain Wyblin was carrying Medlicott's colours on a pole. Someone hit him, and, waving his pole around, he contrived to knock Stonehouse off his feet. Stonehouse was 'so barbarously used, he could not be at the Election'. A Mr Fletcher had his head broken 'in two or three places'. In spite of, or perhaps because of, the disorders, turnout was low. Medlicott won the poll with 105 votes to 87. He sat, but Stonehouse appealed.[47]

Medlicott was already entering his sixties, and had left his parliamentary debut rather late. Also, he could not know the outcome of Stonehouse's appeal. His tenure might be brief, and he lost no time in making his mark. On 28 January 1689, he called for an immediate vote on the knotty problem of the vacancy of the throne. On 19 February, after the first speech from the throne by the new-made William III, he proposed that the convention declare itself a parliament, which after further discussion it did.[48] But on 7 May, the House considered his position. As in 1660, it wanted evidence that each voter had been a payer of scot and lot, a householder in his own right, and not a recipient of alms. The election was declared void, and a new one was ordered. This time Southby stood in the Whig interest, and was declared elected. Again Stonehouse appealed, and on 8 January 1690 won his seat.[49] He would have less than three weeks to enjoy his victory, since the parliament was dissolved on 27 January.

With the events of 1688-9, the world had changed for Abingdon as for the country as a whole. A Dutch king knew instinctively how to deal with towns and cities, and there would be no further attempts at 'regulating' charters and corporations. The Toleration Act of 1689 removed a major source of irritation in local political life. Protestant Dissenters were freed from the threat of prosecution, without being legally allowed into the political process. For most of them, it was no doubt enough, and the others would find ways around the law. In June 1689, before William Foster as mayor and Thomas Medlicott as recorder, fifty-five Presbyterians and Baptists took the new oaths of allegiance to William and Mary and an additional one to the effect that they did not believe in transubstantiation nor in the invocation of the Virgin Mary. Four Quakers added their marks or signatures, as they were now permitted to do.[50]

But the next mayor, James Corderoy, was a Tory. In October 1689, the corporation dismissed Medlicott from the position of recorder in favour of the rising young lawyer Sir Simon Harcourt from nearby Stanton Harcourt. Harcourt had the support of Rowland Holt, son of the Thomas Holt who had been recorder and MP for Abingdon in the 1650s, and brother of the future Chief Justice, John Holt.[51] He would represent Abingdon in parliament from March 1690 until 1705; he would become Lord Chancellor, and die a viscount.[52] His was a new generation, that would take Abingdon into a new and very different century.

[1] N. Luttrell, *A Brief Historical Relation of State Affairs from September, 1678 to April 1714* (1857) I p. 331.

[2] Tim Harris, *Revolution: The great crisis of the British monarchy 1685-1720* (2006), pp 71-2. The outcome has been calculated as 456 Tory supporters to 57 Whig.

[3] Bodl., Ms Clarendon 153; BL Add Mss 15862 esp fos 215-224, 227.

[4] A. Clark, *Wood's Life and Times* (5 vols., Oxford Historical Society, 1891-1900), III p. 145.

[5] J. L. Malcolm, 'Charles II and the Reconstruction of Royal Power', *The Historical Journal* 35 (1992), pp. 307-330; J. Miller, 'The Militia and the Army in the Reign of James II', *The Historical Journal* 16 (1973), pp. 659-679.

[6] Two Bertie brothers, MPs and militia officers, lost their army commissions for their opposition in parliament to Catholic officers - Clark, *L&T* III p.17; Harris, *Revolution,* pp. 192-3.

[7] O. Sansom, *An Account of Many Remarkable Passages of the Life of Oliver Sansom* (1710), p. 367. In the next three months, some 1200 Quakers throughout the country were freed from their gaols. To the disgust of many, it was a Quaker, William Penn, who was advising James on religious matters.

[8] Harris: *Revolution,* pp. 206-7.

[9] TNA, Crown Book of the Oxford Circuit, ASSI 2/2; Mark Goldie (ed), *The entring book of Roger Morrice, 1677-1691* (CD, Cambridge, 2007)*,* P572, P576, P584; Berks Record Office, Preston Papers, A/JQz 11; A.E. Preston, *St Nicholas Abingdon and other papers* (1928), pp 136-9. The grounds for the dispensations are given, in an obvious fiction, as that the accused or their parents had fought for the king's father in the Civil War; and the document was mistakenly addressed to the authorities of Gloucestershire.

[10] TNA, Privy Council Minutes 1687/8, PC 2/72, p. 428; 'The Humble Adress of divers of your Majesties Loyal Subjects, Nonconforming Ministers and their Hearers, in and about your Majesties Corporations of Reading, Abington and Newbury in the County of Berks', *London Gazette,* 12-15 Sept 1687; 'From the Anabaptists in Oxford, Abingdon and Wantage and places adjacent in the Counties of Oxford and Berks', *London Gazette,* 10-13 November 1687.

[11] TNA, Crown Office Docquet Books C 231/8 p. 166

[12] HMC 79 *Lindsey Ms,* p. 270-2

[13] *CSPD* June 1687-Feb 1689, No 545 (21 Nov 87).

[14] R. A. Beddard, 'James II and the Catholic Challenge', in N. Tyacke (ed), *History of the University of Oxford* (Oxford, 1997), iv, pp. 803-954, esp pp. 907-14.

[15] Clark, *L & T* iii pp. 207, 219. Hobson, *Oxford City Acts 1665-1701,* p. xxv. He was installed as high steward by the Oxford recorder, William Wright, son of the Whig alderman of that name who had been an abject victim of his earlier activities. He was now 'the City's darling' - Bodl., Ms Top Oxon c. 325 fos. 20, 21, 24, 38, 68.

[16] BRO, D/A2 c.163 fos. 9-13; Bodl., Return to commissioners by Chancellor Woodward, Ms Tanner 143, fo. 272 ff.

[17] Harris, *Revolution* p. 197.

---

[18] Above, p. 139; Bodl., Bp Fell to Archbp Sancroft, (22 Aug 1683), Ms Tanner 143, fo 117.

[19] ATCA, Corporation minutes ii fos. 47v, 48; BRO, A/AOzc fo. 1.

[20] ATCA manuscripts; TNA, Privy Council Records, PC 2/72, pp 542, 561.

[21] The Baptists were John Fountaine, Robert Payne, William Wiles, John Tull, John Tomkins, Arthur Hearne, Philip Lockton and probably also Richard Pleydell and John Stevenson; the Presbyterians Charles Hughes, snr and jnr. Several of the others may also have been of those denominations. See BL, Richards collection, Ms Add 24666 fo. 340 for a more complete list than in the Corporation minutes, and A.E. Preston's transcript of the 1689 oath-taking against transubstantiation in BRO A/JQo13. The Catholic was William Weston – Mieneke Cox, *Peace and War* (Abingdon, 1993), p. 146.

[22] Clark, *L&T* iii p. 191; see also Harris, *Revolution*, pp 206, 217.

[23] Manfred Brod, *The Case of Reading: urban governance in troubled times* (2006), p. 94; ATCA, Corporation minutes ii 47v, 48.

[24] 'Humble address of the Mayor and Aldermen etc of Abingdon', *London Gazette,* Thu 16 Feb 1688

[25] Bodleian, Ms Rawlinson A 239B, fos. 187 ff; TNA, PC 2/72 , p. 727.

[26] ATCA, Corporation minutes, ii fo 54 (6 Sept. 1688). Richard Southby had first sat in the Protectorate Parliament of 1654.

[27] S.G. Duckett, *Penal Laws and Test Acts: Questions Touching Their Repeal Propounded in 1687-8 by James II* (1882), p. 237.

[28] ATCA, Corporation minutes, ii 53v (15 Aug 1688); Bodleian, Ms Rawlinson A 239B, fos. 187 ff; *CSPD* June 1687-Feb 1689, No. 1354 (9 Aug 1688), No. 1501 (15 Sept 1688); Goldie, *Roger Morrice,* Q121, Q239, P584 .

[29] Brilliantly deconstructed by the Earl of Halifax in his *Letter to a Dissenter* (1687): 'You are therefore to be hugged now only that you may be the better squeezed at another time'.

[30] ATCA, Corporation minutes, ii 50, 52, 52v. On the County Hall, which had opened for business in 1682, see Peter Gale, *Pride of Place: The story of Abingdon's County Hall* (Oxford, 2006).

[31] ATCA, Corporation minutes, ii 48v, 49v; 50v; TNA, PC 2/72 p. 612

[32] ATCA, Corporation minutes, ii 51v, 52v.

[33] TNA, PC 2/72 , pp. 738, 748.

[34] ATCA, Corporation minutes, ii 54v, 56, 58; ATCA, Mayors' Book, 95, 102. Foster had been mayor at James's accession, and it may be that the Corporation had decided on a constructive misreading of the proclamation.

[35] ATCA, Corporation minutes, ii 56; *London Gazette,* 16-28 Dec 88; Anchitell Grey, *Grey's Debates in the House of Commons: volume 9* (1769), (15 March 1689).

[36] Grey, *Debates in the House of Commons,* 9 (5 March 1689).

[37] J.H. Plumb, 'The Elections to the Convention Parliament of 1689', *Cambridge Historical Journal,* 5 (1937), pp. 235-254. at pp 238-9; Brod, *The Case of Reading* , p. 99.

[38] J. Carswell, *The Descent on England: a Study of the English Revolution of 1688 and its European Background* (1969), p. 192

[39] Although during the years of Danby's disgrace, he had attached himself to the Earl of Halifax, who equally supported William − R. Pickavance. 'The English Boroughs and the King's Government: A Study of the Tory Reaction 1681-85.' Unpub DPhil thesis, Oxford University (1976), p. 192.

[40] S.W. Singer, *The Correspondence of Henry Hyde, Earl of Clarendon and* .... *Rochester* (1828) ii p. 215.

[41] Eveline Cruickshanks, David Hayton, Clyve Jones, 'Divisions in the House of Lords on the Transfer of the Crown and Other Issues, 1689-94: Ten New Lists', *Historical Research,* 53 (1980), pp. 56-87; Bodl., Ms Eng Hist c.299.

[42] Bodl., Draft(?) of a letter Clarendon to Mary, London, (Jan 20 1689), Ms Clarendon 9, fos 11-20. The complex debates that led to William and Mary sharing the throne but with William exercising the royal power are described in numerous standard textbooks, e.g. Harris, *Revolution,* pp. 308-63

[43] BL, Addl Ms 18675 passim

[44] Macaulay, *History of England to the death of William III* (1967 edn) ii 184.

[45] *HoP 1660-1690* i 130.

[46] BL, Addl Ms 18675 fo. 49.

[47] *CJ* x (26 Jan, 7 May 1689).

[48] Philip Yorke, E. of Hardwicke (ed), *Miscellaneous State Papers 1501-1726* (1778) ii 412, 423; 'Debates in 1689: February 13th-20th', *Grey's Debates* 9 (1769), pp. 83-106.

[49] *CJ* x (3 June 1689, 31 Oct 1689, 8 Jan 1690).

[50] Berks RO, A/JQo 13. These must have been only a relatively small proportion of the total number of Dissenters. A generation later, the Abingdon Baptist 'auditory' alone numbered between 300 and 400 − Michael Hambleton, *The Story of the Abingdon Baptist Church 1649-2000* (2000), p. 28.

[51] BL, R. Holt to Robert Blackaller, Richards Collection, Addl Ms 28666, (9 October 1689),.

[52] Mieneke Cox, *Abingdon, an 18th century country town* (Abingdon, 1999), pp. 36-7, 43-4; Stuart Handley, 'Harcourt, Simon, first Viscount Harcourt (1661?–1727)', *DNB*. Harcourt was a grandson of that William Waller whose troops had occupied Abingdon in May 1644 and demolished the market cross.

13. Conclusions

Anthropologists speak of liminality, that state of non-being when the old is no more and what is to come is still unknown. It was in that condition that we found Abingdon in 1548, at the start of our study. As former monastic property, it was now subject to no lord but the king, and the king plainly had no intention of keeping it. Much had been sold, and the rest might be alienated en bloc to anyone with enough money at any time. The principal corporate expression of the town community, the Fraternity of the Holy Cross, had brusquely been dissolved. We have no indication of the state of mind of the townsfolk, but a degree of existential anxiety would have been natural. As we saw, the crisis was quickly overcome, and a new phase in the town's history began with two charters constituting respectively the Hospital and the town's corporation. At the end of 1688, those charters, little changed, still gave legal definition to the town. And yet, Abingdon in 1688 was a very different political entity from what it had been four or five generations previously. It was no longer possible to recount its history in isolation; rather, the later chapters of this study have had to start by describing aspects of contemporary national politics and then zoom in to focus on Abingdon's part in them. The aim of this concluding chapter will be to recapitulate the town's history through our chosen period, and to highlight and understand the most significant changes as they occurred.

The sixteenth century had conceptual difficulties with towns. It was understood that they were important to governments as sources of financial wealth which could be borrowed or taxed. No doubt in recognition of this, they, rather than the shires, sent the greater proportion of members to the House of Commons. It was also understood that they were dangerous; it was in towns that murmurings could most easily turn to riot and riot to insurrection. And yet there was a great reluctance to say very much about them. Mason's friend Sir Thomas Smith, in his *Discourse on the Commonweal,* was concerned with their productive function and the need to keep this harnessed and controlled in the public interest. But in his later *De Republica anglorum,* which purports to be a straight description of the working of contemporary government, towns are dismissed in a few lines which do, nonetheless, express their anomalous status. In towns, men who are sufficiently wealthy may be regarded almost as gentlemen, even if elsewhere they would not be:

> Next to Gentlemen be appointed Citizens and Burgesses, such as not onely be free, and receiued as officers within the Cities, but also be of some substance to beare the charges. But these Citizens and Burgesses, be to serue the common wealth, in their cities and burrowes, or in corporate townes where they dwel. Generally in the shires they be of none account ...

Even artisans in towns take up functions which would not otherwise be open to them:

> ... all Artificers, as Taylers, Shoomakers, Carpenters, Brickmakers, Bricklayers, Masons, &c. These haue no voyce nor authoritie in our Commonwealth, and no account is made of them but onely to be ruled, not to rule other, and yet they bee not altogether neglected. For in Cities and corporate townes for default of yeomen, enquestes and Juries are impaneled of such maner of people ... [1]

One function of the charter was to resolve the anomaly by bringing the town into an accepted legal framework. In line with Smith's description, the townsmen were divided into two general classes: burgesses – including the burgess to be sent to parliament – and 'Men of the Inferior sort in the said Borough, Inhabitants'. These would roughly equate, in current social thinking, to gentlemen and yeomen or husbandmen in the country. The former might be 'received as officers'; the latter 'to be ruled', yet 'not altogether neglected'.

The English state in Smith's time was still at an early stage of its long evolution towards the dense tangle of prescription, control and influence that is its twenty-first century form.[2] His snapshot description of its workings was limited to the formal structures of parliament and the law; the political actors he described were qualified by commissions or patents What will have been so obvious to contemporaries that it needed no comment was that influence and authority were functions of personal and usually territorially-bounded status, and that the commissions of sheriffs, justices, or lords lieutenant were confirmations as much as they were conferrals of such status. It was occasions like assizes and sessions that were the great clearing houses of regional politics; men of the political class in its widest definition, from the merest petty constable to the judge of assize or the great territorial magnate, would come together; the wishes of central government would be transmitted downwards, suitably tailored for local consumption; local problems and preoccupations would be noted and, again suitably tailored, transmitted upwards. The problem for towns was their exclusion from such events. Burgesses were 'of none account' in the shires. Parliaments, in principle, would fulfil the same role and the towns would be represented, but they were on too large a scale, held too infrequently, and, as we have seen, the 'burgesses' that attended were often outsiders to the towns that nominally sent them.

Hence the importance to towns of magnate patronage, whether as high stewards or in a less formal relationship. John Mason performed this function admirably, using his position on the Privy Council to obtain Abingdon's two charters on what appear to be remarkably advantageous terms. Neither the leading townsmen nor Roger Amyce could have achieved this by themselves. But this was the time when Mason was at the peak of his political influence; he was owed favours by the Duke of Northumberland for switching support to him from Somerset at the optimum time, and by Mary for his switch from Northumberland to her. There is no record of any services he rendered Abingdon after the grant of the charter and the promulgation of his rules for the Hospital. Abingdon moved into a period of its history when support from outside was consistently either lacking or unhelpful. At Mason's death, the Earl of Leicester moved fast to replace him as high steward, but it would take the corporation another fifteen years to recognise his status to the extent of paying him for his services. Leicester's motive would seem to have been the consolidation of his otherwise weak territorial influence, especially over the nomination of members of parliament, rather than any benefits he could bestow on the town or receive from it. Francis Little was always keen to commemorate benefactions, but found nothing to say about Leicester. His main legacy would seem to have been the religious factionalism that begins to be visible in the 1580s, and there are indications that he patronised the Tesdale family who were always at the heart of the Puritan grouping.

From Leicester's time onward, Abingdon often shared its high steward with other towns in Berkshire and Oxfordshire – Reading almost always, Wallingford, Oxford, and even Banbury on occasion. Only once before the Restoration period is there clear evidence of a high steward performing the sort of service that might have been expected; this is in 1610 when William, Lord Knollys was instrumental in the charter revision that extended the town's legal prerogatives and worked, by its promotion of Walter Dayrell to the office of recorder, in favour of the Little and Mayott party and against the Tesdales. Knollys was no fool, and it must be assumed that he understood the implications of what he was doing.

However, when conflict developed in the 1580s in the corporation and in the Hospital, the parties had no patron to turn to. The relationship with Leicester was apparently not good. He died in 1588. He may have been replaced by Sir Henry Norris, but this is not certain and there is no sign of any action Norris may have taken on the town's behalf. There was so little magnate involvement with Abingdon in the 1590s that the corporation was left to send its own members to parliament; it is not clear whether they were happy at this or regretted the cost and the time spent away from their private affairs. In the later 1590s, Francis Little twice found it necessary to appeal to Lord Egerton, who was Lord Keeper and head of Chancery. This may have been a decision based on legal advice, since Chancery was the court that decided matters of custom, and the question to be asked was whether a particular election had been according to the rules. But no petition in the usual form can now be found, and the surviving documents make it seem that the appeals were by informal contact. Egerton was implicitly being asked to fill the office of visitor to the Hospital that Mason's rules had provided for but had not set up. One possibility is that Knollys served as an intermediary; he was close to Egerton, who was adviser to the Earl of Essex, his nephew.[3] However the matter came to his attention, Egerton set up the usual commissions of local gentlemen, including in each case at least one prominent lawyer, which vindicated Little. The next petition to higher authority would be from the Tesdale side and would be to the Privy Council rather than to Chancery. It may be relevant that one of the current clerks of the Privy Council was an Abingdon man, Thomas Smith, son of the recent Abingdon mayor and hospital master of the same name, sometime a protégé of Leicester, and apparently of Puritan opinions in religion.[4] Later, and until the Civil War, the Privy Council would tend to the opposite view, and it was to that institution that the Mayotts and their party too often appealed. It is indicative of the limitations of the Tudor and early Stuart state that matters of such relatively minor local importance should have to be dealt with at such a high level.

The 1590s was a period of epidemics and high prices, with social unrest throughout the country. Not coincidentally, it was a time of increasing pressure from central government on local authorities, mainly in the form of legislation calling on them to preserve employment, repress vagabondage, and care for the poor.[5] Inflation of money values meant that more people than before were expected to contribute to local funds, and perhaps that more achieved levels of nominal income where they would be expected, or might expect, to take on the burdens of local office.[6] Decisions of the corporation and of the Hospital governors could make or break individuals and households. We do not know what trouble there was on the streets of Abingdon, nor exactly how this was linked with the faction fighting in the council chamber. But the new 'chapters' that Little and his successors introduced into the working of the Abingdon corporation show that the 'inferior sort, inhabitants' who should have had 'no voyce nor authoritie' were finding at least the first of these, and that the corporation, or a majority of its members, was not in favour. Francis Little, as we have seen, had his own platonic ideal of how a town council should work, and was no democrat. Abingdon joined a general trend towards the reinforcement of urban oligarchy and the recruitment of corporation members exclusively by co-option.[7]

The 'increase of governance' of the late Elizabethan period would continue under the Stuarts. It was not so much that offices and institutions were multiplied or reformed; rather that there was increased insistence on functional competence and efficiency.[8] The Abingdon charter revision of 1610 may be seen as an example. It rewarded the town with economic advantages and a new lucrative office, the recordership, that the corporation could henceforth award at its pleasure. But at the same time it named three outsiders to the town bench of justices. This must be seen as a positive development for the town, permitting a closer coupling of local with central preoccupations. Two of the new JPs were judges, and judges were traditionally among the points of contact between central government and the rulers of the localities. It is unlikely that Parry and Williams will ever have wanted to sit in the local magistrates' court, but they will have served as a source of information and advice for the new recorder Walter Dayrell, and through him for the mayor and corporation.[9] Their nomination may well have been among the corporation's requests, and will certainly have been greeted with satisfaction.

The structure of the Tudor state is hard for the modern reader to comprehend. It has been described as a network which was 'integrated and weakly centralised', meaning that the centre was responsive to the localities, finding out what they wanted and ordering them to do it. 'While Elizabeth lived, it worked'.[10] It still worked, if less well, under James I. But it did require a broad agreement between the centre and the provincial rulers on what was meant by good governance – general peace and quiet, dissent muted, opposition repressed, taxes low. Little's 'chapters' express a late sixteenth century ideal. Elizabeth's forceful actions against the Puritans – the suspension of Archbishop Grindal, the promotion of Whitgift – inhibited the development of an alternative conception. To the Puritans, the purpose of government was not to preserve but to improve society. It was a sure recipe for division and disorder. Charles I was the most inept of rulers and his choice of advisers catastrophic, but it is hard to see how disaster could have been avoided when every town and village might have its Edward Roode and its Christopher Newstead, its Tesdales and its Mayotts. Abingdon by 1641 was the whole realm in microcosm, and both town and realm were in more trouble than they probably realized.

Charles and his advisers were not interested in a 'weakly centralised' polity. The centre was to command, local office-holders to enforce. But in reality the localities decided for themselves which commands would be obeyed; traditional measures to mitigate the effects of trade depression or food shortages were accepted; non-parliamentary taxes were refused and military conscription side-stepped. The parliamentary elections of 1640 were the first where ideology was a major deciding factor, and the fiascos of the Bishops' Wars must have totally discredited Caroline government. The battlefield of Newburn was far in the north, but the Abingdon militiamen who had to march to Wadley to confront the rabble that were the best the king could recruit will have learnt a political lesson that would still be remembered two years later.

Thus by 1642 opinions in Abingdon must have shifted under the influence of events. But until then the town was still under its own government within the terms of its charter. With the coming of the Civil War, this changed. The first breach in its liberties was the summoning of the mayor and the serjeant to the House of Commons for a tongue-lashing from the Speaker, for the crime of posting a proclamation from the king they all claimed to serve. What will have made it worse was that the Speaker was William Lenthall, who had property in the vicinity and whom they must have known well.[11] The second breach was made in the next year by the king's chief justice, Sir Robert Heath, when he ordered the removal from the corporation of the man who had reported them to parliament, William Castell. Under war conditions, the charter was effectively in suspense. There were further purges, which may well have been carried out by corporation members themselves, but probably under pressure from outside. Under parliamentarian rule, a county committee was supreme over towns and rural areas alike, and corporation members found themselves either ex officio or in their own right members of this or its subsidiary bodies. No longer was it the case that burgesses were 'of none account' in the shire. Later, a plethora of institutions developed with national or regional remits. Towns like Abingdon ceased to be administratively isolated from the surrounding region. Abingdon men joined in making tax assessments throughout the county, and in controlling the militia. They might have been recruited, although no names have emerged, to the committees that mulcted royalist or papist gentry according to the degree of their 'delinquency', or that surveyed and valued sequestrated property. Both town and county men participated in the enquiry into St Nicholas church, and were involved in the decision that it should not be demolished. A Committee for Plundered Ministers subsidised the stipend of John Pendarves, the vicar at St Helen's. When the same vicar became a sectary, he led a congregation that came in from villages all over the Vale. His successor at St Helen's was on the Berkshire Committee of Ejectors, sitting in judgement over the orthodoxy and morality of clergymen elsewhere in the county. Francis Allen, an army officer not on the corporation, sat as a JP and solemnised civil marriages.

The Restoration regime tried hard to restore the status quo ante, but the lessons of the war and the Interregnum could not be unlearned. The trend towards a greater intensity of government was not reversed. The new-fangled committees and their relatively plebeian personnel disappeared, but the familiar institution of justices' sessions took on a new professionalism and acquired an interlocking hierarchy of levels.[12] If the catastrophes of the past twenty years were not to be repeated, it was felt, there must be a tighter control. Townsmen, it was imagined, had been allowed to assume responsibilities for which they were patently unfit. No longer could they be left to their own devices, subject only to the haphazard supervision of a chronically disorganised Privy Council. The Corporations Act of 1661 was designed to put boroughs such as Abingdon under the tutelage of reliable gentry from the surrounding countryside. The corporation was purged, but it was not the intention of the new rulers to take on themselves the burden of local administration. Instead, the commissions of association of 1664 added Stonehouse and his colleagues to the town's commission of the peace. The presence of even one of them at the quarter sessions would have a salutary effect, but they also had indirect means of encouraging conformity. It was mainly in the petty sessions that matters such as the licensing of victuallers and the regulation of apprenticeships came within their purview, and townsfolk might find that their livelihood depended on keeping on the right side of the local gentlemen. Unfortunately, petty sessions by their nature were informal, and no local records seem to have survived.

Thus, after 1660, towns were not any longer to be seen as standing outside the body politic; they had been brought into it, and subjected to the same controls as the countryside. Charters and the immunities they granted could be ignored or set aside. In Abingdon, a small group of county gentry were in a position to exert authority whenever and to the extent they wanted to.

It is a commonplace that provincial England after the Restoration was under gentry control. But this period also saw the resurgence of the nobility from their political impotence in the Interregnum, when the House of Lords had been abolished and later replaced with an 'Other House' noteworthy mainly for the public acceptance it lacked. The nobility of the Restoration was not necessarily of ancient lineage, but it was one which saw its function as service to the state. It stood between the local gentry and the central government, typically in the office of lord lieutenant of the county. Stonehouse owed his local status to his relationship by marriage to the lord lieutenant of Berkshire, Lord Lovelace of Hurley. In the troubled 1680s, Abingdon found itself within the sphere of interest of the aggressive Lord Norreys of Rycote, who in 1682 assumed the earldom of Abingdon.

If, earlier in the century, Abingdon had felt the lack of magnate interest, it could now complain of a surfeit. As so often, an increase in the intensity of government showed itself less in the development of institutions than in the thoroughness and sense of purpose with which existing institutions operated. The Earl of Leicester in his time had used his high stewardship of Abingdon, as of other towns, to improve his own standing with the central government; but there is no evidence that he interfered in, or even sought great influence over, the workings of the corporation. Lord Norreys, as lord lieutenant of Oxfordshire, saw it as his duty to bring the Whig-dominated corporation of the city of Oxford round to the Tory side, which he achieved by bullying, ruining, or imprisoning its leading members.[13] He had no formal standing in Abingdon, but seeing that Lord Clarendon, its high steward, was inactive, he began to work with the Tory minority and with his main contact in the central government, Leoline Jenkins, to the same end. The revised charter of 1686, with its remodelled corporation and its freight of outside JPs, was the result. The earl will have risen accordingly in the estimation of his political masters in Whitehall and Windsor. He does not seem to have concerned himself with the well-being of the town, which was left to Clarendon's care.

Abingdon's charter of 1556, with a gap between 1686 and 1688 and a few modifications, remained nominally valid until the nineteenth century reforms; but by 1688 its spirit had departed. No longer could the town even be imagined as a closed community of merchants and artisans under the benevolent authority of the wisest among them, and even less could it be considered as standing half outside the structures of a predominantly rural society. Both town society and the corporation that represented it were riven with the same conflicts that divided the nation as a whole, and the strategy and tactics applied

CONCLUSIONS

locally were driven by central party and religious leaderships. The magnates who took an interest in the town were not acting for their personal honour and credit, and only incidentally for the town's benefit, but as agents of a state which was now more strongly centralised than ever before. They were dependent for their career progression on the approval of their political masters, and vulnerable when policy, or mastership, changed. It would be possible to write a political history of Abingdon after 1688, but the interest would be minimal. The corporation and the Hospital would continue to administer their properties, elections would continue to be rowdy and hard-fought, but local initiative had ceased. Like the generality of small towns, Abingdon was no longer any more than a small cog in a great political machine.

---

[1] Sir Thomas Smith, *De Repvblica anglorvm: The maner of governement or policie of the Realme of Englande.* (ca. 1562, 1583), Book 1, Chapters 22, 24. The book was originally written for William Cecil, the future Lord Burghley, another member of the network that connected Smith with Mason and many others.

[2] There is an extensive literature on 'state formation'. The arguments used in this chapter owe much to Philip Corrigan and Derek Sayer, *The Great Arch: English State Formation as Cultural Revolution* (1985); Michael J. Braddick, *State Formation in Early Modern England c.1550-1700* (2000); Paul Withington, *The Politics of Commonwealth: Citizens and Freemen in Early Modern England* (2005).

[3] *HoP 1558-1603*, II, pp. 80-83..

[4] Paul E. J. Hammer, 'Smith, Sir Thomas (*c.*1556–1609)', *DNB*. He should not be confused with the earlier Sir Thomas Smith, friend of Mason and Amyce, and also in his time a clerk to the Privy Council.

[5] G.W. Prothero (ed), *Select statutes and other constitutional documents illustrative of the reigns of Elizabeth and James I* (4th edn, 1913), pp. 93-105.

[6] John Guy, *Tudor England* (1988), p. 454.

[7] Withington, *The Politics of Commonwealth*, pp. 69-75.

[8] Braddick, *State Formation,* p. 17

[9] Braddick, *State Formation,* pp. 37-8.

[10] Braddick, *State Formation,* p. 19; Guy, *Tudor England*, p. 458.

[11] The corporation had spent 40s on repairing the road between Abingdon and Besselsleigh at Lenthall's request. What they got in return is not recorded – ATCA, Corp Minutes i fo. 158v (15 Aug 1635).

[12] For a discussion of 'the increase of governance' in this period, see Anthony Fletcher, *Reform in the Provinces: The Government of Stuart England* (1986), especially Chapter 4 and p. 370.

[13] R. Pickavance. 'The English Boroughs and the King's Government: A Study of the Tory Reaction 1681-85.' Unpubl. PhD thesis, Oxford, (1976), p. 202.

Part Two

14. Abingdon People

Captain, later Lieut-Col, Francis Allen

Allen's origin is unknown, although he was almost certainly from the Abingdon region. He was serving as a captain in Colonel Ingoldsby's regiment in 1644 when it transferred to the New Model Army. The House of Lords committee considering the changes wished to remove him, presumably because he was already known as a radical or Independent in religion. In fact, he stayed. At the Putney debates of October 1647, he, together with his fellow-captain Consolation Fox, attended as representatives ('agitators') from their regiment, and in his one recorded speech he advocated removing the power of veto over the Commons from the king and the Lords, which was the position of the Levellers at the time. He was with the army units that marched into London at the beginning of December 1648, and was a member of the Council of Officers that decided on the trial and execution of the king, though he seems rarely or never to have attended.

In September 1653, in the time of the Barebones parliament, he was made a JP for Berkshire, and was soon conducting civil marriages (introduced in August of that year) at St Nicholas. He was now politically active, defending sectaries and harassing Presbyterians in the county; he used his London army connections to reverse a decision that kept Baptists from worshipping in public halls in Wantage and Grove, and incurred the virulent hatred of the Reading cleric and pamphleteer Christopher Fowler for his defence of the mystical Dr Pordage of Bradfield. In 1656, he was living in Ock Street and paid 4d to the St Helen's church tax, a larger amount than anyone else in the street. He became a county commissioner under Major-General Goffe, and in 1657 a Chancery commissioner investigating the Wrigglesworth charity. By now a lieutenant-colonel and second in command of his regiment, he was purged from it early in 1660 when John Lenthall took it over. Thereafter he is lost to the record, although Anthony Wood says (unreliably) that he 'died but in a sorry condition'.

Sources: R. K. G. Temple, 'The Original Officer Corps of the New Model Army', *Bull Inst Hist Res,* 59 (1986), pp. 50-77; TNA, C 93/24; C.A. Firth (ed), *The Clarke Papers,* Vol 1 (1891); TNA, Crown Office Docquet Books, C 231/6; St Nicholas registers; *CSPD* 1651; Christopher Fowler, *Sathan at Noon*, Part 2 (1656).

Roger Amyce

Roger Amyce was born about 1515, probably in Somerset. Little is known of his family, but his father may have been a financial expert under Henry VII. His wife's father was a senior financial official under Henry VIII who by the early 1530s was reporting to Thomas Cromwell, and this was probably what gave Amyce his own entry to Cromwell's service. By 1538 he was a 'daily waiter' – in full-time employment – in Cromwell's 'household'. Cromwell was a good judge of men, and Amyce will have been one of a generation of administrators he trained in rational managerial techniques and indoctrinated with the prevailing humanistic principles of government in the interest of those governed. In 1539, he was made receiver for the dissolved abbeys of Glastonbury and Reading; he would have £40 per year plus 1% of 'issues' – presumably the money passing through his hands, which would have totalled a few thousand pounds per year. This was within what would become the Court of General Surveyors, since these monasteries had been dissolved ostensibly for the treason of their abbots and not by virtue of the general legislation. In 1547 there was a reorganisation, from which he emerged as surveyor for Berkshire in the Court of Augmentations. (Note that a surveyor at that time dealt with financial rather than trigonometric calculations.) The new position paid £13 6s 8d per year plus undefined but no doubt substantial perquisites, and he was awarded an annuity of £66 in compensation for the receivership. He could thus become a tolerably wealthy man.

In 1548, after the act for the dissolution of the guilds and chantries, he was named to the commission that was to survey and value the government's new acquisitions in Berkshire and Hampshire. Both Sir John Mason and Thomas Denton were fellow-members, although it is probable that Amyce will have been the man doing the actual work. His credentials as a commonwealthman were shown by his naming to the Hales Commission of 1548, enquiring into the perceived rise in sheep farming as a cause of rural depopulation and vagrancy. He carried out various other formal and informal tasks under Edward VI, including a valuation of the remaining lead at Reading Abbey for Protector Somerset, which the latter at his fall was accused of embezzling. He

169

had been a Member of Parliament for Reading in 1545, was an alderman of New Windsor – where he was presumably living – in 1552, and was MP for that borough in the following March and again in 1558. It was at the same time that he was working with Mason and, very probably, Denton, on the setting up of Christ's Hospital. In 1558, he was even more directly involved in the building of an almshouse in Windsor Castle, being employed as site manager, working 130 days, and claiming a modest 7s per day for himself, two assistants and horses for all of them. He also personally selected the building stone from the ruins of Reading Abbey. At the end of the work, he was treated to a celebratory meal for which the corporation paid 14s.

The Christ's Hospital charter allowed Mason and Amyce, but none of the other governors, to reside away from Abingdon. On the death of John Mason in 1566, Amyce succeeded him as Master, but as an absentee since by then he was living at an estate which by 1559 he had bought at Wales Colne, Essex. He was already an Essex JP in 1561. A letter of 1566 shows that he was accustomed to visit Abingdon for important occasions such as audits. His governmental position of surveyor of Berks must also have been carried out by deputies, but he resigned this in 1567, and passed on the Hospital mastership to Richard Mayott in 1568. Surprisingly, he reappears as Master in 1573-4, the year of his death.

Amyce never reached the elevated social status of Mason or Denton. They may have seen his facility with numbers, his technical skills, and his formal penmanship as admirable talents but essentially demeaning. However, his will shows that he was, by the end of his life, a considerable and respected landowner. His funeral sermon was to be preached by 'his good and especial friend', Bishop Freake of Rochester. One of the two overseers was to be Mr Edward Fettiplace, a stepson of Thomas Denton, and the other 'my well-beloved and trusty friend, the right honourable Sir Thomas Smith, knight, Principal Secretary to our Sovereign Lady, the Queen's Majesty'. This was the commonwealth theorist, who had found a solution for the dissolution of the ruling guild in his own home town of Saffron Walden, and had written extensively on the economic problems of towns. It is very tempting to imagine Smith, Mason, and Amyce sitting down together in 1552 to discuss the problems of Abingdon.

A son, Israel Amyce, became surveyor to Robert Cecil, the future Earl of Salisbury, and a noted cartographer.

Sources: *L&P; HoP 1509-1558* and *1558-1603*; TNA, E 315/218 fo. 59; Preston Papers D/EP7 94; A. E. Preston, 'The Demolition of Reading Abbey', *Berks Arch J.,* 39 (1935), pp. 107-144; DNB (on Smith); TNA PROB 11/56 fos 265-6; R.R. Tighe and J.E. Davis, *Annals of Windsor* (1858), i 603-7, 615.

William Ball

The great uncertainty about the William Ball who represented Abingdon in parliament from 1646 to his death two years later is whether he is or is not the pamphleteer William Ball of Barkham, in south-eastern Berkshire. The pamphleteer is plainly a lawyer and expresses opinions compatible with republicanism. The MP is likely to have been a lawyer and, in view of his working relationship with Henry Marten, was almost certainly a republican. He seems to have been put on the parliamentary Berkshire Committee to maintain contact with the London militiamen sent to that county, whose well-being was always a touchy point with the metropolitan authorities. Some of the pamphlets are datelined London, and they show that the author was acquainted with personalities in both Berkshire and London: Sir Francis Pyle, nominal head of the Berkshire Committee; General Philip Skippon; and Speaker William Lenthall. Not all the Ball pamphlets name the author as of Barkham, but there can be little doubt that they are all from the same hand. The arguments for these men to be one and the same seem overwhelming – but the clincher against the identity is simply that that the MP died in 1648 and pamphlets bearing the name of William Ball appear throughout the 1650s.

One or other of the Balls was of Lincoln's Inn and an attorney of pleas in the Court of Exchequer. What we do know about the future Abingdon MP is that at the end of 1645 he had stood apparently successfully in a parliamentary by-election at Reading, but the election had been quashed and after much dispute his Presbyterian opponent had been allowed to sit. In the following March, presumably as part of his Committee duties, he made a fact-finding tour of Berkshire and reported to Speaker Lenthall on the depredations being committed by the unpaid soldiery:

> The soldiers having almost starved the people where they quarter and are half starved themselves and for want of pay are themselves desperate ranging about the Country and breaking and robbing houses and passengers and driving away sheepe and other Cattell before the tribunes faces. Every day brings forth more instances of their outrages.

Later in the year, when Marten was able to return to the Commons from which he had been dismissed by John Pym three years previously, he commended Ball to the electors of Abingdon to replace the excluded George Stonehouse. So far as is known, he was accepted unopposed.

Sources: Bodleian, Letter William Ball to Speaker Lenthall, 1 March 1645/6, Ms. Tanner 60, fo. 491; C. Durston. 'Berkshire and Its County Gentry, 1625-1649' (Reading PhD thesis, 1977); M. Brod, *The Case of Reading* (2006), pp. 37-8.

James Bertie, 5th Baron Norreys and 1st Earl of Abingdon

James Bertie was born in June 1653. He was the son of the Earl of Lindsey by a second marriage, but his mother was a descendant of Lord Williams of Thame and was Baroness Norreys in her own right. He would succeed to this title at her death in March 1657. In April 1674, while still legally a minor, he was made lord lieutenant of Oxfordshire. He owed his early promotion to his half-sister, wife of Thomas Osborne, Viscount and later Earl of Danby, and the latter's strategic need to capitalize on the political decline of the Duke of Buckingham.

His political prominence started in 1681, with the Oxford parliament and the campaign of repression against the Whigs that it inaugurated. His task was to bring the strongly Whiggish city of Oxford to the Tory obedience. Working closely with the secretary of state, Leoline Jenkins, and with the university, he engineered a forced surrender of Oxford's charter and harassed the leading Whig members of the corporation almost to extinction with trumped-up lawsuits, arbitrary imprisonment, and destruction of their businesses. At the same time he promised improved terms in the replacement charter. Here he found himself at odds with the university, which refused to compromise its traditional primacy in local affairs. The improvements, to his great chagrin, did not materialize. Nonetheless, his struggles won him credit with the city, which made him its high steward in September 1687 and reconfirmed him in that function after the Revolution.

Against this, his work with Abingdon was almost a sideshow, but was sufficiently important to him to justify taking the title of Earl of Abingdon when he was promoted in November 1682. His relationship with the Earl of Clarendon does not seem to have suffered, and during the emergency of the Monmouth revolt, when he was in charge of military and security operations in

Oxford and Clarendon was active in London as Lord Privy Seal, their almost daily correspondence was friendly in tone.

He refused to support James II in his desire to abrogate the Test Acts, and was dismissed from all his offices. When William landed at Torbay, he was among the first of the English nobility to rally to him. But in the crucial debate in the House of Lords he was one of those who voted that the throne was not vacant. Nonetheless, he made his peace with the new regime and served it until his early death in 1699. He was never high steward of Abingdon since Clarendon, though older, outlived him. His successors, however, would be hereditary high stewards until the reorganization of 1835.

Sources: http://thepeerage.com/p917.htm#i9164; *VCH Oxon*, Vol 4, pp. 74-180; A. Crossley. 'City and University', in N. Tyacke ed., *History of the University of Oxford*, (Oxford, 1997), pp. 105-134; Oxford University Archives, W/P/R. 13; Bodleian, Ms Clarendon 153, 155; A. Clark (ed), *Life and Times of Anthony Wood* Vol III (Oxford, 1892); HMC vol 79, *Lindsey Papers*, pp. 270-2; Eveline Cruickshanks and Clyve Jones, 'Divisions in the House of Lords on the Transfer of the Crown and Other Issues, 1689-94: Ten New Lists', *Historical Research,* 53 (1980), pp. 56-87

The Blacknall family

William Blacknall, a miller, came from Swallowfield (near Reading, but a Wiltshire enclave in Berks) in 1553 and purchased the whole of the abbey precinct, in which it seems that workshops developed. Both William and his son, also William, were tough entrepreneurial individuals, aggressively protecting their rights by legal and occasionally extra-legal methods, sometimes in conjunction with the saddler and fishery owner, Richard Tesdale. In the third generation, John Blacknall trained as a lawyer but lived on his considerable inheritance. He and his wife both died in 1625, leaving two daughters of whom the younger died soon after. The survivor, Mary, was made a ward of court and a most valuable property. After various legal moves, she was awarded to the Verney family and married at thirteen to Ralph Verney. After the Civil War, her husband felt it safer to spend much of his time on the continent, leaving her to deal with the commissioners seeking to sequestrate their estates. It was while travelling, pregnant, to deliver legal papers to him that she died at Blois in 1650, aged thirty-four.

Sources: A.E. Preston, *St Nicholas Abingdon and other Papers* (1929); BRO D/EP 7/93; James Townsend, *A History of Abingdon* (1910); Miriam Slater, 'The Weightiest Business: Marriage in an upper-gentry family in seventeenth-century England' *P&P* 72(1) (1976) pp. 25-54.

The Bostock family

An early member of the Bostock family, John, was a master of the Holy Cross fraternity about 1520. His son Humfrey was a governor of Christ's Hospital from 1553 till his death in 1579, and one of the first mayors. Grandson Lionell was a governor from 1575 to 1600, twice master and four times mayor. He was stated at different times to be a woollendraper and a maltster, but eventually became wealthy enough to give up trade and become a landowner with an extensive estate in Wiltshire. However, he seems to have continued to be resident at Fitzharris. Anthony Bostock, whom Lionell expelled from the governorship, was his first cousin. Lionell's son William was known as 'mad William Bostock', much addicted to lawsuits. He also became a governor and was once master, but was dismissed for holding back his father's legacy to the Hospital. A nephew of Anthony, Edmund Bostock, was a governor 1624-43, as was his grandson William 1668-77.

Sources: A.E. Preston, *St Nicholas Abingdon and other Papers* (1929), pp 458-66; BL, Richards Collection, Add Ms 28666 fols 275-331.

The Braunche family

The Braunches were already substantial townsfolk in Abingdon in the fifteenth century. Richard Braunch, a woollendraper who died in 1544, had been a master of the Holy Cross fraternity. He profited in a small way from the dissolution of the abbey; in 1538, with two others, he acquired from the Court of Augmentations the right to the next presentation to the vicarage of Marcham. One of his sons, Thomas, migrated to London, where in 1557 he lent 40s to the Abingdon corporation to help pay off the costs of the charter and in 1563 witnessed Roysse's gift for the refoundation of the school. There seems to have been some difference in religion within the family; when a Goodwife Braunche died in Mary's time, her funeral cost the significant sum of 12s 4d, but her month's mind was limited to a pair of tapers at 4d each.

Richard's other son, William (1522-1601), a maltster and draper, remained in Abingdon. He was a hospital governor from 1557, four times master and four times mayor. One of his concerns, with Francis Little, was to commemorate his predecessors, and there is in the Christ's Hospital archives a poem apparently of his own composition in praise of John Mason. Deeply involved in the internecine conflicts of his time, he supported his cousin Lionell Bostock and bitterly opposed John Fisher and his faction. As William Braunche gent, he represented Abingdon in the parliament of 1593.

William's son Thomas (1557-1603) was a bailiff in 1586, but was kept out of the hospital governorship until 1600 by the adverse faction and died in 1603. He was never either master or mayor. Thereafter, the family seems to have declined. A John Braunche, saddler, apprenticed to his father of the same name, received his freedom in 1637, but there is no further mention in the local records. A grandson ventured to Virginia and started a branch of the family there, which still recalls its Abingdon connection. William's political mantle, such as it was, seems to have passed, with the Bull Inn, to his son-in-law Robert Payne.

Mieneke Cox gives a fuller account in her *Peace and War*, pp 49-52.

Sources: Bodl., Mss Gough 6; ATCA, Chamberlains' Accounts; and Corporation minutes; Christ's Hospital minutes; St Helen's registers; Carolyn Branch, *Branch Family History: Abingdon-Virginia-Missouri* (Missouri, 2007), pp. 10-29.

Major-General Richard Browne

Born ca. 1602 and originally from Wokingham, Browne was a successful London merchant dealing in timber and coal and active in city politics. Like many other leading parliamentary soldiers, he had gained his military experience in the Honourable Artillery Company and the London trained bands. In 1643, he became infamous for the vigour with which he suppressed peace demonstrations. After the capture of Reading and Abingdon in 1644, he was named commander-in-chief in Berkshire, Oxfordshire and Buckinghamshire, but constant friction with William Waller restricted his activity in practice to the governorship of Abingdon. Returning to field command, he also managed to antagonise Oliver Cromwell. He entered parliament in 1645, and in 1647 was a commissioner negotiating with the king.

At this point, infuriated with the Independent take-over of the Army and their abduction of the king from Holmby, he changed sides, and was imprisoned for five years in Wallingford Castle.

Nonetheless, by 1659 he was again in parliament. At the Restoration, he had the place of honour at the head of the king's ceremonial escort into London, was made a baronet, and became Lord Mayor in the same year. He died in 1669.

Sources: *DNB*

William Castell

Linendraper. Became principal burgess 1636; mayor 1638, when he also became a hospital governor and, almost immediately, master. In 1642, he informed parliament of a royalist proclamation posted in Abingdon. Ejected from the corporation in November 1643 on grounds of absence but apparently on the instructions of the royalist authorities. He returned with the parliamentarian take-over and took over as mayor when Richard Barton died in March 1645. He also died in office in July of the same year.

Sources: ATCA, Corp Minutes.

The Cheyney family

The Cheyney family were lessees of the Crown and Thistle in Bridge Street from before 1624. William Cheyney was a brother-in-law of Robert Mayott of St Nicholas, and in 1658 joined with him and others to guarantee a salary for a minister at that church and ensure its survival. He was presumably the man of that name who became a secondary burgess in 1643 under the royalist occupation and was dismissed on 11 December 1655 as 'illegally elected'. He may be the William Cheyney who became a hospital governor in 1659 and was three times master and five times mayor before his death in 1678.

Richard Cheyney 'of Fitzharris', possibly a brother, became a principal burgess in 1643. In 1647, he and John Mayott were obliged to make a formal resignation, and were immediately re-elected. He was mayor later that year, but resigned 'voluntarily' in December 1655. He died in 1659, and was buried in St Nicholas church.

A William Cheyney, milliner, became a governor in 1683 and was master in 1690; he was also a principal burgess in 1688. Robert Cheyney, one of the bailiffs, was among the councilmen removed by order of James II in 1687.

Sources: ATCA, Corp minutes; Preston, *St Nicholas;* Jacqueline Smith and John Carter, *Inns and Alehouses of Abingdon* (1989).

Richard Croke

Croke, still in his early twenties, was briefly a deputy to Bartholomew Hall as recorder in the late 1640s. He was of a large and successful legal family based in Oxford, at that time politically allied with Bulstrode Whitelocke. His younger brother, Unton jnr, as a young parliamentarian officer, had distinguished himself as a member of the Abingdon garrison. Richard would later be recorder of, and MP for, Oxford.

Sources: *DNB*

The Curten family

The name of the Curten family was spelled in a great variety of ways, but members served on the corporation and in the hospital almost continuously through several generations. Richard Curtyn, gent, was mayor in 1612 and 1626, and died in 1627 during his second period as hospital master. Another Richard Curten, no doubt his son, was noted in a petition to the privy council in 1628 as belonging to the Tesdale faction in the corporation. He was once master, but does not seem to have been mayor, and died in 1643. Henry Curtyn was an elector and a secondary burgess, but died in 1644. James Curtaine, woollen draper, got his freedom at the age of 25 in 1637, having been apprenticed to his father of the same name. One or other of them made the mistake of lending some £366 to the king's empty treasury during the Civil War, although they later managed to convince the parliamentary authorities that the sum had been only £26. It must have been the younger man who became a principal burgess and a hospital governor in 1645, and would be mayor twice before the Restoration and twice after. It seems that his value to the corporation was his readiness to lend to it; he was owed money in 1646, and in 1660 helped with the second purchase of the fee farm. He was not among those removed from the corporation by Lovelace's commission. When under the Test Act of 1673 it became necessary to swear a new set of oaths of allegiance, both he and his son, James jnr, were among the signatories. The third James Curtaine was an alderman in the new corporation of 1686, but was dismissed when it was 'regulated' by the king in the next year. He was presumably a Tory. After the Revolution, there was constant conflict between him and his colleagues on the corporation; the basis is not obvious, but he may have been suspected of Jacobite sympathies.

Sources: Corp Minutes; Mieneke Cox, *The Story of Abingdon vol 3*; Preston, *St Nicholas*; CCAM; *The English Reports*, Rex v. Mayor of Abingdon 90 ER 1142, 1143.

Thomas Danson

Danson, who was the Presbyterian minister in Abingdon from Langley's death in 1679 to his own retirement in 1692, was born in London about 1629. A prominent academic, he was a fellow of Magdalen College, Oxford, from 1652 to 1657, after which he held various parish livings but lost them after the Restoration. He returned to London, preaching at his house in Spitalfields. His move to Abingdon was doubtless encouraged by his wife Ann, daughter of Tobias Garbrand who was living there.

Danson's reputation rests on a number of controversial tracts against targets in all regions of the theological spectrum. He maintained a strict predestinarian Calvinism, which was coming to look somewhat blinkered by the 1670s when intellectual fashion was moving towards a more liberal interpretation of the doctrine of grace. His works are therefore more noteworthy for the responses they elicited than for their own merits. According to his biographer William Lamont, it was his fate to suffer at the hands of nimbler wits than his own, and he was devastatingly satirised by Andrew Marvell among others. Whether such high-flown matters impinged greatly on the minds of his flock is doubtful, and he was said in 1690 to have at Abingdon 'a great people, a comfortable Supply'.

Sources: Preston, *St Nicholas*; *DNB*.

The Dayrell family

The Dayrells are said to have originated in Lillingston Darrell, Bucks, but Paule Dayrell esq was one of the new men Francis Little brought on to the Hospital's board of governors after his victory over the Tesdale faction in 1598. Dayrell was master in 1601, but had to resign two years later as he was living out of town; he was then replaced by his son Walter.

Walter was a lawyer of Gray's Inn, and husband of Alice who was daughter and sister of two Thomas Mayotts, both several times mayor. He resigned as governor in 1606 to become Hospital auditor and legal advisor to the corporation. In the new charter of 1610, he was formally named as recorder.

Walter Dayrell's legal practice seems to have extended to Oxford, and in 1615 he was giving advice to William Laud, then president of St John's. Samuel Fell, later dean of Christ Church, was a friend. The memorial tablet that Alice had put up in St Nicholas after his death in 1628 left no doubt about where he stood in the current religious controversies: '...the advancement of the clergy being his joy, and the beauty of God's house his delight'. Such sentiments would never have been allowed at St Helen's. They also seem to have descended in the family; in 1653, his son Paule relinquished the family home at Lacies Court to Laud's friend and biographer Peter Heylyn, who had been expelled from his church livings and wanted a home convenient to the libraries and bookshops of Oxford.

Walter Dayrell started a Berkshire legal dynasty; his son-in-law Charles Holloway would succeed him as recorder, and *his* son-in-law would be Edward Dalby, steward of Reading, whose descendants would be active there into the next century.

Sources: Preston, *St Nicholas*; Cox, *Peace and War*; St John's and Christ Church archives.

Thomas Denton

There is probably no one among the personalities that figure in the history of Abingdon who has been as seriously underrated by local historians as Thomas Denton. He was the lawyer who became under-steward of the dissolved abbey in 1539, made a number of judicious purchases of abbey properties, and later married the widow of Sir Edmund Fettiplace of Appleton and Besselsleigh. But he was much more than that. Fortunately, the meticulous researchers at the History of Parliament have pieced together the whole story.

Thomas Denton was born before – and probably well before – 1515, second son of Thomas Denton originally of Fyfield but now of Caversfield, Oxon, a substantial landowner who would be sheriff of Oxon and Berks in 1526. As a younger son, he was destined for the law, and at some unknown date entered the Middle Temple. Here he came to the notice of the king himself, and was honoured with a position in the royal chamber. But at the same time he was becoming active in Berkshire; holding property in Wallingford, he sat for it in parliament in 1536, agreeing to serve without pay. Three years later, he sat for Oxford. He is listed as mayor of Wallingford in 1543.

In the king's chamber, he will have made the acquaintance of John Wellesborne, and in December 1639, within a few days of Wellesborne's nomination as steward of the dissolved abbey, he was named under-steward. He may already have been carrying out the under-steward's duty of holding local courts. His legal career was now taking off; in 1540, he was one of three prominent lawyers commissioned by the king to investigate legal education, with the intention of reforming it. The plan was never carried out, but the reports remain of interest. One of Denton's colleagues on the enquiry was Nicholas Bacon, the future Lord Keeper. He was now moving in the same social circles as John Mason himself. Throughout the 1640s he served on numerous commissions mostly concerned with dissolutions of monasteries and chantries, and in 1551 cooperated with John Mason in suppressing the local political unrest after the fall of Protector Somerset.

In 1554 Denton, together with Lord Stafford, was a prime mover in obtaining a charter for the town of Banbury. Like Abingdon, Banbury would send only a single member to parliament. Denton duly sat for that constituency in April 1554, and entries in the corporation minutes there suggest that he continued to act as its legal advisor and political patron.

All this time, Denton had been making extensive land purchases, many of them from the Abingdon Abbey estates. His wife Margaret was of a Buckinghamshire family, and he was building up an interest in that county. In November 1554 he sat as knight of the shire for Buckingham, and by then was resident at Hillesden. In 1557, he was recorder of Oxford and his elder brother John, as county sheriff, returned him (illegally) to a county seat, himself sitting for Banbury

In 1554, he was treasurer of the Middle Temple, and when he died in October 1558, he was being considered for promotion to Master of the Rolls. His will has a strongly Protestant preamble, but shows the concern for commemoration and prayers for the soul that resisted the English reformers for several generations. He gave directions for an elaborate monument which still stands in All Saints Church, Hillesden. His descendants would be a prominent county family until the line became extinct in 1714.

Sources: *HoP; VCH Oxon* X; *VCH Bucks* IV; BRO, Preston Papers D/EP 7/74; *L&P* XV; XXI ii; *CPR* Edw VI vol IV, p. 392. TNA, Will, PROB 11/41/77 (available on microfilm only); Clare Rider and Celia Charlton, 'The 16th century Inns of Court in Context', in http://www.innertemplelibrary.org.uk/news/conference.doc

Richard Dolphin

Dolphin seems to have been born at Pusey in the Vale circa 1626. He may have benefitted from the educational facilities set up at nearby Longworth by Henry Marten. He comes to notice about 1669 when he acted as an intermediary for Dissenters in Abingdon and elsewhere in the Vale who needed to get excommunications lifted.

At about the same time, he is mentioned as curate in Appleton, Longworth and other Vale villages, and in 1670, aged 44, matriculated as a student at Magdalen Hall, Oxford. He vanishes from the records about 1675.

Sources: E. Kitson, 'Notes on Some Rectors of Appleton, Berks', *Oxoniensia,* Vol XXVI/XXVII (1961/2); BRO, Preston papers, D/A2 c. 188; D/A2 c.1.

Henry Forty

Forty was Baptist minister in Abingdon from 1675 till his death. Born in 1615, he first comes to notice as curate of Newnham Murren, Oxon, in 1641. At some time, he became minister at St Mary's, Wallingford, but by May 1647 had been ejected from there, rather surprisingly in view of his later career, by the parliamentary authorities. Moving to London, he became associated with William Kiffin in the new Particular Baptist church and was signatory to various tracts and declarations. By 1656, he was Baptist minister in Totnes and in that capacity attended Pendarves's funeral in Abingdon. After the

Restoration, he fell foul of the heresy-hunting Seth Ward, then Bishop of Exeter, and is said to have spent twelve years in prison. On his release at the king's Declaration of Indulgence in 1672, he returned to London, and in 1675 moved to Abingdon.

In spite of his age, he continued very active, reviving Pendarves's Abingdon Association and rallying his congregation to face the renewed persecution of the 1680s. He was one of the Dissenters rescued by Medlicott with a royal dispensation at the 1686 assizes. His death in 1692 was seen as the breaking of one of the last links with the great early days of the Baptist sect, and his obsequies at Southwark were observed with laudatory sermonising and elegiac verse.

Sources: BL, Plundered Ministers, Add Ms 15671 fo. 14; Preston, *St Nicholas*; Ernest A. Payne, *The Baptists of Berkshire* (1951).

Captain Consolation Fox

Fox may have come from Staffordshire; he was a prisoner of war at Dudley Castle in 1645 and was part of a prisoner exchange. The Christian name suggests that his parents had been godly people, but such names were not common among the puritans in Berkshire. In 1559, he represented the Baptists of Wallingford at a meeting of the Abingdon Association of Particular Baptists, which had been set up by Pendarves. He first appears in Abingdon in early 1660, when he is noted as an elector for the convention parliament, but again represented Wallingford at the Association meeting in June of that year. He was active as a maltster and by 1663 was living in Ock Street, possibly (from the order of properties in tax lists) in the same five-hearth house that his former comrade Francis Allen had occupied.

In 1647 Fox had been, with Allen, one of the 'agitators' sent to represent their regiment at the Putney debates. He is not known to have spoken. He reappears on the strength of his regiment after the return of the Rump Parliament in 1659, along with Allen and with several other officers whose names suggest a deliberate attempt to pack it with Independents and religious sectaries. All were comprehensively purged when the regiment was handed over to John Lenthall in early 1660; there was a brief mutiny, but discipline was quickly restored.

Fox and his wife were frequently prosecuted for religious dissent. In 1669, his house was being used for Baptist meetings, and he was under sentence of excommunication in 1670, using the services of Richard Dolphin to get it lifted. His son, Discretion Fox, died young.

Sources: *CJ* iv (7 Oct 45); C.A. Firth (ed), *The Clarke Papers,* Vol 1 (1891); BRO, Preston Papers A/AEp 1, D/A2 c.1; St. Helen's churchwardens' accounts; TNA, Hearth Tax, E 179; *CJ*; Cox, *Peace and War*; B.R. White (ed). *Association Records of the Particular Baptists of England, Wales and Ireland to 1660,* (nd) pp. 189, 195, 203, 214.

The Garbrand family

Tobias Garbrand (Garbron, Garberon) was a descendant of Garbrand Herkes, a sixteenth-century Dutch refugee who flourished as a Protestant bookseller in Oxford. He was principal of Gloucester Hall, a not very distinguished Oxford college of the time, but was expelled at the Restoration. His first wife had come from Culham, and he moved to Abingdon and practised as a physician. He lived in a town centre house with six hearths, and in the 1661 'voluntary gift' to the king subscribed 20s, putting him in the upper middle rank of inhabitants for wealth. Along with Henry Langley, he was a member of the intellectual circle of Samuel Hartlib, which produced ideas for social and educational reform; he was a patron of John French, the alchemist, but seems not to have published anything of his own. He was a Presbyterian, and his daughter married the future minister, Thomas Danson. A son, Joshua, was among the children of Dissenters expelled from Roysse's school, in 1671. He died in 1689 and was buried, in spite of being excommunicate, in St Helen's.

Another son, John, became a barrister and in the early 1680s published tracts in favour of the Duke of York. Tobias jnr, a linendraper in London, married in 1663 Margaret Mayott, of the Mayotts of St Nicholas. In 1681, her brother Robert died unmarried in Oxford, leaving a considerable fortune, of which £600 was to go as charity to sixty dissenting ministers who had been expelled from their livings under the Uniformity Act of 1662, and by then will have been aged and in poverty. Such a bequest was unthinkable at the time; the executors refused to act, and the court of Chancery ruled for forfeiture under Elizabethan anti-papist legislation. Tobias claimed the bequest on his wife's behalf, though it is unclear whether he hoped to have the benefit of it or whether he was trying to protect it from the king's rapacious hands. The terms of the will show that Mayott distrusted his brother in law, and the former possibility seems the more likely. Proceedings dragged on for many years, until after the Revolution when the ruling was reversed.

Sources: Preston, *St Nicholas*; *DNB* (John Garbrand and Garbrand Herkes); St Helen's registers; *CSPD* 1684-5 p. 95; TNA, PROB 11/348; Mark Goldie (ed*), Roger Morrice's Ent'ring Book* (CD, 2007), P 360, P 435.

Matthew Griffith

Griffith was briefly vicar of St Helen's at the Restoration, but resigned the living almost immediately. The connection with Abingdon probably lies in the fact that Edward Roode, when he left the town during the Royalist occupation, had been intruded into two London livings, those of St Mary Magdalen and St Benet Sherehog, from which Griffith had been ejected. His crime was to have preached at St Paul's in October 1642 on the text 'pray for the peace of Jerusalem'. He was at the siege of Basing House, where, fortunately for him, he was severely wounded. When the parliamentarians stormed the fortress, they massacred the uninjured defenders, and when Griffith's daughter remonstrated they killed her too. After the war, he returned to London and preached clandestinely, but was imprisoned in 1659 for being too forward in advocating a Restoration. He eventually returned to St Mary Magdalen and died in his pulpit in 1665.

Sources: *DNB*; Preston, *St Nicholas,* pp. 179, 226; Matthew Griffith, *A pathetical persuasion to pray for publick peace* (1642); Joshua Sprigge, *Anglia rediviva* (1647), pp. 138-9.

John and Robert Hanson

William Lee was a prominent Abingdon citizen, four times mayor and four times master of the Hospital between 1590 and 1624. When he died, according to a tablet in St Helen's church, he had almost two hundred descendants. One of his daughters, Isobel, married John Hanson, from Blewbury but a citizen of London, in 1594. Two baptisms are recorded in St Helen's to 1598, and three more after 1608. It would seem that the family had moved to London and later moved back. John Hanson will have been born in London about 1600; he was a Bennett scholar at Roysse's School in 1612. Robert, born in Abingdon in 1608, followed him in 1620.

The younger John Hanson, apparently a brewer and tobacconist, took a puritan/parliamentary line; he was mayor successively in 1654 and 5, and his tract of 1656 shows a deep spiritual sensibility as well as a politic courtesy to his critics. He may later have moved to London, in which case he was probably the John Hanson who died there in 1679. Robert, at least after the Restoration, was a royalist and Tory. He was a London sheriff in 1665 after which, as was usual, he was knighted; and was lord mayor in 1671. There was always a shortage of parliamentary seats in London; in 1675 he tried his luck in Abingdon, but was defeated by Sir John Stonehouse's electoral organisation and, it may be feared, dirty tricks. His appeal to the House Committee for Elections got nowhere, and he eventually withdrew it. He died in London in 1680.

Sources: TNA, PROB 18/11/70; 11/360-1; 11/367; J.R. Woodhead, *The Rulers of London 1660-1689* (1966), pp. 81-95; St Helen's Registers; Nigel Hammond, *A Record of Tesdale Ushers & Bennett Scholars 1609-1870* (Self-published, 2004); John Hanson, *A Short Treatise Shewing the Sabbatherians Confuted by the New Covenant* (1658).

Bartholomew Hall

Hall was recorder of Abingdon from 1649, when Bulstrode Whitelocke resigned the post, until 1656. He was a friend of Whitelocke from the Middle Temple, and a neighbour, living at Harpsden near Henley. He inherited several positions that Whitelocke, by 1649, had become too grand to be troubled with, and was dismissed from the Abingdon recordership because of his concentration on the affairs of the Duchy of Lancaster.

Sources: R. Spalding, *The Diary of Bulstrode Whitelocke 1605-1675* (Oxford, 1990); *VCH Oxon* 'Texts in Progress' on Harpsden; *CJ* 10 Feb 1647.

Peter Heylyn

Peter Heylyn or Heylin, born in Burford in 1599, was an academic and polymath who was ejected from his clerical livings during the Interregnum and resided from 1653 till the Restoration at Lacies Court in Abingdon. He probably benefited from the tacit protection of his Burford neighbour William Lenthall and of John Lenthall at Besselsleigh. Although his geographical works were highly regarded, his main significance was as a Laudian and royalist polemicist and – to use an anachronistic term – spin-doctor. It is largely to Heylyn and his parliamentarian opposite number William Prynne that we owe the traditional oversimplified view of the Civil War as a struggle between moralising Puritans and debauched blaspheming cavaliers. In fact, his loyalty was always to his patron William Laud and to the monarchical ideal rather than to the Stuart dynasty; one of his publications while in Abingdon optimistically aimed to convince Oliver Cromwell to take the throne and restore the Laudian church. His influence on Abingdon affairs can be seen in the successful defence of St Nicholas and, perhaps, in the local interest that developed in the doctrine of the seventh-day Sabbath, a subject on which he had written extensively and was still writing. At the Restoration he was expected to get a bishopric but, being by then almost completely blind, was passed over. He died as a sub-dean of Westminster in 1662.

Sources: DNB; Preston, St Nicholas; Anthony Milton, *Laudian and royalist polemic in seventeenth-century England : the career and writings of Peter Heylyn* (2007).

The Holloway family

Charles Holloway was briefly recorder in 1628, Christ's Hospital auditor 1628-9, and was deeply involved in the political factionalism of the time. He was an Oxford man, son of the town clerk, and was born in 1595. He entered the Inner Temple in 1611, was called to the bar in 1620, and a bencher in 1640. He married Alice Dayrell, a Mayott granddaughter, at St Nicholas in 1624. He was a friend of Anthony Wood, who approved of him for appearing in 1661 on behalf of the university to counter the objections of Unton Croke (actually by then his son Richard Croke), recorder of the city, against its privileges. Wood nonetheless describes him as 'gravely dull' and 'a very covetous man'. He died in 1679. Wood also refers to the son of Charles and Alice, also named Charles and a lawyer, who died in Oxford in 1695 at sixty-six. This was probably the Charles Holloway who was put out of the Oxford Corporation in the quo warranto crisis of 1682. He was, says Wood, nicknamed 'Necessity' because 'necessity knows no law'. A daughter of

Charles and Alice, also Alice, married Edward Dalby, later recorder of
Reading and progenitor of a line of local lawyers and politicians. The Richard
Holloway who was sometime recorder of Oxford and Wallingford and later a
judge seems to have been unrelated.

Sources: BRO, D/EP 7/71; Anthony Wood, *Life and Times; City of Oxford;* St
Nicholas registers.

Thomas and John Holt

A barrister of Gray's Inn, Thomas Holt was recorder of Abingdon from 1656
and its MP during the Interregnum. He was dismissed as recorder in 1676 in
favour of Thomas Medlicott, ostensibly for residence in Reading, but probably
because his political views were towards the royalist and proto-Tory end of the
spectrum while Medlicott would be sympathetic to Dissenters and Whigs. He
remained steward of Reading, where the corporation was strongly Tory. As a
lawyer, he was eclipsed by his son John, who was admitted to his father's inn
in 1652 when not yet ten years old, and in his career at King's Bench managed
to please both sides of the growing political divide. James II made him
recorder of London but later dismissed him. In 1688 he supported William,
and became chief justice in the following year. His brother Rowland, to whom
he was close, wrote to Robert Blackaller, mayor of Abingdon, in October
1689, expressing the pleasure of both of them at the final dismissal of
Medlicott as recorder. John Holt died in 1710, leaving a legacy of legal
decisions of enduring importance.

Sources: *DNB;* BL Richards Collection, Addl Ms 24666, fo. 342.

The Hyde family

The Hydes were county gentry of middling status and, as a family, prolific.
They had been settled in Berkshire since the mid-thirteenth century. William
Hyde, who died at Denchworth in 1557, owned a number of estates in the
Vale. He was high sheriff in 1551, and a knight of the shire in three
parliaments. He was a cousin of John Yate of neighbouring Lyford, a future
recusant, and many of the Hydes would continue in the old faith throughout

the seventeenth century. William was a member of the Fraternity of the Holy Cross, as had been some of his forbears. His younger son, Oliver, migrated to Abingdon, acquiring through his first wife Banbury Court in West St Helen's Street. Roger Amyce noted him in 1547 as a trustee of the Guild of Our Lady; and he was one of the first governors of the newly founded Christ's Hospital in 1553. John Mason named him as his deputy, and he was Abingdon's first parliamentary burgess, serving in 1558 and 1563. He was mayor in 1561. He died in 1566.

Oliver's nephew Humphrey inherited Banbury Court, and, through his wife, acquired Northcourt. He was four times mayor between 1579 and 1601, dying in 1608. Another nephew, George, became stepson of Richard Lovelace, and the two of them sat for the county in the parliament of 1601. It was probably George's son and grandson, both named Humphrey, who were member of the second Lord Lovelace's commission under the Corporations Act of 1661. The elder died in 1678, specifying in his will that the dole to be handed out to the poor at his funeral was to exclude 'anabaptists, quakers, and phanatiques'. The younger was probably the JP who repeatedly prosecuted Oliver Sansom and his fellow-Quakers in the 1680s.

A branch of the family at Sutton Wick and at Blagrove (between Abingdon and Wootton) was Catholic. Wood notes Richard Hyde of Blagrove as saddler to the Duke of York in 1665.

Sources: *HoP*; TNA, PROB 11/39, 11/344, 11/380; Wood, *L&T* ii 41; O. Sansom, *An Account of Many Remarkable* Passages (1710).

Edward and Henry Hyde, first and second Earls of Clarendon

Edward Hyde (1609-1674) and his elder son Henry Hyde (1638-1709) were successively high stewards of Abingdon from the Restoration till Henry's death, although the father was in exile after 1667 and the son in disgrace from 1689. They were from Wiltshire, not related to the Berkshire gentry family of the same surname. Edward was the chief minister to Charles II throughout his long exile, and lord chancellor from 1658; Henry's political education came as a teen-ager when he served his father as secretary. Soon after the Restoration, the king's brother, the Duke of York, secretly married Henry's sister Anne who was pregnant by him. There was general embarrassment, but the older

Hyde was created an earl so as to minimize the *mésalliance*. It is unclear why Abingdon chose him as high steward, unless there was some thought that the position went with the ownership of Cornbury House, near Woodstock, which had a hundred years earlier been in the hands of the Earl of Leicester, or with the chancellorship of Oxford University, which had previously been held both by Mason and Leicester. He proved unable to dominate political affairs for long, and in 1667 was forced into exile by his political enemies.

Henry and his younger brother Laurence went into opposition, but returned to the centre of affairs in the late 1670s. Laurence, the more able of the two, became Earl of Rochester in 1682. Both loyally supported their brother in law, the Duke of York, throughout the exclusion crisis, although their sister was dead; they were close to their nieces, the future queens Mary II and Anne. The second Earl of Clarendon found himself drawn into some unsavoury local politics, with the aggressive Lord Norreys, later Earl of Abingdon, encroaching on his regional authority. When York acceded to the throne as James II, Clarendon became Lord Privy Seal and then lord lieutenant of Ireland, but both Hydes were soon sidelined as James developed his pro-Catholic policies and preferred Catholic advisors. When William invaded, Clarendon, with great reluctance, joined him; he seems to have believed, or wished to believe, that William would simply force a change in James's policy and then return home. In the end, he refused to swear allegiance to the new monarchs, and spent the rest of his life in seclusion and occasionally in the Tower.

Sources: DNB; S.W. Singer (ed), *The Correspondence of Henry Hyde, Earl of Clarendon and ... Rochester* (1828); Bodl, Ms Clarendon 90, fos 11-20; Ms Clarendon 155, fo. 33; Ms Eng Hist c.99.

Robert Jennings

Robert Jennings (1622-1705) was a rather paradoxical individual; it is not every schoolmaster whose career culminates in the shrievalty of his county.

In July 1651, Bulstrode Whitelocke was asked by an acquaintance, a Mr Libbe of Pangbourne, to recommend Jennings to the vacant schoolmastership at Reading. He had an appropriate certificate from St John's College in Oxford. Whitelocke may not have been aware that he had lost his college fellowship for having fought on the Royalist side in the Civil War. The job went to another man, but four years later, in the context of the intense Presbyterian-Independent conflict in Reading, the Independents were able to eject the current schoolmaster and put Jennings into his place. He proved very popular, especially, and remarkably given his record, among the religious sectaries. Six months later, with a swing in the political pendulum, the position was reversed and Jennings was expelled. He appealed, but without success. Jennings and Libbe had taken the precaution of having the recommendation renewed with Abingdon in their sights instead of Reading, and in 1657 Jennings became head master of Roysse's.

Jennings was not in holy orders, and had a businesslike approach. By 1663, he was being referred to as a 'gent', and was extending the school buildings with the approval of the corporation but as a private venture. By 1677, he was lending money to the corporation. Jennings retired in 1683 to an estate he had bought at Shiplake, and in 1694 was pricked as high sheriff of Oxfordshire although he was permitted on grounds of age to have his son carry out the duties. He died in 1705.

Sources: Spalding, *Diary of Bulstrode Whitelocke*; BRO, Reading records, R/HMC/LXI(61); Brod, *The Case of Reading;* Preston, *St Nicholas;* Thomas Hinde and Michael St John Parker, *The Martlet and the Griffen* (1997).

The Knollys family

The Knollys family traced their descent from a line of London merchants of the 14th and 15th centuries, but Robert Knollys (d. 1521) was in the service of Henry VII. Henry VIII granted him the manor of Rotherfield Greys for the rent of one red rose each year at midsummer. Francis Knollys (1512-96) continued to benefit from royal patronage. He was knighted on the battlefield of Pinkie in 1547, was master of the horse to Edward VI, and became constable of Wallingford Castle and a Berkshire JP. By 1551 he was a member of the circle of advanced Protestants that met at the house of William Cecil, the future Lord Burleigh, and found it necessary to go into exile in Switzerland when Mary came to the throne. Under Elizabeth (who was first cousin to his wife), he became a privy councillor and a trusted household official. He was used in delicate tasks like the reception of Mary Stuart when she came to England and the arrest of the Duke of Norfolk for his involvement with her, but his most important role was as parliamentary manager for the crown. He became a fixture as knight of the shire for Oxfordshire, joined in later life by his son William. His career was hampered by his extreme Protestant views, frequently unwelcome to the queen, but he was able to amass large landholdings especially in Berks and Oxfordshire; he died as the dominant magnate between Henley and Reading.

Francis Knollys and his wife had at least eleven children, of whom the most important were their daughter Lettice (1543-1635) and the oldest surviving son William (c.1545-1632), later Earl of Banbury. Lettice became the mother of Elizabeth's future favourite, the second Earl of Essex; as her second husband she married the earlier favourite, the Earl of Leicester, whose mistress she had been probably even before her widowhood. William succeeded to most of his father's political and court functions, closely allied with Leicester and Essex in their lifetimes. He was an active patron, succeeding Leicester to at least five high stewardships. His career continued into James's reign, but by a second marriage in 1605 he imprudently allied himself with Thomas Howard, Earl of Suffolk, and in 1619 would share in his downfall. Although deprived of his functions in central government, his authority in Oxfordshire and Berkshire would continue almost to the end of his long life.

Sources: *DNB*, *HoP*

Henry Langley

Henry Langley was born in 1610, the son of an Abingdon shoemaker. He was sent to Roysse's school, and matriculated at the newly-founded, or refounded, Pembroke College in 1629 although somewhat above the usual age. He took his BA degree in 1632, and remained in Oxford as a preacher and college tutor.

He seems to have found favour in high places, because during the Civil War, when Oxford was the Royalist capital, a resolution of Parliament gave him the London living of St Mary Newington, where the previous incumbent had been driven out for his political views. But his chance to return to Oxford came in April 1647. He was one of a group of seven 'godly preachers' sent by parliament to expose students and staff to what would now be the only acceptable ideology.

In July, Dr Thomas Clayton, the Master of Pembroke College, died. The fellows resolved to pre-empt whatever changes were in store by a rapid election, and within three days had chosen Henry Whitewicke, a kinsman of the co-founder. Langley alerted his contacts. It was probably the fourth Earl of Pembroke, whose late brother was commemorated in the college's name, and who was now chancellor of the university, who on 18 August placed before the House of Lords the following missive 'from the inhabitants of Abingdon':

> The election to the place of master of Pembroke College is of great importance to them, as above twenty fellows and scholars are supplied to the college from Abingdon freeschool; the fellows intend suddenly to elect a new Master now that Dr Clayton is dead, whose virtues may not, perhaps be answerable to that place. The petitioners therefore pray that Mr Henry Langley, M.A., born in Abingdon and indulgent tutor to many gentlemen's sons, an ancient member of the College, pious in his religion, excellent in learning and judgement, and of honest and blameless conversation, may be appointed master.

Langley had a successful, if brief, career as Master. He took his advanced degrees, and added to his emoluments by becoming a canon of Christ Church. Under his rule, Pembroke became as godly as anyone could wish, and even the undergraduates are recorded as spending their spare time in religious exercises. In the wider world, with his friends Henry Cornish and Tobias Garbrand, he was a member of the intellectual circle of Samuel Hartlib, much concerned with social and educational reform. He preached, as would be expected, although opinions of his ability as a preacher tended to be uncomplimentary. At the Restoration in 1660, he was unceremoniously expelled and Wightwicke was restored.

A staunch Presbyterian, Langley fell foul of the laws the Cavalier Parliament introduced against non-conformism, and especially of the Five-Mile Act, which forbade former preachers from residing within five miles of any town. He made his home in Tubney and opened a school there for the sons of dissenting families. His career as a schoolmaster will no doubt have taken off in 1671 when Dr Jennings, the head of Roysse's, expelled his dissenting pupils.

Langley died in 1679, and, in spite of his religious deviance, was buried in St Helen's. An amusing, if scurrilous, personal description survives:

He hath a bowsing nose, standing somewhat awry, with a wert at the end of it, and little peeping eies: an infallible note of an envious and malitious person. He walks with his shoulders as other men do with their legges, one before another. He loves a whore as well as his country-man *Martin* [Henry Marten of Longworth, currently MP for Berkshire]. His belly is his God; he is a second *Marriot* [William (or John) Marriot, 'the great eater of Gray's Inn', about whom extravagant tales were told]: where he is, there is always famine, and a plague. From which curses good Lord deliver Pembroke Colledge.

Sources: Douglas Macleane, *Pembroke College* (1900); *LJ* ix p. 497; HMC, *House of Lords Mss,* 6th Appx, (1877), p. 192; M. Burrows, *Register of the Visitors of the University of Oxford from A.D. 1647 to A.D. 1658* (1881); (George Wharton), *Mercurius Elencticus* (5-12 November 1647), pp. 14-15.

Francis Little

Little was not a native of Abingdon, but became a freeman in June 1587. He is likely to have had a connection with the Tesdale family. He used both the names Little and Brooke, as did the first husband of Maud Stone, who afterwards became the wife of the Thomas Tesdale who was the effective patriarch of that clan. Edward Little had hanged himself in 1566. But the name of Little does not appear in the wills of either Thomas or Maud Tesdale, nor indeed in any other Tesdale will that survives. It seems unlikely, therefore, that he was a son of Maud, and more probable that he was a more distant relation.

Little was made a secondary burgess only three months after attaining the freemanship, and immediately became the bailiff selected by the outgoing mayor, Lionell Bostock. Principal burgess in 1589, his first spell as mayor started in 1592, and in the same year he became a governor of Christ's Hospital, of which he was master in 1596. He was Abingdon's MP in the parliament of 1597-8.

His business interests were varied. He was noted as a woollendraper, and later as a brewer and innholder. He was tenant of The Two Brewers in Stert Street and the White Hart, where the Old Gaol would later stand. He also held several leases in St Nicholas parish, mostly from members of the Blacknall family, residing in the former vicarage at the east end of the St Nicholas chancel. He seems to have made a career out of leasing properties, often from the borough, improving them, and then cashing in on the improvements by exchanging the leases for better ones. Such practices would obviously lend themselves to exactly the sort of accusations of corruption that were being made by both sides in the conflicts of the late sixteenth century. There were also property transactions further afield; one at Appleton in 1616 seems to show him as not over-scrupulous in his dealings, and opposed him in consequent lawsuits to Richard Wightwick, the future co-founder of Pembroke College.

In August 1631, after over forty years of service, Little was given peremptory notice of expulsion from the corporation, on the grounds that he was 'dysabled in estate' and that he had not been carrying out his duties. He died in the following January.

Sources: AE Preston, *Christ's Hospital, Abingdon* (1929); A. C. Baker, *Historic Abingdon: Parliamentary History* (Abingdon, 1963); Preston, *St Nicholas; VCH.*

Henry Marten

Marten was a knight of the shire for Berkshire in the Long Parliament, and highly influential in Abingdon. It will have been in Abingdon that he was elected in 1640, and he was able in 1646 and 1649 to secure the election of his friends, Ball and Neville, to the borough seat.

Marten's father, Sir Henry, was a leading civil lawyer who made a fortune in the church courts and in the court of admiralty. He bought a number of estates in north-west Berkshire, near his Catholic kin, the Yates of Lyford. Henry was brought up in London and in Longworth, and when he came to adulthood was given Becket House, near Shrivenham, as a home of his own. By the time Sir Henry died in 1641 his son was a professional politician in London, and although he moved his family to Longworth, he himself never lived there.

Marten was a great parliamentarian, a master of wit and repartee. He was leader of the 'fiery spirits' in the Commons who saw the struggle as one to bring England into line with the ideals of the Roman republican writers. His greatest influence was in the period of the Commonwealth, 1649-1653, when he could imagine the sovereign unicameral parliament as equivalent to the Roman senate in its most glorious phase; and he was never reconciled to the rule of Cromwell as military dictator. He had been an enthusiastic regicide in 1649, and was duly condemned to death by the Cavalier Parliament. However, he had never carried political opposition into the personal sphere, and could call in sufficient favours in the restored House of Lords (which he had abolished) for the sentence to be commuted to life imprisonment.

Marten had an unfortunate reputation as an inveterate womaniser, but this was largely political caricature. It is true, however, that he left his second wife and the children of his two marriages to remain at Longworth, while he lived in London, apparently very happily, with a lady he wasn't married to. The abandoned wife, according to some writers, was a daughter of the first Baron Lovelace, which would make him a brother in law to George Stonehouse. It is certainly the case that the Lovelace family helped support him in his imprisonment. He died in 1680 at Chepstow Castle, where he had been confined.

Sources: C. M. Williams, 'The Political Career of Henry Marten' (Unpub. DPhil thesis, Oxford, 1954); Sarah Barber, *A Revolutionary Rogue: Henry Marten and the English Republic* (2000); A.L. Rowse, 'Henry Marten, republican and regicide' in *Four Caroline Portraits* (1993).

Sir John Mason

Probably no other native of Abingdon has ever climbed as high up the political pole as John Mason, and since that pole in his time was perhaps more greasy than in most, the fact that he died of natural causes is evidence of a significant achievement.

His origins are remarkably cloudy. He was born about 1503. There is general agreement that his mother was sister of a monk at Abingdon Abbey, but nothing is known of a Mr Mason beyond a vague statement that he was a cowherd. The mother would have a second family with the surname Weekes or Wykes. The last abbot, Thomas Rowland or Pentecost, saw to his education. There were certainly rumours after the Dissolution that the abbot had lived in incest with his sisters and had fathered children with them. The coat of arms that Mason eventually acquired is unusually uninformative on his genealogy. Whatever the truth, it is now unlikely to emerge.[*]

---

[*] There is a letter, in Latin, from the abbot to Mason, dated 20 March 1533. In a transcript, it seems to be avuncular in tone, and to speak of his father as living but also of his widowed mother. But the original is so blotched and faded that it is mostly unreadable and the transcription must be approached with extreme scepticism. The letter is TNA, SP 1/75 f.33, and the transcript is in *L&P* Vol IV, p. 114. Hurd, *Sir John Mason 1503-1566* (Abingdon, 1975), pp. 3-4, gives a translation.

Mason's first patron after studies at Oxford was Sir Thomas More, who started his training for a diplomatic career and sent him abroad to learn languages. At More's fall he showed for the first time the survival skills that would be brought into use several times during his later career, moving easily from the ambit of the disgraced chancellor into that of his supplanter, Thomas Cromwell. When Cromwell went to the block in 1540 he was brought back from an embassy and briefly imprisoned; but his abilities were in demand and he soon returned to governmental service as a clerk to the privy council and in various other administrative roles. At the accession of Edward VI he was knighted and soon after became a privy councillor in his own right; but he carefully chose his time to abandon Protector Somerset, continued to prosper under Northumberland, and duly deserted him in his turn to take up the cause of Mary against Lady Jane Grey. Mary made him comptroller of her household, a post in which he continued under Elizabeth. Throughout the time, he was frequently abroad on diplomatic embassies. He died in 1566.

Mason owed his successful career to a fortunate combination of business and social skills. He frequented the humanist circles that were a feature of the intellectual life of the time, notably that around William Cecil, the future Lord Burleigh. A diplomat and negotiator to his finger tips, his conversation was always witty and pleasing, although rarely exposing his true opinions. He knew when to surrender gracefully, as when he had to relinquish his chancellorship of the University of Oxford first to Cardinal Pole and, having recovered it under Elizabeth, to the Earl of Leicester. He feathered his nest as was appropriate, but was not so shamelessly avaricious as a Lord Williams or a Sir Richard Rich. He was competent and honest in financial matters, or he would not have retained his household function under Mary into Elizabeth's reign. The sound strategic sense evident in his diplomatic dispatches and his linguistic abilities made him all but indispensible. And, most important of all, he never showed any ambition to rise to the top echelon of government, challenging those already there and braving the thunder round the throne of which his friend Wyatt wrote so feelingly. Mason, like his closer friends, was among the less unsavoury of the ruling élite in the Age of Plunder.

Sources: DNB; HoP 1509-1558; 1558-1603; D.G.E. Hurd, *Sir John Mason, 1503–1566* (1975); P.F. Tytler, *England under the Reigns of Edward VI and Mary with the Contemporary History of Europe* (1839); Sir Thomas Wyatt, *Circa Regna tonat.*

The Mayott family

The Mayotts were without doubt the leading family of mayoral status in Abingdon throughout the sixteenth and seventeenth centuries. Roger Mayott, who died in 1509, enriched a whole regiment of priests and chantry clerks with legacies for the good of his soul. Thomas was a master of the Holy Cross fraternity in 1520, and his son Richard, also a master in his time, must have been a leader among the townsmen working towards the charter. He would become the first mayor in 1556 as well as the first local master of the hospital in 1569 once Roger Amyce had stepped down. By the mid-seventeenth century, the Mayotts were a clan with two separately armigerous branches that defy genealogical analysis. One branch in 1664 refused to pay the herald, Elias Ashmole, his no doubt heavy fee, and was duly omitted from the visitation.

Richard Mayott married Eleanor Roughton in 1530; she would survive him by thirty-five years, dying in 1614 at 104 – an unusually great age for the time. They had at least six children. Through the daughters, they were connected with the Orpwoods and the mayoral Smith family of Oxford. Their son Thomas was twice mayor and once master, and his son, also Thomas, was mayor and master in his turn. It was the grandson John, mayor in 1659, who had the misadventure of being imprisoned by the House of Commons in the Lenthall affair and was removed by the Lovelace commission from both the corporation and the hospital in 1663. The elder Thomas also had a son John, who died in 1644 and who seems from his will (BRO, D/ER T154/2) to have been an industrialist, leaving his son Robert 'my right in the pottage worke with the vates and other things thereto belonging'.

But there was also a Robert Mayott jnr who was mayor in 1640 and died as hospital master in 1643, and there was the John Mayott who married Joan Payne, was mayor during the fateful election campaign of 1640 and, re-elected in 1643, also died in that year. They seem to have come from another branch. The latter John and his long-lived wife started a separate dynasty of Mayotts of St Nicholas. Their eldest son Robert, born in 1606, married Anne Winch, of a wealthy Reading clothmaking family. The first son of Robert and Anne, also Robert, born about 1630, was presumably the man who worked with his brother-in-law William Cheyney in the defence of St Nicholas's church against the godly faction that wished to see it demolished. By 1658, he owned an estate at Fawler in Oxfordshire, and in 1660 resigned as governor of Christ's Hospital because he was now living there full-time, turning himself from a tallow-chandler into a country gentleman. He was a neighbour, and would become a friend and confidential agent, of the second Lord Clarendon, high steward of Abingdon. He would be high sheriff of the county in 1682. The charter of 1686 would bring him back to Abingdon as a JP, and he would eventually return to his birthplace to be buried at St Nicholas in 1714.

Sources: CH Governors and Masters Book; Abingdon Town Council, Mayors' Book; St Helen's and St Nicholas registers; Berks RO, D/EP 7 61; Wills at BRO and TNA; Singer, *Clarendon Correspondence;* Preston, *St Nicholas*; Cox, *Peace and War*; Harleian Society, *Visitations of Berks.*

Thomas Medlicott

Recorder of Abingdon, 1675-86 and 1687-9. Born in London, 1627, and educated at Merchant Taylors, Christ's College Cambridge, and the Middle Temple. Called to the bar 1653. Little is known of his career before 1675, when he was made a JP for Middlesex. Came to Abingdon 1676 replacing Thomas Holt as recorder; the corporation paid his legal expenses when Holt sued. His appointment was welcomed by his future political opponent John Stonehouse, and he and Stonehouse worked together in 1678 on the prosecution of the half-mad MP for Milborne Port (Somerset), Michael Malet, for alleged lese-majesty during the Berkshire county by-election of that year. He was made a Berkshire JP in 1678, but dismissed in the purge of 1680 as politically unreliable. He was described on that occasion as 'of a great estate in the county' but this would seem to have been financial rather than landed. In the new charter of 1686 he was replaced by William Finmore, but was reinstated by the king's 'regulation' of November 1687. In the meantime, he made a reputation by his defence of Dissenters prosecuted under the repressive acts. When William invaded in 1688, he came out in support, and William stayed briefly at his house in East St Helen's Street on his erratic route from Exeter to London. He was elected to parliament for Abingdon in 1689 after a somewhat chaotic campaign against Stonehouse, and made an immediate impression, but was unseated on appeal. It seems to have been by the machinations of the Holt family that he was dismissed as recorder in October 1689 in favour of the future Lord Harcourt.

His son Thomas jnr had meanwhile bought an estate at Malet's old constituency of Milborne Port, which he would represent in parliament, and it was there that the father died in 1716.

Sources: HoP; *CSPD* 5 Dec 1675 and 17 Sept 1678; Corporation minutes; Medlicott family history website: http://users.chariot.net.au/~ace/0013.htm; HMC, *House of Lords* II App. 2, p. 173; *CJ* 1689.

Henry Neville

Henry Neville was Abingdon's MP from 1649 to 1653, the only one of its parliamentary representatives to have gained a solid historical reputation as a leading political theorist of his time. Neville was a republican, and on occasion a writer of politically-barbed pornography.

He was born in 1619, a younger son of the manorial family of Billingbear, East Berkshire. His step-father owned Italian books and Neville probably learnt the language from him. Any such library at the time will have included the works of Machiavelli, from which he may have imbibed the republican ethos. At twenty, he was forced into a sham marriage with a twelve-year-old heiress, intended to keep her property out of the rapacious hands of the king's Court of Wards. There is no evidence the couple ever cohabited, or that Neville was ever able to enjoy a normal married life with a wife of his choosing. This will not have endeared him to the practices of monarchy. Soon after, as the Civil War was starting, Neville went off to Italy, where he would spend the next several years making intellectual friendships and studying the politics of the various city-republics. Returning to England just in time to fight on the parliamentary side, he became a drinking companion and political ally of Henry Marten of Longworth, then approaching the peak of his parliamentary career. It was probably Marten's influence in Abingdon that got him elected in 1649.

At about this time Neville was publishing a series of pamphlets under titles like 'The Parliament of Ladies'. On one level, these were exposés of the sexual shenanigans of the great and powerful. But they were, and were intended to be, deeply subversive of established authority. The basic trope was that the wives of national leaders had taken over their places in parliament, and were debating matters of national importance. But each debate quickly declined into a discussion of the sexual prowess of the men concerned, on which all the women were supposed to have first hand knowledge. The conclusion the reader would take away was that there was no difference between the women's lust for sex and their menfolk's for power, and that both were equally irrelevant to the public interest that parliament was supposed to be furthering.

And also, that men who couldn't control their wives were unlikely to do much better with a fractious and divided post-war society.

Neville lost his seat at Cromwell's coup of 1653, and his career thereafter does not particularly concern Abingdon. He would be a leading member and financial backer of the republican 'think-tank' the Rota Club, and author or co-author of a number of political treatises and tracts. After the restoration of the monarchy, he would be forced into exile and spent several more years with his friends in Italy. His later work was an attempt to reconcile his form of republicanism with the evolving Whig-liberal consensus, and this was one of the strands that would lead, in the next century, to the American constitution. The style of political pornography that he pioneered would become a major form of political comment under the libertine Charles II. Neville died in 1690.

Sources: *DNB;* Gaby Mahlberg, 'Henry Neville and English Republicanism in the Seventeenth Century' (Unpubl PhD thesis, U of East Anglia, 2005).

The Norris family

The Norris family was based at Yattendon in the fifteenth century; William Norris may have fought at Bosworth, and Henry VII made him lieutenant of Windsor Castle. His grandson, Henry, born before 1500, made his career in Henry VIII's privy chamber, becoming chief gentleman, groom of the stool, and keeper of the privy purse. This gave him effective control of royal patronage, and was a very lucrative but also a dangerous position. His home was at Bray, and among the offices he amassed was a stewardship of Abingdon Abbey. He was a witness to the king's at first clandestine marriage to Anne Boleyn, and in 1536 shared the fate of that unfortunate queen, refusing to save himself by adding to the accusations against her. His infant son, also Henry (ca 1525-1601), had some of his father's estates restored to him in 1539, and in 1544 benefited from further grants which included lands of the dissolved abbey of Reading. By then, he had married Margery, daughter and co-heiress of Sir John, later Lord, Williams of Thame. He was strongly protestant and an adherent of Northumberland under Edward VI; when Mary came to the throne he kept his head down, but he and his wife frequently entertained the young Elizabeth when her future was uncertain, and the friendship that developed would be lifelong.

At Elizabeth's accession, he gained further properties, was employed occasionally as ambassador to France, and was frequently knight of the shire for Berkshire until called to the Lords as Baron Norreys of Rycote in 1572. He remained patron of a number of parliamentary seats in Oxon and Berks, filled by his six sons when they could spare the time from the military occupations in which they delighted. Although a frequent visitor to court, his main functions were local. He shared with Francis and then William Knollys the lord lieutenancy of the two counties. He succeeded Leicester as high steward of Wallingford in 1588, and probably also did so at Abingdon, although there is no conclusive evidence. There are conflicting opinions on the extent to which Norrises and Knollyses were in competition for local influence, but there is no evidence of serious hostility between them.

All of Henry Norris's sons were soldiers, but it was the second, John, who was to become one of the greatest generals of the age, campaigning in France, Ireland, and especially in the Netherlands. The ungovernable temper which seems to have been common to all members of the family was always a disadvantage; John quarrelled with Leicester, his superior in the Netherlands, and after Leicester's death relations with his stepson, Essex, remained uneasy. The third son, Edward, sometime MP for Abingdon, would be the only one not to die on active service.

Edward died childless in 1603. The first Baron Norreys had only one male grandchild who died without a male heir. The barony would then descend in the female line until the fifth baron, James Bertie, succeeded his mother in 1657.

Sources: *DNB*; HoP; J. S. Nolan, *Sir John Norreys and the Elizabethan military world* (1997).

The Payne family (and other Paynes)

The surname Payne is prominent in Abingdon history. At the visitation of 1664, the twelve principal burgesses included three Paynes, two of whom were also serving as hospital governors. But it does not seem that all Paynes were related. The Nicholas Payne who is noted as assisting Amyce in his valuation of guild and chantry properties in 1549 was probably an outsider. So apparently was the Robert Payne who was usher at Roysse's school from 1645 and reader and later rector of St Nicholas, and so certainly was George Payne, who succeeded Major-General Browne as garrison commander in 1645.

Robert Payne, a woollen draper, married Martha Braunche; he was mayor four times and hospital master three times before his death at the age of seventy-five in 1628. Of his sons, John was once mayor and Richard, Thomas and William were each once master of the hospital. Richard lent £75 13s 6d to the king in 1643, dying immediately after; his executor, another Richard, tried, no doubt vainly, to get it back. Francis, a maltster, became son-in-law of John Tesdale and was twice mayor. It was he who was removed by Lovelace's commission from the mayoralty and the hospital governorship, but later recanted, took the necessary oaths, and was reinstated. Another son, Robert, was a clergyman who was ejected after the Civil War from his living in Tadmerton and his canonry of Christ Church, returned miserably to Abingdon, and died in 1651. One daughter married the Parliamentarian and future mayor William Castell, while the other became the wife of a John Mayott, probably the mayor who died in office in 1643, and matriarch to a whole dynasty of Mayotts of St Nicholas.

Another Robert Payne, whose relationship is unclear, became a secondary burgess on 3 June 1650, just in time to sign the resolution for the involuntary purchase of the fee farm from the commonwealth government eight days later. It may be assumed that he helped finance it. He was later chamberlain and bailiff, but disappears from the records after 1653. He may be the Robert Paine who was buried in St Helen's in 1659. Yet another of the same name, also a woollen draper, was a Baptist, frequently in trouble with the law, and noted as one of the leaders of the Whig marching demonstration at midsummer 1682. He was put by James II on to the short-lived 'regulated' corporation in 1687. A John Payne, apothecary, was brought into the corporation in 1660; he was four times hospital master between 1669 and 1694 and mayor in 1695.

Sources: Corp. and Hospital Minutes; Cox, *Peace and War*; Preston, *St Nicholas*; Wills at BRO; TNA, PROB 11/348; CCAM; BRO, D/EP7 94; Bodleian, Ms Ashmole 851.

John and Thomasine Pendarves

John Pendarves was born in Crowan, Cornwall, in 1622; he matriculated at Exeter College, Oxford, in 1637 as a servitor (meaning he would have to work his way through college) and graduated B.A. in early 1642. Exeter College was Puritan in a largely Laudian university. He left Oxford at the start of the Civil War, presumably to join the parliamentary army as a chaplain, and appears in Abingdon after its capture by the parliamentarians in May 1644 as vicar of St Helen's and, later, as chaplain to Colonel Rainsborough's regiment which was stationed there. By the late 1640s, he was in contact with William Kiffin and the developing Particular Baptist denomination. He resigned from St Helen's and moved to Wantage as vicar there, developing personal followings in both towns. By 1650, he was back in Abingdon as minister to a separated Baptist congregation. He died of dysentery in London in 1656; his body was brought back to Abingdon for burial, and his funeral was the occasion of serious disturbances which had to be put down by the militia.

Thomasine Pendarves, b. 1618, was of the substantial Dartmouth family of Newcomen. She was a woman of strong character and a more mystical strain of religion than her husband, linked with controversial characters like the 'Ranter' Abiezer Coppe and the prophetess Elizabeth Poole. Their domestic life may have been difficult. Six children were born between 1647 and 1654 but none thereafter. Pendarves at that time was travelling extensively on Baptist business and they may have ceased to cohabit. None of the children survived infancy. Thomasine remained in Abingdon as a widow until 1671, occasionally being fined for religious nonconformity, but then disappears from the record.

Sources: *DNB*, B.R. White, 'John Pendarves, the Calvinistic Baptists and the Fifth Monarchy', *Baptist Quarterly* 25 (1973-4) 251-71; G.F. Nuttall, 'Abingdon Revisited, 1656-1675', *BQ* 36 (1996) pp. 96-103; Manfred Brod, 'Doctrinal Deviance in Abingdon: Thomasine Pendarves and her circle', *BQ* 41 (2005) 92-102; Abiezer Coppe, *Some sweet sips of some spiritual wine* (1649), pp. 39-61.

Elizabeth Poole

The prophetess Elizabeth Poole first comes unambiguously into the spotlight in the fraught month of December 1648, when, as 'the gentlewoman from Abingdon', she seems to have had a fixed status in the Council of Officers sitting in Whitehall and debating the fate of the king and the settlement of a divided and war-weary nation. She had access to the soldiers singly or in small groups, and was allowed to speak in their plenary sessions. But when, on 5 January 1649, she advised that the king should be imprisoned but not executed, her prophetic gifts were called into question and she was dismissed. The full background remains unclear. Her own theology came from the small group of Familists and assorted mystics around Dr Pordage of Bradfield, but the political aspects of what she was expounding will have been agreeable to the Levellers whose attempts to influence the army were being fended off and who would soon be driven into an impotent opposition. Who got her her entry into the Council is unknown, but a possible candidate would be the Abingdon soldier and Leveller Francis Allen.

Almost certainly, Poole is to be identified with an infant baptised in the London parish of St Gregory by St Pauls in 1622. At some point in her youth she joined a Baptist congregation, but, it seems, was expelled. One can only guess that there had been some allegation of sexual impropriety, and that her migration to Abingdon was in search of the boy-friend among the London troops sent there in 1644. If this is correct, she didn't find him, but she did become a friend of Thomasine Pendarves and a member of John Pendarves's proto-Baptist following. At some time after the Whitehall debacle, she returned to London.

St. Gregory was a centre of printing and publishing where production of tracts and newspapers was an expanding industry in the mid-century. Poole seems to have had good connections there and a flair for publicity. At one of her meetings with the Council of Officers, she was even able to circulate a pre-printed handout. In 1653, she staged an early version of a media event at the Army chapel at Somerset House. While accomplices caused a distraction, she climbed into the pulpit and proceeded to preach for more than two hours to a delighted audience that frustrated all attempts to stop her. After the Restoration, she helped to run an underground press in Southwark, and was arrested in 1668. A woman who was arrested with her was released three weeks later, but there is no further mention of Poole in the records.

Sources: *DNB*; Manfred Brod, 'Politics and Prophecy in Seventeenth-Century England: The case of Elizabeth Poole', *Albion* (1999), 395-412; M. Brod, 'The Seeker Culture of the Thames Valley', in M. Caricchio, G. Tarantino, eds., *Cromohs Virtual Seminars. Recent historiographical trends of the British Studies (17th-18th Centuries)*, 2006-2007: Sections 2, 4, (http://www.cromohs.unifi.it/seminari/brod.html).

The Reade family

The Reade family originated in Reading, where a William Rede was mayor in the fifteenth century. What brought Thomas Reade to Abingdon in the 1530s or '40s seems to have been a family relationship with Katherine Audlett, widow of the last steward of the abbey, who had died a significant landowner in spite of the ruinous lawsuit with the abbey that had needed the intervention of Thomas Cromwell to settle. Thomas Reade was one of the trustees of Audlett's will, and after the death of Katherine in 1540 seems to have inherited most or all of the Audlett estates. He based himself at Barton, just outside Abingdon on the far side of the Abbey precinct. He was a master of the Holy Cross fraternity and one of the first governors of the Hospital, but died in 1556, and none of his successors seems to have taken an active role in town affairs. While building up his interests in Abingdon, Reade continued to nourish his connections with the Reading district. One of his daughters married Richard Beake of Whiteknights, Leicester's nominee for Abingdon's MP in 1572, and Leicester himself occasionally stayed at Barton on his travels between London and Kenilworth. Another daughter married Sir Thomas Vachell of Coley; his executors were Sir Francis Engelfield of Engelfield and Edmund Plowden of Shiplake. Thomas's son, also Thomas, married Mary, daughter of George Stonehouse of Radley. Their son, again a Thomas, was knighted in 1606, accepted a baronetcy in 1619, and died in 1637.

The family owned a number of properties in several counties, and the next generation spread itself among them. The next Sir Thomas lived at Appleford and, like his Stonehouse kin, was a royalist. His twenty-year-old brother Compton remained at Barton and, according to tradition, defended it against the parliamentarians until 'it was burnt over his head'. The house was certainly destroyed in the war, and the Reades never returned to it. Sir Thomas of Appleford would be one of the county JPs intruded into Abingdon under the charter of 1686, but removed again in James II's 'regulation'.

Sources: Cox, *Peace and War*; Compton Reade, *A record of the Redes of Barton Court, Berks* (Hereford, 1899).

The Roode Family

Edward Roode, who brought the Puritan-conservative conflict in Abingdon to a head, became vicar of St Helen's in 1624. His antecedents are unknown, and there is no evidence that he had attended either of the universities. His opponents secured his ejection in 1629, but he returned in 1640 when the political climate changed. His widow would later claim that he had spent the intervening time in the bishops' prison, but this seems unlikely, since such a long imprisonment would certainly have been commented on elsewhere. The corporation gave him the lease of a house and garden in St Edmund's Lane at 5s per year and with no recorded entry fine; and when in 1637 his son Onesiphorus matriculated at New Inn Hall in Oxford the father was said to be of Thame.

Leaving Abingdon again in 1642, he was, again according to his widow Margaret, sent by Parliament to preach in Essex, Kent and Suffolk. In fact, he seems to have had powerful friends. He was given the two London livings of the expelled royalist Matthew Griffith, and also put by Sir William Constable in charge of collecting contributions in those counties for Lord Fairfax's army in Yorkshire. The actual collecting was done by deputies, and seems to have been remarkably efficient. At Roode's death in October 1643, the deputies had in their hands £611 14s in money, 631 oz of silver and 11 oz of gold, three geldings, a mare, and three cases of pistols.

After the war, Margaret Roode applied to the Committee for Plundered Ministers for a pension, and in 1648 was awarded a lump sum of £100 and a half share in a parsonage being given to a Mr Hughes – presumably the William Hughes intruded into the living of Hinton Waldrist, Berks. She later complained she had been deprived of this by the malice of William Prynne, positioning her husband as a proto-Independent. The protector's council in 1654 ordered her to get the £100 and 20s per week with arrears, but this was never paid and in the following year there was another order for 15s per week. It is not clear that this was ever paid either, and in March 1660, as one of the last acts of the Long Parliament, it was reconfirmed. Unfortunately, payment seems to have been expected to be made by debenture – government-issued paper of fluctuating and dubious value – and it is to be feared that the widow never did get her deserts.

A second son, Edward Roode jnr, was forced upon Merton College by the parliamentary visitors to the university, and finished as minister of Gamlingay, Cambridgeshire.

Sources: *4th Report of the Deputy Keeper of the Public Records* (1843), p. 193; *CSPD*; *CJ*; Venn, *Alumni Cantabrienses* (1924) I iii p. 485.

Sir Thomas Smith and the Smith family

There were, of course, several families surnamed Smith in early modern Abingdon. A Richard Smith married Eleanor Mayott of the mayoral family and, apparently, deserted her and their children. For twenty-one years from 1618, her brothers arranged for her maintenance from the tolls of stallage and piccage in the town's market. But the most important Smiths were the descendants of the Richard Smith who had been gentleman-usher to Elizabeth and bailiff of her manor of Radley before it was sold off, and was mayor of Abingdon in 1564. He and his wife Alice, née Bostock, had two sons, Richard jnr and Thomas.

It was either Richard jnr or his son, Richard the third, who was living at Fitzharris and was involved in the 1571 affray in the market square. The grandson married a Dayrell, probably a sister of Walter, the recorder. It will have been he who was on Francis Little's list of potential hospital governors who had been kept out by the machinations of the Tesdale faction, but he was a principal burgess until 1606 when he was allowed to resign as he was leaving town. He appears in the heralds' visitations of London as a gentleman of Abingdon and of the City of London.

The gentleman-usher's second son, Thomas, was three times mayor and twice hospital master, dying in 1597. Thomas's eldest son, also Thomas, was born in 1556 and will have been one of the earliest pupils at Roysse's refounded school. He went on to Christ Church, Oxford, and won the patronage of the Earl of Leicester, chancellor of the university. By the late 1580s, he was private secretary to Leicester's stepson the Earl of Essex, acting for him in a number of delicate matters that included pacifying the queen when he had displeased her, as he often provocatively did. Essex got him a clerkship of the Privy Council, where one of his roles was managing the difficult interface between the rival interests of his patron and Robert Cecil, the future Earl of Salisbury. As Essex's influence declined, he moved gradually into the Cecil camp, gaining a number of lucrative offices and marriage to a baron's daughter half his age. He was knighted at the accession of James, and seemed on the verge of a career that might have surpassed that of John Mason himself, apparently being groomed as successor to Salisbury. But by 1607 his health was giving way and he died two years later leaving a 'young fayre' widow and a large fortune.

Sources: Corp. Minutes; Cox, *Peace and War*; Harleian Society, *Visitations of Berks*; *DNB,* Carolyn Branch, *Branch Family History* (Missouri, 2007), pp. 22, 24 (on the 'unnaturall father' Richard Smith).

Edward Stennett

Some facts about Edward Stennett are uncertain. According to the *DNB*, he was born in 1629 and died in 1705, but these dates are hard to reconcile with service as a chaplain in the Civil War and with a funeral sermon preached by his son in 1695. He is listed at different times as a brazier and as a physician. The two-hearth house he occupied in Abingdon in 1663 suggests the former rather than the latter as a calling.

The question of the seventh-day Sabbath was being debated by the Abingdon Association of the Particular Baptists even before Pendarves's death. The belief was strong among the Baptist communities of the towns and villages along the Icknield Way, between Wallingford and Princes Risborough. Stennet may have been introduced to the idea by his father in law, Richard Quelch, the Oxford watchmaker and Fifth Monarchist, who came originally from Wallingford. It may also be relevant that Peter Heylyn at Lacies Court was writing on the subject at an elevated academic level, although it seems unlikely that there can have been much direct contact between the two.

Stennett was one of the Abingdon Baptists excommunicated in 1670. He moved from Abingdon to Wallingford in 1671, taking up residence in the castle precinct which had a special jurisdictional status and where he would be out of reach of the local magistrates. His house was licensed for worship under the Indulgence of 1672.

His sons were well educated. One of them was named, meaningfully, Jehudah, and fittingly became a Hebraist. Under another son Joseph and *his* son Joseph and grandson Samuel, the Seventh Day Baptist denomination developed to a peak in the nineteenth century. It still had 55,000 members in 1992, mostly in America.

Sources: DNB (under Joseph Stennett); E. Stennett, *The Royal Law Contended for* (1658); J. Hanson, *A Short Treatise Showing the Sabbatharians Confuted by the New Covenant* (1658); B.W. Ball, *The Seventh-Day Men: Sabbaterians and Sabbaterianism in England and Wales, 1600-1800.* (Oxford, 1994); *B.R. White (ed). Association Records of the Particular Baptists of England, Wales and Ireland to 1660* (nd), pp. 210, 214.

The Stonehouse family

George Stonehouse was a merchant of the staple and a financial official in the royal household who had served four sovereigns. In 1560 he purchased the lordship of the manor of Radley from Elizabeth, who had been granted it by Edward VI after the attainder of Lord Seymour of Sudeley. If he expected an untroubled retirement he would be disappointed, for in 1570 fighting broke out between his tenants and employees of William Blacknall and Richard Tesdale. The latter were penning the waters of the Thames ever higher at Abingdon lock the better to work their mills, and the traditional grazing meads of the Radley men were being submerged. The lawsuits that resulted would continue well into the next century.

On George's death the property passed to his eldest son William. Another son, James, moved to Amerden Hall, Essex, and started a cadet branch of the family. William seems to have involved himself in ineffectual plotting to put Arabella Stuart on the throne instead of James I, but was pardoned. He was county sheriff in 1606 and created a baronet in 1628. His elder son John represented Abingdon in the parliament of 1628-9 but died unmarried in 1632. The third baronet was John's brother George, who married in 1633 Margaret, daughter of the first Lord Lovelace of Hurley. George was high sheriff of the county in 1637, and was returned to parliament for Abingdon in both the elections of 1640, in which year he was also a deputy-lieutenant. Ejected from parliament in 1643, he kept his head down during the interregnum but made his come-back as MP in 1660 and retained his seat in the Cavalier Parliament until his death in 1675.

The date and manner of his dismissal from the House of Commons suggests that he may have chosen to attend the counter-Parliament that the king called in Oxford. While many of his colleagues were ruined by sequestrations and compounding, he remained a wealthy man; he was allowed by the victorious side to compound for his estates at the minimum level of one-tenth of their assessed value. In 1649, he was one of two benefactors who financed the new pound lock on the Swift Ditch by which barges could bypass the shallow waters of the Thames at Abingdon, a development that would incidentally simplify the management of his water-meadows on the far side of the river, at Thrupp. About the same time, he came to the rescue of a distant cousin at Amerden, whose dealings with the sequestrators were proving enormously costly, with a loan of no less than £10,000. And on the positive side, he may have pulled off the property deal of a lifetime when he bought a parcel of confiscated ecclesiastical land that made him owner of great tracts of Knightsbridge in London.

He was a member of his brother in law the second Lord Lovelace's commission in 1663, and by a commission of association in that year became an Abingdon JP. He sat occasionally in the local sessions until 1670.

George Stonehouse disinherited his oldest son. The reason is uncertain, but there seems to have been a scandal involving a widow, Mrs Anne Scarlett, who claimed he had married her. He denied it, but their offspring seems nonetheless to have been considered legitimate. The father took out a new patent of baronetcy in favour of his second and third sons. Thus John was the second baronet of the new creation. He would be Abingdon's MP in all the parliaments from 1675 to 1690, and it would be he who would bring in the new charter in 1686 and be named as JP in it. In his magisterial duties he would be helped by his younger brother James of Tubney.

John's son, also John, would be an MP − for Berkshire, not Abingdon − in his turn and also Comptroller of the Household and a privy councillor. James's grandson, also James, would be seventh baronet and achieve eminence as a physician and as author of *Admonitions Against Drunkenness, Swearing and Sabbath-Breaking* (1769) and other improving tracts.

Sources: *VCH;* Cox, *Peace and War;* notes by A.E. Preston and Agnes Baker in Radley College archives (by courtesy of Mr A.E. Money, archivist, 2003); TNA, REQ 2 89/51, STAC 5 576/26; *CCAM* p. 1081; *CCC* p. 1629; TNA, Close Rolls, C 54/3359/180; H.G. Davis, C. Davis, *The Memorials of the hamlet of Knightsbridge* (1859), p.15.

The Tesdale family

The Tesdales seem to have come to Abingdon early in the sixteenth century when John Tesdale was prior of the abbey and master of its school, and his brother Thomas settled at Fitzharris. Thomas's son and heir, Thomas II, married three times with a strong preference for well-endowed widows, and became wealthy. He and his brother Richard were deeply involved with Christ's Hospital. The family seems to have kept the religious piety that will have underlain John's dedication to the religious life. This is indicated by the involvement of Thomas II's son and heir, Thomas III, in the affray of 1571 on the side of the Untons of Wadley, who were known for their godliness, and by indications (admittedly inconclusive) of a connection with the Earl of Leicester through his subordinate Richard Beake. In spite of their residence at Fitzharris, they preferred St Helen's to St Nicholas as their place of worship. Thomas III became rich enough to move away from Abingdon to country estates at Kidlington and then at Glympton, and the hospital and the corporation had perforce to accept his resignation. Thomas III's children died young, and when he died in 1610 he provided by his will the £5000 that would eventually go towards the foundation of Pembroke College for the further education of boys from Roysse's school at Abingdon.

A comprehensive account of the early Tesdales is given by AE Preston in *St Nicolas Abingdon and other papers,* pp. 412-457.

The factional strife that would pit Tesdales against Francis Little and the Mayotts started with the sons of Thomas II's brother John, Anthony and Christopher. Richard Tesdale, their uncle, was a governor for part of the time but seems to have stood aside. The Thomas Tesdale of Gray's Inn who was forced in as recorder in 1628 over the prior claim of Charles Holloway was a son of Anthony, and the Lawrence Stevenson who was accused of offering bribes to ensure Christopher's election to the corporation was a son-in-law. Benjamin and Joshua Tesdale, who kept the feud going through the 1630s, were brothers, but their parentage is unclear. John Tesdale, several times mayor in the same period and in 1648, was a son of Christopher; and Francis Payne, who was dismissed by the Lovelace commission in 1663 but later reinstated, was John Tesdale's son-in-law. The names of Joshua Tesdale and of various Tesdale in-laws – Arthur Hearne, Philip Lockton – appear in the lists of those prosecuted for religious dissent in the Restoration period.

Sources: ATCA, Corp. minutes; CH, Minute Book; Cox, *Peace and War*; Preston, *St Nicholas*; Wills at BRO and TNA.

John Tickell

Born in Tavistock, Tickell went up to New Inn Hall, Oxford in 1646 as a servitor. He took his BA in 1649, and a fellowship at New College. But in 1650, in the purge of Christ Church by the parliamentary visitors, he was forced on that college as a student (equivalent to a fellow elsewhere). Some sources identify him with a 'Tecle' mentioned as chaplain of Christ Church at that time, but in fact the chaplain there was Thomas Danson (above). In February 1652, Tickell was made MA by virtue of a special dispensation from the chancellor of the university, Oliver Cromwell, presumably because he had not kept the usual number of terms since matriculation; this may be taken as evidence of service in the Civil War.

He is generally described as a Presbyterian, probably because of the company he kept on the Berkshire Commission of Ejectors and for his hostility to spiritualists like John Pordage, for whose ejection from the Bradfield rectory he was primarily responsible, and Abiezer Coppe, whose recantation he castigated, no doubt correctly, as insincere. However his published works seem rather to position him as an Independent, insisting on the rights of a congregation to regulate its own membership.

After his departure from Abingdon, he was a supernumerary minister in Exeter. He conformed, after some hesitation, after the Restoration, and was vicar of Barnstaple and then of Widdecombe, Devon, 1674-1690. He died in 1694, having passed on the living to his son, also John.

Sources: Foster *Alumni*; Wood, *Fasti* and *Athenae*; John Tickell, *The bottomles pit smoaking in familisme* (1651); Tickell, *Church-rules proposed to the church in Abingdon and approved by them* (1656); Manfred Brod, 'A Radical Network in the English Revolution: John Pordage and his Circle, 1646-54' *English Historical Review*, cxix, 484 (2004), 1230-1252.

Thomas Trapham

Trapham was born in Maidstone. He was licensed by the University of Oxford to practise surgery in March 1633, and two months later was received into the Company of Barber-Surgeons in London. He was probably already living in Abingdon before the outbreak of the Civil War in 1642, because he later complained that he had lost property there during the royalist occupation. Benjamin Tesdale's will of 1647 mentions 'my cousin Trapham'. He became surgeon to John Hampden's regiment which recruited in Abingdon, and then transferred to that of Major-General Skippon. Trapham seems to have fought in the disastrous Lostwithiel campaign in 1644, and, in the following year, at the victorious battle of Naseby. In 1649, it was he who prepared the executed Charles I for burial, making a comment that became famous: 'he had sewn on the goose's head'. Later in the same year, the newly-purged University awarded honorary degrees to a number of distinguished soldiers; Trapham became a Bachelor of Physick. A doctorate would follow in 1658.

He was Cromwell's personal surgeon on his Irish and Scottish campaigns, and at the decisive battle of Worcester in 1651. When the fighting was over, he was appointed surgeon of the military hospital at the Savoy in London, responsible for an average of 350 patients. During 1658, with an English army fighting in Flanders, he set up reception facilities for the sick and wounded at the ports, and, no doubt as a private venture, sent over £200-worth of medical supplies.

At the same time, he was becoming a leading local citizen. In October 1648, he was made a principal burgess. He was active enough in the town, although he never became mayor, but his principal field of action was the county. Under the controversial rule of Cromwell's major-generals, Trapham was one of the county commissioners and a land-tax assessor under William Goffe. Yet always his deepest interest was in religious affairs. He was a strong and aggressive Presbyterian, and a member of a committee which endeavoured to reorganise the Berkshire parishes so as to eliminate those seen as either too conservative or too radical and scatter their congregations. Among others, St Nicholas in Abingdon, which continued using the forbidden prayer-book, was to be pulled down and its congregation transferred to St Helen's. There was enormous opposition and none of the proposed changes stuck.

Trapham was also an active member of the Commission of Ejectors, which was set up in 1654 with the task of rooting out unsatisfactory clergymen. Here he was allied with John Tickell, the vicar of St Helen's. The commission was quickly captured by the Presbyterians and used as a latter-day inquisition, searching not for drunkenness but for heresy. Their record was mixed, but their greatest triumph was in their action against Dr Pordage of Bradfield. Pordage's mystical 'society' catered especially to female spirituality throughout the region, and its influence was felt in Abingdon through Thomasine Pendarves, wife of Tickell's predecessor at St Helen's, and Elizabeth Poole, 'the

Abingdon prophetess'. Pordage's disbelief in the Trinity was undeniable, and the proceedings against him were marked with anger and deadly hatred. Trapham himself drew his sword and threatened to kill Pordage with his own hands. Pordage's ejection struck what was probably a decisive blow against the tradition of spiritualist religion that had previously flourished in the middle Thames Valley.

Immediately after the Restoration in 1660, Trapham was dismissed from the Abingdon corporation; and when Presbyterianism was banned in its turn he appears from time to time with his wife in the court records, paying fines for attending illegal assemblies. He died in December 1683, and in spite of his record was buried at St Helen's.

Sources: Eric Gruber von Arni, *Justice for the maimed soldier* (2001); *DNB* on Skippon; *CSPD* 1644-5; HMC 13th Rept Part I Vol 1; Lambeth palace, Ms 985 COMM IV/10; Ms 1000 COMM XIIC/1; Bodl., Ms Rawlinson A33 f.73; Bodl., Ms Gough Berks 5, f.176; Wood's *Fasti*; Corporation minutes.

Bulstrode Whitelocke

Whitelocke's historical reputation has suffered from Thomas Carlyle's damning description of him as 'wooden' and 'dryasdust', but this says more about Carlyle than about Whitelocke. He was, indeed, much given to long-winded self-examination and preaching, but was nonetheless urbane and sociable, and a keen musician. In many of his actions he was, as a recent biographer has described him, an improbable Puritan. As a young man at the Middle Temple, he became Master of the Revels, and fell heavily into debt. After the death of his first wife, he courted a young woman whose relatives disapproved of him. He hired a gang of toughs, bundled her into his coach while his men kept her family from pursuing, and she was wedded and bedded before her angry kinsfolk could catch up with them. His third wife was a rich and attractive widow with many hopeful suitors; he swept her away to a secret wedding, and there was much nocturnal tiptoeing in the house where they were both staying as guests. His social skills were most in evidence when Cromwell's government sent him as ambassador to the court of the glamorous Queen Christina of Sweden; he became the queen's constant dancing partner, and the first foreigner to learn of her sensational decision to abdicate.

Whitelocke's father, Sir James Whitlock, was an assize judge on the circuit that included Abingdon, and Whitelocke's early experience was on that circuit. His wife, when he became Abingdon's recorder in 1632, had been born Rebecca Benet and may therefore have been related to the Tesdales, but she died two years later. His diaries frequently record his frustrations with 'Abingdon which was att this time, & too often [,] overwhelmed with different & fierce factions.' In the conflict over the mayoral election of 1634, he supported the Tesdale interest, leading to the enmity of the Mayott side. He was summoned to attend the Privy Council to account for his alleged failure to prosecute local Puritan non-conformists, but argued that this was the job of the ecclesiastical, not the common-law, courts. It was the Tesdales who initiated and supported his candidacy for the Abingdon parliamentary seat in the Spring 1640 election, and the Mayotts who ensured his defeat. Eventually, his rise to political prominence after the civil war led him to resign the recordership, but he continued to take an interest in the town.

Whitelocke was a convinced parliamentarian, but his actions during and after the civil war were often independent and principled, which made him more enemies than friends on both sides. Sent in 1644 to negotiate with the king, he went beyond his brief, privately advising Charles on the reply he should make to bring about a settlement. Charles, characteristically, took no notice, but Whitelocke himself was in danger of being tried by his own side for treason. He took no part in the trial or execution of the king, but afterwards occupied several elevated legal and governmental positions, Keeper of the Great Seal and deputy-speaker of parliament among them. The Restoration was a turning-point in his fortunes: he had to pay heavily in bribes and blackmail to avoid being excepted from the Act of Oblivion; his public career was at an end, and his health was failing. Nonetheless, his abilities and integrity continued to command respect, and he was consulted professionally by no less a worthy than Prince Rupert. He died in 1675.

Sources: *DNB* (1st and 2nd editions); Ruth Spalding, *The diary of Bulstrode Whitelocke, 1605–1675* (1990); Ruth Spalding, *The improbable Puritan; a life of Bulstrode Whitelocke 1605-1675* (1975).

The Wickham family

A William Wickham esq. was living in Abingdon in 1632, and must have been wealthy because he paid more tax than anyone else − 50s − towards the steeple works at St Helen's. He was listed as a mayoral 'elector' in 1636. In 1638, he petitioned the Court of Star Chamber to agree that he was a descendant of William of Wickham and thus his family should have preferential rights at Winchester College and New College, Oxford. The court was polite but left the decision to the institutions themselves.

John Wickham (1618-83) of Garsington, Oxon, was probably William's son. He was a candidate at the Abingdon parliamentary by-election in 1675, but was unsuccessful. He was sheriff of Oxfordshire 1682-3. His sister Martha in 1628 married Richard Mayott of the Abingdon mayoral family, who died in 1644. They had five children. Her second husband was William Finmore of South Hincksey, and her daughter Jane married William's son Richard. Their son William would be Abingdon's recorder 1686-7.

Sources: Corp minutes; St Helen's Churchwardens' accounts; CH, Governors' and Masters' book fo 25; CH Register of Ordinances; *CSPD* 31 Jan 1638.

APPENDIX 1

Abingdon Book of Ordinances, folio 13: 'Chapter 41' (see page 35)

An acte and order made by the Com'on Counsell for this Boroughe of Abingdon the xxiiith day of August, in the second yere of the raigne of our sov'aigne Lord James by the grace of God kyng of Englande Scotland France and Ireland defendor of the fayth etc. Anno Dom 1604.

In the tyme of John Blacknall gent Maior. Anno Dom 1604

An acte concerning the elec'on of the Maior and Bayliffe
ca. 41

Whereas Kyng Phillipp and Quene Mary by their lres patente bearing date the Twentieth day of November in the Third and fourth yeres of their raigne made unto this borough touching the incorporating of the same have (amongst other thinges therein conteyned) graunted unto the Maior Bayliffe and Burgesses of this Borough and their Successors. That they the said Maior Bayliffe and principall Burgesses, and Sixtene or more other persons called secundary Burgesses, shall make and be called ye Com'on Counsell of the said borough for all thinge causes matters Acte ordynances and busynesses touching this Borough and the gov'ment thereof and profitt of the same. And further that they and their successours by their said Comon counsell or by the greater or more parte thereof have auethorytie power and lycence to make constitute ordayne and establishe good wholesome honest ordinances lawes and constitutions Aswell for the better regiment govmt and gov'nance of the Maior Bayliffe and burgesses and other officers, artificers and Inhabitants of the Borough aforesaid for the tyme being howe and in what sorte they behave and use them selves in their offices and busynesses and for the victualling of the same borough for the publique good and com'on profitt and weale thereof and of the Country adjoyning. As also for the better pres'vac'on of the landes tenem'ts possessions and revenewes of the Maior Bayliffe and Burgesses of the borough aforesaid and their Successors by the said l'res patente geven graunted or assigned, or otherwise afterward to be geven graunted or assigned and for other causes and busnesses touching or conc'ning the said borough And that the said ordynances lawes and constitutions should be invio'ably kept so as they were not repugnant to the lawes and statute of the Realme nor prerogatyves of hir said heighnes hir heires or successors. **And wheras** synce the making of the said Ch're especially nowe of Latter yeres Certayne disordered p'sons within this Borough some of them neither having wherw'th all to lyve, nor yett using any honest or lawfull course or trade of life wherby to manteyne themselves, but lyving in riott and disorder offensyve to the godlie quiet and peaceable estate and gov'ment of the said Towne; Yett not w'thstanding att such tymes and place as the said Maior and Bayliffes or any of them are by and according to the p'port of the said Charter to be chosen, The said Disordered p'sons have and doe use to repaire unto ye said ellec'on and not only Intrude and make themselves as principall partyes in the said Nominac'on allowaunces and elecc'ons: But also very often tymes Do combyne and confederate them selves to no'iate, chuse and assigne such person or p'sons unto the said Offices or places as either they suppose or ymagine will more favorably tollerate and beare w'th their disorders and misrule Orells suche as for some other sinister and undewe respectes they shall like to prefer therunto, And the said disordered p'sons and their adherentes by their Combinac'ons and other practizes often tymes carry and rule the same elecco'ns as seemeth best unto them selves so as then the best and discreetest sorte of men of the said Townesmen and Inhabytantes could prevaile litle therin , But were as yt were in effect excluded as yf they had no voyces att all touching the same. And therby yt came to passe That sometymes not only undewe and unfitt elections, allowaunces, nominacions and assignations were made of the said Maiors and bayliffes sometyme p'ferring, electing and nominating suche as were not fitt, and rejecting those w'ch were fitt, sometymes in ymposing those offices and charge and burthen of them uppon some especiall p'sons more often then was fitt or p'happs then they or their Estates were well able conveniently [to] beare. But also as in assemblies of such people is very usuall some mutinous tumultes, uprores, quarellinges, civil! Dissentions and other disorders have happened and befallen the said elections and are like more and more to growe and happen to the p'judice of the said Towne and disturbans of the peaceable and good gov'ment therof; For Reformac'on wherof and the better prevenc'on of all such populer Disorder, confusion & mischeefe as are like daylie to ensewe yf so muche power and auchthorytie be p'mitted and conteynewed unto people of that rank, qualitie and condic'on. YT IS therfore this p'nte day ordered and decreed by the Maior, bayliffes and burgesses and the Coman Counsell here assembled, that from hensfourth no such disordered p'son as before ys menco'ed shall have any Voice, power or aucthoritie to make any elecc'on, allowaunce, nominac'on or assignac'on in the said l'res patentes especified, But that all and ev'y such elecc'on, allowaunce, nominac'on or assignac'on of all and ev'y maior and bayliffes as in the said l'res patentes ys lymitted or graunted to be made either yerely or upon the death or amoveall of any such Maior or bayliffe or otherwise by the secundary Burgesses, other burgesses and ye lnhabitantes of the Inferior sorte shall allwayes herafter from hensfourth be had and made by the said

Secundary Burgt'sses and by the best, gravest and discreetest of the said other Burgesses and the lnhabitantes of the lower sorte only and by no others in such manner as herafter ys expressed. That is to say That ther shalbe chosen by the said Maior, bayliffes and burgesses and Secundary Burgesses, or the more p'te of them w'ch shalbe present then for yt purpose, Forty persons or more at their pleasure, of the gravest, wisest and most sufficient men of the said other burgesses and inhabitantes of the lower sorte inhabiting w'thin the said borough, W'ch said Forty persons so presentlie to be chosen, and all others herafter from tyme to tyme to be elected shall allwaies be called the Comons Electors or Electors for ye Comons. And that the said Secundary Burgesses and those Electors for and in behalf of all the said other Burgesses and men of the lower sort inhabiting the said borough att all and ev'y tyme and. tymes herafter when such election, nominac'on, assignac'on or allowaunce of the said officers or any of them ys or ought to be made by or according to the purporte of the said l'res patentes shall or may assemble and mete together, and that they or the more part of them so assembled shall have full power, liberty and aucthorytie at all such tymes both to no'iate and assigne such two p'sons of the Principall burgesses to be chosen maior, and to geve allowance unto the Baylieffes which from tyme to tyme shalbe chosen by the Maior, As also to make, chuse and elect one Baylief for the Comons in such and in as ample mann'r and forme to all intentes, Constructions and purposes as the said secundary Burgesses and men of Inferior sort inhabiting the said Towne have lawfully heretofore used to doe or as they or any of them might by virtue of the said l'res patentes heretofore lawfully have don or used. AND lastly yt is ordered that when and as often as yt shall fortu'e any of the said Electors to dy or not dwell in this Borough or be removed from his said place of Electorshipp, That after ev'y suche avoydance of the said Electors place by any meane whatsoev'r, That then and so often the said Maior, Baylieffes and burgesses for the tyme being, together w'th the said Secundary burgesses or the more part of them shall assemble and mete together before they proceed to the election of any Maior or Baylieff. And that they or the more p'te of them soe assembled, shall chuse one or more electors in the Rome or roomes of him or them whose place so shall be voide as aforesaid, so as ther shalbe al waies att the tyme of ev'y such election of Maior or baylieff the Nomber of Fortie electors at the lest then lyving and inhabiting in the said borough for to make & joyne in such nominac'on and election as aforesaid yf they will.

APPENDIX 2

John Richardson:
In honour of ABINGDON, or On the seventh day of September's solemnization.
1641.

Not farre from faire *Calena* placed is
A pleasant Towne, neere silver Thamisis;
Where you may view the ruin'd Battlements
Of old king cissas ancient Monuments
Where struts th'unparall'd, harmlesse, threaten'd Crosse
(Yet lately blest from Babylonish drosse)
Where *Aarons* bels in *Helens* Church doe ring
 Peales, that doe blesse us from the poyson'd sting
Of death eternall. Neere the Church-yard Wall
Stands the faire structure of Christs Hospitall,
Where *Royse* his fruitfull Nurceries supplie
Great *Pembrooks* Gardens insufficiencie.
Of things of late, that in this Towne befell,
Something my oblieg'd Muse is forc'd to tell;
(Though but in rustick phrase) yet Ile expresse
To A B I N G D O N my love and thankfulnesse:
Yet Ile not Barber-like hyperbolize
And sell my Customers a Chest of Lies:
No this Ile banish, thus I will not sin,
Il'e write no more but truth, and now begin.
Tuesday (the seventh day of this last September,)
(Which day I'me sure our Children will remember)
Was by the King, and Court of Parliament
Proclaim'd a Festivall, and to be spent
In sacred wise; because 'twixt Scots and Vs,
A joyfull peace is now concluded thus.
So soone this welcom'd newes was heard off here,
Griefe shrunk aside, no sorrow did appeare;
Each Man by's Cheerefull Visage you would think
Nought but *Nepenthes* liquour then did drink.
The day being come, (Ile barre to complement)
And tell you briefly how the time we spent.
Ith'dawne of day, before *Hyperions* son
Bridl'd his horses, or his Course begun,
Old *Helens* trowling Bells such peales did ring,
And to our drowsie eares such tunes did sing,

(When honest *Nick* began to sympathise,
Striking up's Lowbells in melodious wise)
That we no longer in our beds could lie,
But each prepar'd for this daies jubilie.
To *Helens* Courts (ith' morne) at seven oth' Clock,
Our Congregation in great numbers flock;
Where we till Twelve our Orizons did send
To him, that did our Kingdomes Quarrels end.
And there two Sermons two Divines did preach,
And most divinely gratitude did teach.
At twelve the Priests lips blest us; home we came,
And sung sweet Anthems to *Iehova's* name,
At Two againe (in Clusters) we did pack,
And fill'd the Church as full as it could thwack,
Till foure we staid, and Sermon being ended,
Towards our triumphant Crosse our course was bended.
 And thus we march'd. First with my golden Mace
('Tis fit I put my selfe ith' formost place)
I pac'd along, and after follow'd mee
The Burgesses by senioritie.
Our Prætour first (let me not misse my Text)
I think the Clergie-men came marching next;
Then came our Iustice, with him a Burger sage,
Both march'd together in due equipage:
The rest oth' Burgers, with a comely grace,
Walk'd two, and two along to th' Market-place;
And after them, hundreds both young, and old
Crowding along, that time you might behold,
(Being come to th' famous Crosse, our journies end),
Her mounting Stayres in state we did ascend;
The Clerk was call'd, and he a Bible took,
The hundred and sixt Psalme he out did look,
Two thousand Quoristers their notes did raise,
And warbled out the great Creatours praise,
Their thundering Eccho gave so great a shout,
Nicklas and *Helen* were quite baffl'd out.
Over my head, I saw King *David* stand,
Listning toth' Musick, with his Harp in hand,
Sure when the Psalmist liv'd, with's sacred Lire,
He seldome play'd, or sung to such a Quire.
If either King could speake, hee'd sweare by's Crown
No haire-braind Separatist would pull him downe:

For why, this heavenly joy, we had so late,
Did seeme, in part, the Crosse to consecrate.
The Psalme is ended; but the Folke begin
Lowder and lowder crie, God save the K I N G,
While Bonfires blaze, their caps are throwne away,
All to expresse the triumph of the day.
The *Helvian* liquor, and rich Maligo,
And English beere, our Senate did bestow:
No cost was spar'd, and yet I must confesse,
I saw no shew of brutish drunkennesse:
Sure some diviner hand, that day did guide
The Vulgar, that they should not slip aside,
And further to set forth a greater joy,
Out comes the skillfull Sergeant *Corderoy*,
With's his ratling Drummes, and Fife, and Colours flying,
With's Musketteeres (and yet ther's none fear'd dying)
Bravely they march'd about; but made a stop,
When they drew neere the well knowne Antelop;
A fiery peale they rung ith' Senats Eares;
(Gallantly done by warlike Musketteeres)
Anon they made a Guard, my noble Master,
March't through them to the front, (but yet no faster
Then my Mace and I) safely did they guard
The King's Lieutenant home, when in his yard,
Or Court, another peale they out did thunder,
Which made the thronging people shout and wounder;
Their Muskets having shot out all their powder
They made their Throats their Muskets, and shot lowder,
Such was their joy (a Barrell being spent)
In sober manner every man home went.
And them with speed followed my Muse and I,
To learne what further newes we could descrie.
And now 'tis supper time. In every street
Neighbours with Neighbours at some house did meet.
Their monies joyn'd together for a Feast,
And each to other is a welcome Guest,
(Supper being done) anon they 'gin to sing
Some joyfull Hymne (a joyfull revelling)
Travell my Muse, goe, wander up and downe,
Search into City, Village, Hamlet, Town,
Tell me at thy returne (if thou canst tell)
Where any Feast with ours could parallell.

And yet this was not all, for what was spent
On *Irus* Crue, made the full complement
Of this daies jubilie, this was the best
Of Sacrifice, this season'd all the rest.
Vpon this day the poore were not neglected,
Thirteene or Foureteene pounds were here collected
And some (no question) out of Charitie,
In private gave to their necessitie.
Thus have I shew'd you in a home-spun way,
(Yet true enough) how we this happy day
Did from the morning to the evening spend;
But I am weary, and I'le make an end.

POSTSCRIPT

Thus to th' generall view a Seriants quill,
Ventur'd at last to show her weaker skill.
Such friends, that at her Errours will connive,
Humbly to thank, and gratifie sheele strive,
But let detracting fooles about them look,
Her Master is a subtile Tenter-hook;
Hee'le quickly snap them, if such chance to be
Within the Verge of his authoritie
But if sh'ath written any blamefull act,
'Twas her dull ignorance, and no wilfull fact. Sic ex officio allusit IOH:
RICHARDSON Serviens ad Clavam Burgi de *Abingdon* in Come Berks.

Mock-learned references:

Calena: Oxford
King Cissa: Supposed founder of Abingdon Abbey.
Nepenthe: A potion to allay grief.
Hyperion: father of Helios, the sun-god.
Helvian: (in Roman times) wine from the present Ardèche region.
Irus's crew: beggars.

Conventions and abbreviations

- Many of the standard calendars have now been digitised, and page numbers of the paper versions are no longer helpful in identifying references. In such cases, page numbers have been dropped in favour of item numbers or operative dates.
- Place of publication is London unless otherwise stated.

A&O	C.H. Firth and E.S. Rait, *Acts and Ordinances of the Interregnum, 1642-1660*, 3 vols, (1911).
APC	*Acts of the Privy Council of England, 1542-1631*, 46 vols (1890-1964).
ATCA	Abingdon Town Council Archives, Abingdon.
BL	British Library, London.
Bod or Bodl	Bodleian Library, Oxford.
BRO or BerksRO	Berkshire Record Office, Coley, Reading.
BQ	*Baptist Quarterly*
CCalSP	*Calendar of the Clarendon State Papers*, 5 vols (Oxford, 1872-1970).
CCAM	*Calendar of the Committee for the Advance of Money*, 1642-56, 3 vols (1888-92).
CCC	*Calendar of the Committee for Compounding*, 1643-60, 5 vols (1880-92).
CH	Christ's Hospital, Abingdon.
CJ	*Journals of the House of Commons*.
CPR	*Calendar of Patent Rolls*.
CSP	*Calendar of State Papers*
CSPD	*Calendar of State Papers Domestic*.
DNB	*The Oxford Dictionary of National Biography* (on-line).
EHR	*English Historical Review*
HMC	Historical Manuscripts Commission.
HoP 1509-1558	*The House of Commons 1509-1558,* ed. Bindoff, 3 vols (History of Parliament Trust, 1982).
HoP 1558-1603	*The House of Commons 1558-1603,* ed. Hasler, 3 vols (History of Parliament Trust, 1981).
HoP 1660-1690	*The House of Commons 1660-1690,* ed. Henning, 3 vols (History of Parliament Trust, 1983).
JP	Justice of the Peace

L&P	*Letters and Papers, Foreign and Domestic, of the Reign of Henry VIII, 1509-47,* 21 vols (1862-1932).
L&T	*The life and times of Anthony Wood, antiquary, of Oxford, 1632-1695* (ed. A. Clark), 5 vols (Oxford, 1891-1900).
LJ	*Journals of the House of Lords*
MP	Member of Parliament
NA	The National Archives, Kew.
ODNB	*The Oxford Dictionary of National Biography* (on-line).
OED	*The Oxford English Dictionary*
P&P	*Past and Present*
RO	Record Office.
SR	*Statutes of the Realm*, 12 vols (1810-28).
TNA	The National Archives, Kew.
ThSP	*Collection of the State Papers of John Thurloe* (ed. Birch) 7 vols (1732).
VCH	*Victoria County History* (of Berkshire, if not otherwise stated: 4 vols (1906-27)).

INDEX

Note: No attempt has been made in this index to discriminate among individuals of the same name. Places are in Berkshire unless otherwise specified.